WOMEN WRITERS
FROM PAGE TO SCREEN

GARLAND REFERENCE LIBRARY
OF THE HUMANITIES
(VOL. 687)

WOMEN WRITERS
FROM PAGE TO SCREEN

Jill Rubinson Fenton
Charles G. Waugh
Jane Russo
Martin H. Greenberg

GARLAND PUBLISHING, INC. • NEW YORK & LONDON
1990

Library of Congress Cataloging-in-Publication Data

Women writers: from page to screen / Jill Rubinson Fenton . . . [et
al.].
     p. cm. — (Garland reference library of the humanities ; vol.
687)
    Includes bibliographical references.
    ISBN 0-8240-8529-9 (alk. paper)
    1. Film adaptations—Catalogs. 2. Literature—Women authors—
Adaptations—Film catalogs. 3. Motion pictures—United States—
Catalogs. 4. Motion pictures—Great Britain—Catalogs.
5. Literature—Women authors—Bibliography. I. Fenton, Jill, 1948–
II. Series.
PN1997.85.W58   1990
016.79143'75'082—dc20   89–23479
                                                              CIP

Printed on acid-free, 250-year-life paper
Manufactured in the United States of America

DEDICATION

To our mothers and daughters.

TABLE OF CONTENTS

PREFACE

Our volume presents a comprehensive listing of more than two thousand two hundred British (English speaking dominions included) and American feature films and television movies inspired by women's writings. Over seventy-five years of cinematic history are covered: from the emergence of four-reel silent feature films in 1913 to the flourishing of cable television movies by the end of 1988.

In our research, we came across many women considered literary giants and hundreds more widely read years ago, but neglected now. Many of their works, and the films based on them, while not classics, offer interesting insights into the values and dreams of their times. Serious researchers can also note differences between the authors' filmed and unfilmed works, the manner in which works have been translated into film, and the ways in which various film versions differ.

The heart of our book is the alphabetically-by-author index. All authors are credited in the case of collaborations, with female authors receiving separate entries. Known pen names are identified, with the real names of female authors cross-indexed. Authors known to be listed under multiple names are cross-indexed. Adaptors of foreign language works are listed; translators are not.

The filmed literary works of each author are indented beneath her name, with multiple literary works listed alphabetically. When a film has multiple literary sources by women, double listing and cross indexing are utilized. To the right of each literary work, except for novels, is a one or two-letter notation indicating type of work. These are listed below and appear in the glossary.

        A..........short non-fiction article
        CS.........collected stories
        D..........diary (only those of literary merit are
                    included)
        MP.........musical play
        NF.........book length non-fiction, including biography and
                    autobiography
        O..........opera or operetta
        P..........play
        Po.........poem
        RS.........related short stories
        S..........short story
        So.........song

Two notations (such as [S/N]) indicate the orginal literary work was later converted to another form by the same author.

Because the term story is often used to designate story concepts and story (or screen) treatments as well as short stories, we omit all unpublished story references. But we do include unproduced plays (known to be plays and not just screenplays) and unpublished novels.

Indented beneath the literary work is the title of the film. Films are listed only under their direct sources, though in most cases the secondary source is cited. When multiple tiles exist, we list the title preferred by the country of origin. When several films have been adapted from one work, they are listed chronologically -- then alphabetically for those few instances when two films of the same work were released in the same year. Next to the title of appropriate films, additional classification notations appear. These are listed below.

     (*)..........silent film
     (G. B.).....country or countries of origin. See glossary
               for abbreviations. Only when coproduced with
               other countries are U. S. productions noted.
     (TVM).......film (fewer than five hours) produced for a
               television network
     (AF)........anthology film, consisting of two or more
               separate stories
     (Anim.).....animated film

The name of production companies and distributing companies (or networks of first appearance) and years of release appear beneath the film titles. Information about distributing companies, networks of first appearance, and release date, are listed, whenever possible, for country of origin.

A sample entry follows:

Lestrange, David (also see Constance Collier and Ivor Novello)
    (joint pseud. of Constance Collier and Ivor Novello)

   When Boys Leave Home (P)

      <u>Downhill</u> (*) (G. B.)
      Gainsborough Prod./World Wide Films, Ltd., 1927

For convenience's sake, we have also included film and title indices near the end of our book.

In the two years spent compiling our master list, we encountered difficulties of elusive titles; problems in determining gender and country of origin; inconsistency of information among sources, especially about distribution companies and film release dates; copyrighted under-crediting and public domain over-crediting; and a lack of differentiation between screenplays and plays and story concepts,

GLOSSARY

```
A..............article (short work of nonfiction)

AF.............anthology film (composed of two or more
               separate stories)

aka............also known as

anim...........animated

Austr..........Australia

Cal............California

Can............Canada

Co.............company

Col............Colorado

comp...........compiler

comps..........compilers

Corp...........corporation

CS.............collected stories (book of unrelated stories
               by single author or collaborating authors)

D..............diary

D. C...........District of Columbia

Dist...........distributor/distributors

ed.............edition/editor

eds............editors

Eng............England

Fra............France

Ger............Germany

G. B...........Great Britain

Inc............Incorporated

Ind............India
```

```
Ire..............Ireland

Ita..............Italy

Jp...............Japan

Jr...............junior

Ltd..............Limited

M. D.............doctor of medicine

Mich.............Michigan

Mme..............madame

MP...............musical play

N................novel (used only when title is unknown)

NF...............non-fiction book (except for book length
                 diaries)

N. J.............New Jersey

N. Y.............New York

N. Z.............New Zealand

O................opera or operetta

P................play

Penn.............Pennsylvania

Phil.............Philadelphia

Po...............poem

Prod.............Producing/Production

pub..............publisher/publishers/publication/
                 publications/publishing

q. v.............see that which was mentioned

RS...............related stories

S................short story/novelette/novella

S. Afr...........South Africa

So...............song
```

```
Spa............Spain

St..............saint

Swed...........Sweden

TVM............television movie

univ...........university

U. S...........United States  (used only when movie is a
                              multicountry production)

U. S. A.........United States of America

V. C...........Victoria Cross

vols...........volumes

Vt.............Vermont

Wisc...........Wisconsin

Yugo...........Yugoslavia

*..............silent movie

?..............information is in doubt
```

Women Writers
From Page to Screen

Aberson, Helen and Harold Pearl

    Dumbo

        Dumbo
        Walt Disney Prod./RKO Radio Pictures, Inc., 1941

Abbott, Eleanor Hallowell [Eleanor Hallowell]

    Little Eve Edgarton

        Little Eve Edgarton (*)
        Bluebird Photoplays, Inc., 1916

    Molly Make-Believe

        Molly Make-Believe (*)
        Famous Players Film Co./Paramount Pictures Corp., 1916

    Old Dad

        Old Dad (*)
        Chaplin-Mayer Pictures Co./Associated First National,
        1920

Abrahall, Clare Hoskyns

    Prelude (NF)

        Wherever She Goes (Austr.)
        Ealing Studios, Ltd./Mayer-Kingsley International
        Pictures, Inc., 1950

Abrahams, Doris Caroline (see Caryl Brahms)

Abrams, Margaret

    The Uncle

        The Uncle (G. B.)
        Play-Pix/British Lion, 1964

Adams, Harriet Stratemeyer (see Carolyn Keene)

Adams, Jane

    Sex and the Single Parent (NF)

        Sex and the Single Parent (TVM)
        Time-Life Television Prod./Columbia Broadcasting
        System, 1979

Adamson, Joy

    Born Free (NF)

        Born Free (G. B.)
        Open Road-Atlas-Highroad/Columbia Pictures Corp., 1965

    Living Free (NF)

        Living Free (G. B.)
        Open Road-Highroad/Columbia Pictures Corp., 1971

Addington, Sarah

    Bless Their Hearts (S)

        And So They Were Married
        Columbia Pictures Corp., 1936

    Dance Team

        Dance Team
        Fox Film Corp., 1932

Addyman, Elizabeth

    The Secret Tent (P)

        The Secret Tent (G. B.)
        Forward/British Lion, 1956

Adkins, Ella

    Second Chance (P)

        Time is my Enemy (G. B.)
        Vandyke/Independent Film Dist., 1954

Adler, Polly

A House Is Not A Home (NF)

>   A House Is Not A Home
>   Embassy Pictures Corp., 1964

Akins, Zoe (also see the entry below)

Daddy's Gone A-Hunting (P)

>   Daddy's Gone A-Hunting (*)
>   Metro-Goldwyn Pictures, 1925

>   Women Love Once
>   Paramount Pictures Corp., 1931

Declassee (P)

>   Declassee (*)
>   Corinne Griffith Prod./First National, 1925

>   Her Private Life
>   First National, 1929

The Furies (P)

>   The Furies
>   First National, 1930

The Greeks Had a Word for It (P)

>   The Greeks Had a Word for Them
>   Samuel Goldwyn Prod./United Artists Film Corp., 1932

>   How to Marry a Millionaire (also based on the play
>   Loco, by Dale Eunson and Katherine Albert)
>   Twentieth Century-Fox Film Corp., 1953

Morning Glory (P)

>   Morning Glory
>   RKO Radio Pictures, Inc., 1933

>   Stage Struck
>   RKO Radio Pictures, Inc., 1958

The Old Maid (P, based on the novelette "The Old Maid" by
Edith Wharton)

>   The Old Maid
>   Warner Brothers Pictures, Inc., 1939

Pardon My Glove (P)

        <u>Ladies</u> <u>Love</u> <u>Brutes</u>
        Paramount Famous Lasky Corp., 1930

To You My Life (S)

        <u>Accused</u>
        United Artists Film Corp., 1936

Akins, Zoe and Lajos Biro (also see the entry above)

The Moon-Flower (P)

        <u>Eve's</u> <u>Secret</u> (*)
        Famous Players-Lasky Corp./Paramount Pictures Corp.,
        1925

Albert, Katherine and Dale Eunson

Loco (P)

        <u>How</u> <u>to</u> <u>Marry</u> <u>a</u> <u>Millionaire</u> (also based on the play, <u>The</u>
        <u>Greeks</u> <u>Had</u> <u>a</u> <u>Word</u> <u>for</u> <u>It</u>, by Zoe Akins)
        Twentieth Century-Fox Film Corp., 1953

Albrand, Martha
    (pseud. of Heidi Huberta Freybe Loewengard)

After Midnight

        <u>Captain</u> <u>Carey,</u> <u>U.</u> <u>S.</u> <u>A.</u>
        Paramount Pictures Corp., 1950

Desperate Moment

        <u>Desperate</u> <u>Moment</u> (G. B.)
        British Film Makers-Fanfare/General Film, 1953

Alcott, Louisa May

Little Men

        <u>Little</u> <u>Men</u>
        Mascot Pictures, 1934

        <u>Little</u> <u>Men</u>
        RKO Radio Pictures, Inc., 1950

Little Women

        <u>Little</u> <u>Women</u> (*) (G. B.)
        G. B. Samuelson/Moss, 1917

Little Women (*) (also based on the same named play, by
Marian de Forest, which was derived from Alcott's
novel)
William A. Brady/State Rights--Famous Players-Lasky
Corp.--Paramount Pictures Corp.-Artcraft Pictures Corp,
1919

Little Women
RKO Radio Pictures, Inc., 1933

Little Women
Metro-Goldwyn-Mayer, Inc., 1949

Little Women (TVM)
Groverton Prod.-Universal Television/National
Broadcasting Co., 1978

An Old Fashioned Girl

An Old Fashioned Girl
Eagle Lion, 1948

Aldrich, Bess Streeter

Miss Bishop

Cheers For Miss Bishop
United Artist's Film Corp., 1941

The Silent Stars Go By (S)

The Gift of Love: A Christmas Story (TVM)
Amanda Prod., Inc./ Telecom Entertainment, 1983

The Woman Who was Forgotten (S)

The Woman Who was Forgotten (*)
Woman Who was Forgotten, Inc./States Cinema Corp., 1930

Alexander, Elizabeth

Fifty-Two Weeks for Florette (S)

You Belong to Me
Paramount Pictures Corp., 1934

Roles

Changing Husbands (*)
Famous Players-Lasky Corp./Paramount Pictures Corp.,
1924

Second Choice

> Second Choice
> Warner Brothers Pictures, Inc., 1930

The Self-Made Wife (S)

> The Self-Made Wife (*)
> Universal Motion Pictures Co., 1923

Alexander, Shana

Decision to Die (A)

> The Slender Thread
> Athene Prod./Paramount Pictures Corp., 1965

Alison, Joan and Murray Burnett

Everybody Goes to Rick's (P -- unproduced)

> Casablanca
> Warner Brothers Pictures Inc., 1942

Allan, Janet

Little Big Shot (P)

> Little Big Shot (G. B.)
> Byron/Associated British Film Dist., 1952

Allen, Jane (also see the entry below)
(unidentified pseud.)

A Girl's Best Friend is Wall Street (S)

> She Knew All the Answers
> Columbia Pictures Corp., 1941

Allen, Jane and Mae Livingston (also see the entry above)
(Jane Allen: unidentified pseud.)

Thanks, God! I'll Take It From Here

> Without Reservations
> RKO Radio Pictures, Inc., 1946

Allen, Jay Presson

The First Wife (P)

    <u>Wives</u> <u>and</u> <u>Lovers</u>
    Hal Wallis Prod./Paramount Pictures Corp., 1963

Forty Carats (P, based on the foreign language play by
Pierre Barillet and Jean Pierre Gredy)

    <u>Forty</u> <u>Carats</u>
    Columbia Pictures Corp., 1973

Just Tell Me What You Want

    <u>Just</u> <u>Tell</u> <u>Me</u> <u>What</u> <u>You</u> <u>Want</u>
    Warner Brothers Pictures, Inc., 1980

The Prime of Miss Jean Brodie (P)

    <u>The</u> <u>Prime</u> <u>of</u> <u>Miss</u> <u>Jean</u> <u>Brodie</u> (*) (G. B.) (also based
    on the same named novel, by Muriel Spark, from which
    the play was derived)
    Twentieth Century-Fox Film Corp., 1969

Allen, Judy

    December Flower

        <u>December</u> <u>Flower</u> (TVM) (G. B.)
        Roy Roberts-Granada Television, 1984

Allingham, Margery

    Tiger in the Smoke

        <u>Tiger</u> <u>in</u> <u>the</u> <u>Smoke</u> (G. B.)
        J. Arthur Rank Film Prod./ J. Arthur Rank Film Dist.,
        Ltd., 1956

Amen, Carol

    The Last Testament (S)

        <u>Testament</u>
        Paramount Pictures Corp., 1983

Ames, Mildred

    Anna to the Infinite Power

        <u>Anna</u> <u>to</u> <u>the</u> <u>Infinite</u> <u>Power</u>
        Columbia Pictures Corp., 1983

Anderson, Peggy

Nurse

>> Nurse (TVM)
>> Robert Halmi Prod./Columbia Broadcasting System, 1980

Anderson, Verily

Beware of Children

>> No Kidding (G. B.)
>> Gregory, Hake and Walker Prod./Anglo-Amalgamated Film,
>> 1960

Andrews, Daisy H. and John Colton

Drifting (P)

>> Drifting (*)
>> Universal Motion Pictures Co., 1923

>> Shanghai Lady
>> Universal Motion Pictures Co., 1929

Andrews, Mary Raymond Shipman

The Courage of the Commonplace

>> The Courage of the Commonplace (*)
>> Thomas A. Edison, Inc.-Perfection Pictures/George Kline
>> System, 1917

The Three Things

>> The Unbeliever (*)
>> Thomas A. Edison, Inc.-Perfection Pictures/George Kline
>> System, 1918

Angelou, Maya
(pseud. of Marguerite Johnson)

I Know Why the Caged Bird Sings (NF)

>> I Know Why the Caged Bird Sings (TVM)
>> Tomorrow Entertainment, Inc./Columbia Broadcasting
>> System, 1979

Angus, Bernadine

    Angel Island (P)

        <u>Fog Island</u>
        Producers Releasing Corp., 1945

Anholt, Edna and Edward Anholt

    Quarantine (S)

        <u>Panic in the Streets</u> (also based on the short story
        "Some Like 'em Cold," by the Anholts)
        Twentieth Century-Fox Film Corp., 1950

    Some Like 'em Cold (S)

        <u>Panic in the Streets</u> (also based on the short story
        "Quarantine," by the Anholts)
        Twentieth Century-Fox Film Corp., 1950

Annesley, Maude

    Wind Along the Waste

        <u>Shattered Dreams</u> (*)
        Universal Film Manufacturing Co., 1922

    The Wine of Life

        <u>The Wine of Life</u> (*) (G. B.)
        I. B. Davidson/Butcher's Film Service, 1924

Anthony, C. L. (also see Dodie Smith)
    (pseud. of Dorothy Gladys "Dodie" Smith)

    Autumn Crocus (P)

        <u>Autumn Crocus</u> (G. B.)
        Associated Talking Pictures/Associated British Film
        Dist., 1934

    Service (P)

        <u>Looking Forward</u>
        Metro-Goldwyn-Mayer, Inc., 1933

Anthony, Evelyn
    (pseud. of Evelyn Bridget Patricia Stephens Ward-Thomas)

    The Tamarind Seed

The <u>Tamarind Seed</u> (G. B.)
Jewel Prod., Inc.-Lorimar Prod.-Pimlico/Scotia Barber,
1974

Archibald, Gilda Varesi and Dorothea Donn-Byrne (Dorothea Donn-
Byrne is the married name of Dorothea "Dolly" Byrne)

Enter Madame; a Play in Three Acts (P)

<u>Enter Madame</u> (*)
Samuel Zierler Photoplay Corp./Metro Pictures Corp.,
1922

<u>Enter Madame</u>
Paramount Pictures Corp., 1935

Arley, Catherine

Woman of Straw

<u>Woman of Straw</u> (G. B.)
Novus/United Artists' Film Corp., 1964

Armstrong, Charlotte

The Case of the Weird Sisters

<u>The Three Weird Sisters</u> (G. B.)
British National Films, Ltd./Pathe Exchange, Inc., 1948

The Enemy (S)

<u>Talk About a Stranger</u>
Metro-Goldwyn-Mayer, Inc., 1952

Mischief

<u>Don't Bother to Knock</u>
Twentieth Century-Fox Film Corp., 1952

The Unsuspected

<u>The Unsuspected</u>
Warner Brothers Pictures, Inc., 1947

Arnow, Harriette

The Dollmaker

<u>The Dollmaker</u> (TVM)

Finnegan Associates-Independent Pictures Corp. Films,
Inc.-Dollmaker Prod./American Broadcasting Co., 1984

Arundel, Edith

The Persistent Warrior

Green Fingers (G. B.)
British National Films, Ltd./Anglo, 1947

Ashbrook, Harriette

Murder of Stephen Kester

Green Eyes
Chesterfield Motion Pictures, 1934

Ashe, Penelope
(group pseud. of Billie Young and Harvey Aronson, Robert W.
Greene, Mal Karman, Mike McGrady, Bill McIlwain, and 18
others)

Naked Came the Stranger

Naked Came the Stranger
Catalyst, 1975

Ashton, Helen

Yeoman's Hospital

White Corridors (G. B.)
Vic Films/General Film, 1951

Ashton, Winifred (see Clemence Dane)

Ashton-Warner, Sylvia
(pseud. of Sylvia Henderson)

I Passed This Way (NF)

Sylvia (N. Z.) (also based on the nonfiction book
Teacher, by Ashton-Warner)
Southern Light-Cinepro/Metro-Goldwyn-Mayer, Inc.;
United Artists Film Corp., 1985

The Spinster

Two Loves

Julian Blaustein's Prod./Metro-Goldwyn-Mayer, Inc., 1961

Teacher (NF)

Sylvia (N. Z.) (also based on the nonfiction book *I Passed This Way*, by Ashton-Warner)
Southern Light-Cinepro/Metro-Goldwyn-Mayer, Inc.; United Artists Film Corp., 1985

Askew, Alice and Claude Askew

God's Clay

God's Clay (*) (G. B.)
Arthur Rooke, 1919

God's Clay (*) (G. B.)
First National, 1928

John Heriot's Wife

John Heriot's Wife (*) (G. B.)
Anglo-Hollandia/National, 1920

Poison

The Pleydell Mystery (*) (G. B.)
British Empire, 1916

The Shulamite

The Shulamite (*) (G. B.) (also based on the play *The Shulamite*, by Edward Knoblock, which was adapted from the Askews' novel)
London Films/Jury's Imperial Pictures, 1915

Under the Lash (*) (also based on the play *The Shulamite*, by Edward Knoblock, which was adapted from the Askews' novel)
Famous Players-Lasky Corp./Paramount Pictures Corp., 1921

Testimony

Testimony (*) (G. B.)
George Clark/Stoll, 1920

Atherton, Gertrude (also see the entry below)

The Avalanche; a Mystery Story

The Avalanche (*)

12

Famous Players-Lasky Corp./Famous Players-Lasky Corp.--
Artcraft Pictures Corp., 1919

Black Oxen

Black Oxen (*)
Frank Lloyd Prod./Associated First National, 1924

The Crystal Cup

The Crystal Cup (*)
Henry Hobart/First National, 1927

Mrs. Balfame

Mrs. Balfame (*)
Frank Powell Prod. Corp./Mutual Film Corp.-Mutual Star
Prod., 1917

Patience Sparhawk and Her Times

The Panther Woman (*)
Petrova Picture Co./First National, 1918

Perch of the Devil

Perch of the Devil (*)
Universal Motion Pictures Co., 1927

The Tower of Ivory

Out of the Storm (*)
Eminent Authors Pictures, Inc./Goldwyn Dist. Corp.,
1920

Atherton, Gertrude and Vicki Baum, Vina Delmar, Sophie Kerr, and
Ursula Parrott and Polan Banks, Irvin S. Cobb, Zane Grey,
Rupert Hughes, and J. P. McEvoy (also see the entry above)

Woman Accused

Woman Accused
Paramount Pictures Corp., 1933

Atkinson, Eleanor

Greyfriars Bobby

Challenge to Lassie
Metro-Goldwyn-Mayer, Inc., 1949

Greyfriars Bobby (U. S./G. B.)
Walt Disney Prod./Buena Vista Dist. Co., 1961

Auel, Jean M.

> **The Clan of the Cave Bear**

>> The Clan of the Cave Bear
>> Warner Brothers Pictures, Inc., 1986

Austen, Jane

> **Northanger Abbey**

>> Northanger Abbey (TVM) (G. B.)
>> Masterpiece Theater/Public Broadcasting System, 1987

> **Pride and Prejudice**

>> Pride and Prejudice (also based on the same named play,
>> by Helen Jerome, which was derived from Austen's novel)
>> Metro-Goldwyn-Mayer, Inc., 1940

> **Sir Charles Grandison** (P [?], based on the same named novel,
> by Samuel Richardson)

>> Jane Austen in Manhattan
>> Contemporary, 1980

Austin, Anne

> **A Wicked Woman**

>> A Wicked Woman
>> Metro-Goldwyn-Mayer, Inc., 1934

Austin, May and E. V. Edmonds

> **The King's Romance** (P)

>> The King's Romance (*) (G. B.)
>> British and Colonial Kinematograph Co./Kinematograph
>> Trading Co., 1914

Axelson, Mary McDougal

> **Life Begins** (P)

>> Life Begins
>> First National/Warner Brothers Pictures, Inc.-First
>> National, 1932

A <u>Child</u> <u>is</u> <u>Born</u>
Warner Brothers Pictures, Inc., 1940

Ayres, Ruby Mildred

A Bachelor Husband

A <u>Bachelor</u> <u>Husband</u> (*) (G. B.)
Astra Films, 1920

The Black Sheep

The <u>Black</u> <u>Sheep</u> (*) (G. B.)
Progress/Butcher's Film Service, 1920

Castles in Spain

<u>Castles</u> <u>in</u> <u>Spain</u> (*) (G. B.)
Lucoque Films-Taylor/Gaumont, 1920

The Man Without a Heart

The <u>Man</u> <u>Without</u> <u>a</u> <u>Heart</u> (*)
Banner Prod., 1924

The Romance of a Rogue

<u>Romance</u> <u>of</u> <u>a</u> <u>Rogue</u> (*)
A. Carlos/Quality Dist. Corp., 1928

The Second Honeymoon

<u>Second</u> <u>Honeymoon</u>
Continental Talking Pictures, 1930

Babbitt, Natalie

Eyes of the Amaryllis

The Eyes of the Amaryllis
Children's Video Library, 1982

Tuck Everlasting

Tuck Everlasting
Coe Films, 1980

Bacon, Josephine Daskam

The Ghost of Rosy Taylor (S)

The Ghost of Rosy Taylor (*)
American Film/Mutual Film Corp., 1918

Bagnold, Enid

The Chalk Garden (P)

The Chalk Garden (G. B.)
Quota Rentals/Universal International Motion Pictures,
1963

National Velvet

National Velvet
Metro-Goldwyn-Mayer, Inc., 1944

International Velvet (G. B.)
Peerford--Metro-Goldwyn-Mayer British/Cinema
International Corp., 1978

Bailey, Helen Marion Edginton (see May Edginton)

Bailey, Temple
(pseud. of Irene Temple)

Peacock Feathers

Peacock Feathers (*)

Universal Motion Pictures Co., 1925

Wallflowers

>   <u>Wallflowers</u> (*)
>   Film Booking Office of America, 1928

Bainbridge, Beryl

The Dressmaker

>   <u>The</u> <u>Dressmaker</u> (G. B.)
>   Ronald Shedlo-Freeway/Film Four-British Screen, 1988

Sweet William

>   <u>Sweet</u> <u>William</u> (G. B.)
>   Boyd's Co.-Berwick Street-Kendon/Inc. Television Co.,
>   1980

Baird, Marie Terese

A Lesson in Love

>   <u>Circle</u> <u>of</u> <u>Two</u> (Can.)
>   Film Consortium of Canada, 1980

Baker, Dorothy

Young Man With a Horn

>   <u>Young</u> <u>Man</u> <u>with</u> <u>a</u> <u>Horn</u>
>   Warner Brothers Pictures, Inc., 1950

Baker, Jane and Pip Baker

Moment of Blindness (P)

>   <u>The</u> <u>Third</u> <u>Alibi</u> (G. B.)
>   Eternal/Grand National Pictures, 1961

Baker, Trudy and Rachel Jones

Coffee, Tea or Me? (NF)

>   <u>Coffee,</u> <u>Tea</u> <u>or</u> <u>Me?</u> (TVM)
>   Columbia Broadcasting System Entertainment/Columbia
>   Broadcasting System, 1973

Baldwin, Faith (maiden name of Faith Baldwin Cuthrell)

Apartment for Jenny (S)

> Apartment for Peggy
> Twentieth Century-Fox Film Corp., 1948

August Weekend (S)

> August Weekend
> Chesterfield Motion Pictures, 1936

Beauty

> Beauty for Sale
> Metro-Goldwyn-Mayer, Inc., 1933

Comet Over Broadway (S)

> Comet Over Broadway
> First National, 1938

The Gosamer World (S)

> Queen for a Day (also based on the stories "Horsie," by
> Dorothy Parker, and "High Diver," by John Ashworth)
> United Artists Film Corp., 1951

Men are Such Fools

> Men are Such Fools
> Warner Brothers Pictures, Inc., 1938

The Moon's Our Home

> The Moon's Our Home
> Paramount Pictures Corp., 1936

The Office Wife

> The Office Wife
> Warner Brothers Pictures, Inc., 1930

> The Office Wife (G. B.)
> Warner Brothers Pictures, Inc.-First National/Warner
> Brothers Pictures, Inc., 1934

Part-Time Marriage

> Week-End Marriage
> First National, 1932

Portia on Trial (S)

> Portia on Trial

Republic Pictures Corp., 1937

Rosalie's Career

The Way of All Women
World Wide, 1932

Skyscraper

Skyscraper Souls
Metro-Goldwyn-Mayer, Inc., 1932

Spinster Dinner

Love Before Breakfast
Universal Motion Pictures Co., 1936

Wife Versus Secretary (S)

Wife Versus Secretary
Distributed Films, 1936

Balfour, Lady Evelyn

Anything Might Happen

Anything Might Happen (G. B.)
Realart Pictures Corp./RKO Radio Pictures, Inc., 1934

Ball, Oona

Barbara Comes to Oxford

The City of Youth (G. B.) (*)
British University Films, 1928

Banks, Mrs. Linnaeus (married name of Isabella Varley)

The Manchester Man

The Manchester Man (*) (G. B.)
Ideal, 1920

Banks, Lynne Reid

The L-Shaped Room

The L-Shaped Room (G. B.)
Romulus Films/British Lion, 1962

Bannerman, Kay and Harold Brooke

All for Mary (P)

All for Mary (G. B.)
J. Arthur Rank Film Prod./J. Arthur Rank Film Dist.,
Ltd., 1955

Handful of Tansy (P)

No, My Darling Daughter! (G. B.)
J. Arthur Rank Film Prod.-Five Star/J. Arthur Rank Film
Dist., Ltd., 1961

How Say You? (P)

A Pair of Briefs (G. B.)
J. Arthur Rank Film Prod./J. Arthur Rank Film Dist.,
Ltd., 1962

Banning, Margaret Culken

Enemy Territory (S)

Woman Against Woman
Metro-Goldwyn-Mayer, Inc., 1938

Barber, Antonia

The Ghosts

The Amazing Mr. Blunden (G. B.)
Hemisphere/Hemdale, 1972

Barber, Elsie Oaks

Jenny Angel

Angel Baby
Madera Prod./Allied Artists, 1961

Barclay, Florence L.

The Mistress of Shenstone

The Mistress of Shenstone (*)
Robertson-Cole Pictures, 1921

Barclay, Frances and Leon M. Lion

20

The Chinese Puzzle (P)

    The Chinese Puzzle (*) (G. B.)
    Ideal, 1919

    The Chinese Puzzle (G. B.)
    Twickenham/Woolf and Freedman Film Service, 1932

Barcynska, Countess Helene
    (pseud. of Marguerite Florence Helene Jarvis Evans)

The Honeypot

    The Honeypot (*) (G. B.)
    G. B. Samuelson/Granger, 1920

Jackie

    Jackie (*)
    Fox Film Corp., 1921

Love Maggy

    Love Maggy (*) (G. B.)
    G. B. Samuelson/Granger, 1921

Rose O' the Sea; a Romance

    Rose O' the Sea (*)
    Anita Stewart Prod./Associated First National, 1922

Tesha

    Tesha (*) (G. B.)
    British International Pictures-Burlington Films/
    Wardour, 1928

We Women

    We Women (*) (G. B.)
    Stoll, 1925

Bard, Mary

The Doctor Wears Three Faces

    Mother Didn't Tell Me
    Twentieth Century-Fox Film Corp., 1950

Barfoot, Joan

Dancing in the Dark

                    <u>Dancing</u> <u>in</u> <u>the</u> <u>Dark</u>
                    New World Cinema-Simcom, 1986

Barling, Muriel Vere Mant (see Pamela Barrington)

Barnes, Margaret Anne

    Murder in Coweta County (NF)

                    <u>Murder</u> <u>in</u> <u>Coweta</u> <u>County</u> (TVM)
                    Telecom Entertainment/The International Picture Show
                    Co./Columbia Broadcasting System, 1983

Barnes, Margaret Ayer

    The Age of Innocence (P)

                    <u>The</u> <u>Age</u> <u>of</u> <u>Innocence</u>   (also based on the same named
                    novel, by Edith Wharton, from which the play was
                    derived)
                    RKO Radio Pictures, Inc., 1934

    Westward Passage

                    <u>Westward</u> <u>Passage</u>
                    RKO Radio Pictures, Inc., 1932

Barnes, Margaret Ayer and Edward Brewster Sheldon

    Dishonored Lady (P)

                    <u>Dishonored</u> <u>Lady</u>
                    Mars Film Corp., 1947

Barrie, Jane
     (pseud. of Mildred Savage)

    Parrish

                    <u>Parrish</u>
                    Warner Brothers Pictures, Inc., 1961

Barringer, Emily Dunning

    Bowery to Bellevue (NF)

                    <u>The</u> <u>Girl</u> <u>in</u> <u>White</u>
                    Metro-Goldwyn-Mayer, Inc., 1952

                              22

Barrington, E.
    (pseud. of Lily Beck)

   The Divine Lady: a Romance of Nelson and Emma Hamilton

        <u>Divine</u> <u>Lady</u>
        First National, 1929

Barrington, Pamela
    (pseud. of Muriel Vere Mant Barling)

   Account Rendered

        <u>Account</u> <u>Rendered</u> (G. B.)
        Major/J. Arthur Rank Film Dist., Ltd., 1957

   The Big Chance

        <u>The</u> <u>Big</u> <u>Chance</u> (G. B.)
        Major/J. Arthur Rank Film Dist., Ltd., 1957

Barrows, Sydney Biddle

   Mayflower Madam: the Secret Life of Sydney Biddle Barrows
   (NF)

        <u>Mayflower</u> <u>Madam</u> (TVM)
        Robert Halmi/Columbia Broadcasting System, 1987

Barrymore, Diana and Gerold Frank

   Too Much, Too Soon (NF)

        <u>Too</u> <u>Much,</u> <u>Too</u> <u>Soon</u>
        Warner Brothers Pictures, Inc., 1958

Bart, Jean
    (pseud. of Marie Antoinette Sarlabous)

   The Man Who Reclaimed His Head (P)

        <u>The</u> <u>Man</u> <u>Who</u> <u>Reclaimed</u> <u>His</u> <u>Head</u>
        Universal Motion Pictures Co., 1934

   The Squall (P)

        <u>The</u> <u>Squall</u>
        First National, 1929

Barthel, Joan

>   **A Death in California** (NF)

>   >   A <u>Death</u> <u>in</u> <u>California</u> (TVM)
>   >   Mace Neufeld Prod.-Lorimar Prod/American Broadcasting
>   >   Co., 1985

>   **A Death in Canaan** (NF)

>   >   A <u>Death</u> <u>in</u> <u>Canaan</u> (TVM)
>   >   Chris-Rose Prod.--Warner Brothers Television/Columbia
>   >   Broadcasting System, 1978

Bartlett, Virginia Stivers and Lanier Bartlett

>   **Adios**

>   >   <u>The</u> <u>Lash</u>
>   >   First National, 1930

Bartley, Mrs. Nalbro Isadorah

>   **The Bargain True**

>   >   <u>The</u> <u>Lure</u> <u>of</u> <u>Luxury</u> (*)
>   >   Bluebird Photoplays, Inc., 1918

>   **The Bramble Bush** (S)

>   >   <u>The</u> <u>Bramble</u> <u>Bush</u> (*)
>   >   Vitagraph Co. of America, 1919

>   **Cynic Effect** (S)

>   >   <u>The</u> <u>Country</u> <u>Flapper</u> (*)
>   >   Dorothy Gish Prod./Producers Security Corp., 1922

>   **Miss Antique** (S)

>   >   <u>The</u> <u>Amateur</u> <u>Wife</u> (*)
>   >   Famous Players-Lasky Corp./Famous Players-Lasky Corp.--
>   >   Paramount Pictures Corp.-Artcraft Pictures Corp., 1920

>   **A Woman's Woman**

>   >   A <u>Woman's</u> <u>Woman</u> (*)
>   >   Albion Prod., 1922

Bartram, Clara
>   (pseud. of Alice Duer Miller)

Her First Elopement

Her First Elopement (*)
Realart Pictures Corp./Realart Pictures Corp.-a Star
Prod., 1920

Bassett, Sara Ware

The Harbor Road

Danger Ahead (*)
Universal Film Manufacturing Co., 1921

The Taming of Zenas Henry

Captain Hurricane
RKO Radio Pictures, Inc., 1935

Bassing, Eileen

Home Before Dark

Home Before Dark
Warner Brothers Pictures, Inc., 1958

Baum, Vicki (also see entry below)

Berlin Hotel

Hotel Berlin
Warner Brothers Pictures, Inc., 1945

Big Shot (S)

The Great Flamarion
Republic Pictures Corp., 1945

Grand Hotel (N/P)

Grand Hotel (also based on an English language adaption
of the play, by William A. Drake)
Metro-Goldwyn-Mayer, Inc., 1932

Weekend at the Waldorf
Metro-Goldwyn-Mayer, Inc., 1945

Mortgage on Life

A Woman's Secret
RKO Radio Pictures, Inc., 1949

Baum, Vicki and Gertrude Atherton, Vina Delmar, Sophie Kerr,   and
Ursula Parrott and Polan Banks, Irvin S. Cobb, Zane Grey,
Rupert Hughes, and J. P. Mc Evoy (also see entry above)

Woman Accused

Woman Accused
Paramount Pictures Corp., 1933

Baumer, Marie

Penny Arcarde (P)

Sinner's Holiday
Warner Brothers Pictures, Inc., 1930

Bawden, Nina
(pseud. of Nina Mary Mabel Kark)

On the Run

On the Run (G. B.)
Derick Williams/Children's Film Foundation, 1969

The Solitary Child

The Solitary Child (G. B.)
Beaconsfield/British Lion, 1958

Beardsley, Helen

Who Gets the Drumstick? (NF)

Yours, Mine and Ours
Desilu-Walden Prod./United Artists Film Corp., 1968

Beattie, Ann

Chilly Scenes of Winter

Head Over Heels
United Artists' Film Corp., 1979

Beck, Lily (see E. Barrington)

Bell, Mary Hayley

Whistle Down the Wind

            Whistle Down the Wind
            Allied Film Makers-Beaver/J. Arthur Rank Film Dist.,
            Ltd., 1961

Bell, Pearl Doles

     Her Elephant Man

            Her Elephant Man (*)
            Fox Film Corp., 1920

     His Harvest

            Love's Harvest (*)
            Fox Film Corp., 1920

     Sandra

            Sandra (*)
            Associated Pictures/First National, 1924

Belmont, Eleanor Robson and Harriet Ford

     In the Next Room (P, based on the novel The Mystery of the
     Boule Cabinet, by Burton E. Stevenson)

            In the Next Room (also based on the novel The Mystery
            of the Boule Cabinet; a Detective Story, by Burton E.
            Stevenson, from which the play was derived)
            First National, 1930

            The Case of the Black Parrot (also based on the novel
            The Mystery of the Boule Cabinet; a Detective Story, by
            Burton E. Stevenson, from which the play was derived)
            First National/Warner Brothers Pictures, Inc., 1941

Bennett, Dorothea [Dorothea Bennett Young]

     The Jigsaw Man

            The Jigsaw Man (G. B.)
            Evangrove/United Film, 1984

Bennett, Dorothy and Irving White

     Fly Away Home (P)

            Daughters Courageous
            Warner Brothers Pictures, Inc., 1939

<u>Always</u> <u>in</u> <u>My</u> <u>Heart</u>
Warner Brothers Pictures, Inc., 1942

Bennett-Thompson, Lillian and George Hubbard

Where the Heart Lies (S)

<u>The</u> <u>Love</u> <u>Gambler</u> (*)
Fox Film Corp., 1922

Without Compromise

<u>Without</u> <u>Compromise</u> (*)
Fox Film Corp., 1922

Benson, Sally
    (pseud. of Sara Benson)

Junior Miss (RS)

<u>Junior</u> <u>Miss</u> (also based upon the same named play, by
Jerome Chodorov and Joseph Fields, which was derived
from Benson's stories)
Twentieth Century-Fox Film Corp., 1945

Meet Me in St. Louis (RS)

<u>Meet</u> <u>Me</u> <u>in</u> <u>St.</u> <u>Louis</u>
Metro-Goldwyn-Mayer, Inc., 1944

Benson, Sara (see Sally Benson)

Bentham, Josephine (also see the entry below)

A Bride for Henry (S)

<u>A</u> <u>Bride</u> <u>for</u> <u>Henry</u>
Monogram Pictures Corp., 1937

Bentham, Josephine and Herschel V. Williams (also see the entry
    above)

Janie (P, based on the same named novel, by Bentham)

<u>Janie</u>
Warner Brothers Pictures, Inc., 1944

Berg, Gertrude

Me and Molly (P)

> Molly
> Paramount Pictures Corp., 1950

Berman, Susan

> **Easy Street**
>
> > Easy Street
> > Polygram, 1982

Bernard, Judith (see Judith Michael)

Berriault, Gina

> **The Stone Boy** (S)
>
> > The Stone Boy
> > Twentieth Century-Fox Film Corp., 1984

Berteaut, Simone

> **Piaf** (NF)
>
> > Piaf -- the Early Years (U. S./Fra.)
> > Moritz-Weissman/Twentieth Century-Fox Film Corp., 1982

Bialk, Elisa (also see the entry below)

> **The Sainted Sisters of Sandy Creek** (S)
>
> > The Sainted Sisters (also based on the unproduced play
> > The Sainted Sisters, by Bialk and Alden Nash, which was
> > derived from Bialk's short story)
> > Paramount Pictures Corp., 1948

Bialk, Elisa and Alden Nash (also see the entry above)

> **The Sainted Sisters** (P -- unproduced)
>
> > The Sainted Sisters (also based on the short story "The
> > Sainted Sisters of Sandy Creek," by Elisa Bialk, from
> > which the play was derived)
> > Paramount Pictures Corp., 1948

Bibesco, Princess Marthe (see Lucile Decaux)

Biddle, Cordelia Drexel and Kyle Crichton

My Philadelphia Father (NF)

The Happiest Millionaire (also based upon the play The Happiest Millionaire, by Kyle Crichton, which was derived from Biddle's book)
Walt Disney Prod./Buena Vista Dist. Co., 1967

Bird, Carol and John H. Ayers

Missing Men (S)

Bureau of Missing Persons
First National, 1933

Birtles, Dora

The Overlanders

The Overlanders (G. B.)
Ealing Studios, Ltd./Eagle-Lion, 1946

Bjelke-Petersen, Marie

Jewelled Nights

Jewelled Nights (*) (Austr.)
Louise Lovely, 1925

Black, Betty and Casey Bishop

The Sisterhood

The Ladies Club
Media Home Entertainment-Heron/New Line Cinemac, 1986

Blackwell, Nell and Roland Edwards

The Man from Yesterday (P)

The Man from Yesterday
Paramount Pictures Corp., 1932

Blain, Mary D. (see Tats Blain)

Blain, Tats

(pseud. of Mary D. Blain)

Mother Sir

> <u>Navy Wife</u>
> Allied Artists, 1956

Blaisdell, Anne
> (pseud. of Barbara Elizabeth Linington)

Nightmare

> <u>Fanatic</u> (G. B.)
> Hammer Films-Seven Arts/Columbia Pictures Corp., 1965

Bland, Edith Nesbit (see Edith Nesbit)

Bleneau, Adele

The Nurse's Story: In Which Reality Meets Romance

> <u>Adele</u> (*)
> United Picture Theaters of America. Inc., 1919

Blixen, Karen (see Isak Dinesen)

Block, Anita Rowe

Love and Kisses (P)

> <u>Love and Kisses</u>
> Universal Motion Pictures Co., 1965

Block, Libbie

One Hour Late

> <u>One Hour Late</u>
> Paramount Pictures Corp., 1934

Pin-Up Girl (S)

> <u>Pin-Up Girl</u>
> Twentieth Century-Fox Film Corp., 1944

Wild Calendar

> <u>Caught</u>
> Metro-Goldwyn-Mayer, Inc., 1949

Blume, Judy

    Forever

        <u>Forever</u> (TVM)
        Roger Gimbel Prod./Electrical and Musical Industries
        Television Columbia Broadcasting System, 1978

Blyton, Enid

    Noddy in Toyland (P)

        <u>Noddy in Toyland</u> (G. B.)
        Bill and Michael Luckwell/Luckwell, 1958

Bodington, Nancy H. (see Shelley Smith)

Boland, Bridget

    Cockpit (P)

        <u>The Lost People</u> (G. B.)
        Gainsborough Prod./General Film, 1949

    The Prisoner (P)

        <u>The Prisoner</u> (G. B.)
        Facet-London Independent Prod./Columbia Pictures Corp.,
        1955

Bombeck, Erma

    The Grass is Always Greener Over the Septic Tank (NF)

        <u>The Grass is Always Greener Over the Septic Tank</u> (TVM)
        Joe Hamilton Prod./Columbia Broadcasting System, 1978

Bonacci, Anna

    The Fantastic Year [L'Ora della Fantasia] (P)

        <u>Kiss Me, Stupid</u>
        Phalanx Prod.-Mirsch Corp.-Claude Prod./Lopert
        Pictures, 1964

    L'Heure Eblouissant

        <u>Wife for a Night</u>

Edward Harrison, 1957

Bonett, Emery
    (pseud. of Felicity Winifred Carter Coulson)

A Girl Must Live

   A Girl Must Live
   United Artists' Film Corp., 1941

High Pavement

   My Sister and I
   General Film, 1948

Bonner, Geraldine (also see the two entries below)

Miss Maitland, Private Secretary

      The Girl in the Web (*)
      Jesse D. Hampton Prod.-Robert Brunton Prod./Pathe
      Exchange, Inc., 1920

Bonner, Geraldine and Elmer Harris (also see the entry above and
    the entry below)

Sham (P)

      Sham (*)
      Famous Players-Lasky Corp./Paramount Pictures Corp.,
      1921

Bonner, Geraldine and Hutcheson Boyd (also see the two entries
    above)

Sauce for the Goose (P)

      Sauce for the Goose (*)
      Select Pictures Corp., 1918

Boo, Sigrid

Servant's Entrance

      Servant's Entrance
      Fox Film Corp., 1934

Boothe, Clare (maiden name of Clare Boothe Luce) (also see Clare
    Boothe Luce)

Margin for Error (P)

>Margin for Error
>Twentieth Century-Fox Film Corp., 1943

Borden, Mary

>**Action for Slander**

>>Action for Slander (G. B.)
>>London Saville/United Artists' Film Corp., 1937

Borer, Mary C. (also see the entry below)

>**The House with the Blue Door**

>>The Secret Tunnel (G. B.)
>>Merton Park/General Film Dist., Inc., 1947

Borer, Mary C. and Arnold Ridley (also see the entry above)

>**Tabitha** (P)

>>Who Killed the Cat? (G. B.)
>>Eternal/Grand National Pictures, 1966

Bosher, Kate Langley

>**Frequently Martha** (S)

>>Nobody's Kid (*)
>>Robertson-Cole Pictures, 1921

Bottome, Phyllis
(pseud. of Phyllis Forbes-Dennis)

>**Danger Signal**

>>Danger Signal
>>Warner Brothers Pictures, Inc., 1945

>**Heart of a Child**

>>Heart of a Child (G. B.)
>>Beaconsfield/J. Arthur Rank Film Dist., Ltd., 1958

>**The Mortal Storm**

>>The Mortal Storm
>>Metro-Goldwyn-Mayer, Inc., 1940

Private Worlds

> Private Worlds
> Paramount Pictures Corp., 1935

The Rat

> The Rat
> RKO Radio Pictures, Inc., 1938

Boucicault, Ruth Holt

The Substance of His House

> A House Divided (*)
> J. Stuart Blackton Prod., Inc., 1919

Bourbon, Diana

Roaming Lady

> Roaming Lady
> Columbia Pictures Corp., 1936

Bowen, Catherine Drinker (also see the entry below)

Yankee from Olympus

> The Man with Thirty Sons
> Metro-Goldwyn-Mayer, Inc., 1952

Bowen, Catherine Drinker and Barbara von Meck (also see the entry above)

The Music Lovers (NF)

> The Music Lovers
> Russfilms/United Artist's Film Corp., 1970

Bowen, Elizabeth

The Death of the Heart

> The Death of the Heart (G. B.)
> Granada, 1986

Bowen, Marjorie (also see George Preedy and Joseph Shearing)
(pseud. of Gabrielle Margaret Vere Campbell Long)

35

Mistress Nell Gwynne (also see Mrs. Charles A. Doremus for an additional entry based only on the play Nell Gwyne)

Nell Gwynne (*) (G. B.) (also based on the play Nell Gwyne, by Mrs. Charles A. Doremus, which was derived from Bowen's novel)
W. M. Prod.-British National Films, Ltd./First National, 1926

Bower, B. M.
(pseud. of Bertha Muzzy Sinclair)

Chip of the Flying V

Chip of the Flying V
Universal Motion Pictures Co., 1940

The Happy Family

The Galloping Devil (*)
Canyon Pictures Corp.-States Rights, 1920

Bowker, Fanny

Priscilla the Rake (P)

She was Only a Village Maiden (G. B.)
Sound City Films/Metro-Goldwyn-Mayer, Inc., 1933

Boyd, Eunice Mays (see Theo Durrant)

Boyle, Kay

Avalanche

Avalanche
Producers Releasing Corp., 1946

Maiden, Maiden (S)

Five Days One Summer
Ladd/Columbia Pictures Corp.-Electrical and Musical Industries-Warner Brothers Pictures, Inc., 1982

Brace, Blanche

The Adventures of a Ready Letter Writer (S)

Don't Write Letters (*)

Famous Players-Lasky Corp., 1922

A Letter for Evie
Metro-Goldwyn-Mayer, Inc., 1945

Brackett, Leigh (also see George Sanders)

The Tiger Among Us

13 West Street
Ladd/Columbia Pictures Corp., 1962

Braddon, Mary Elizabeth (also see Mrs. Henry Wood)

East Lynne (P, based on the same named novel, by Mrs. Henry Wood)

East Lynne (*) (Note: sources differ as to whether this film was based on Braddon's play or Wood's novel)
Fox Film Corp., 1916

Lady Audley's Secret

Lady Audley's Secret (*)
Fox Film Corp., 1915

Lady Audley's Secret (*) (G. B.)
Ideal, 1920

Bradford, Barbara Taylor

Hold that Dream

Hold that Dream (TVM)
Robert Bradford Prod.-Taft Entertainment Television-Bradford Portman Prod.-Operation Prime Time, 1986

Bradley, Alice

The Governor's Lady (P)

The Governor's Lady (*)
Jesse L. Lasky Feature Play Co./Paramount Pictures Corp., 1915

The Governor's Lady (*)
Fox Film Corp., 1923

Bradley, Lilian Trimble (also see the two entries below)

37

What Happened Then? (P)

>What Happened Then? (G. B.)
>British International Pictures/Wardour, 1934

Bradley, Lillian Trimble and Forrest Halsey (also see the entry
   below and the entry above)

The Wonderful Thing (P)

>The Wonderful Thing (*)
>Norma Talmadge, 1921

Bradley, Lillian Trimble and George Broadhurst (also see the two
   entries above)

The Woman of the Index (P)

>The Woman on the Index (*)
>Goldwyn Pictures Corp./Goldwyn Dist. Corp., 1919

Bradley, Mary Hastings (also see the entry below)

The Fortieth Door

>The Fortieth Door (*)
>Pathe Exchange, Inc., 1924

The Palace of Darkened Windows

>The Palace of Darkened Windows (*)
>National Picture Theatres, Inc./Select Pictures Corp.,
>1920

Bradley, Mary Hastings and Reba Lee (also see the entry above)

I Passed for White (NF)

>I Passed for White
>Allied Artists, 1960

Braeme, Charlotte M. (see Bertha M. Clay)

Brahms, Caryl and S. J. Simon
   (Caryl Brahms: pseud. of Doris Caroline Abrahams)

The Elephant in White

>Give Us the Moon

38

Gainsborough Prod., 1944

No Nightingales

> The Ghosts of Berkeley Square (G. B.)
> British National Films, Ltd., 1947

Trottie True

> The Gay Lady (G. B.)
> Two Cities Films, Ltd./Eagle-Lion, 1949

Brainerd, Mrs. Edith Rathbone Jacobs (see E. J. Rath)

Brainerd, Eleanor Hoyt

How Could You, Jean?

> How Could You, Jean? (*)
> Mary Pickford/Famous Players-Lasky Corp.--Artcraft
> Pictures Corp., 1918

Pegeen

> Pegeen (*)
> Vitagraph Co. of America, 1920

Brancato, Robin F.

Blinded by the Light

> Blinded by the Light (TVM)
> Time-Life Prod., Inc./Columbia Broadcasting System,
> 1980

Brand, Christianna
  (pseud. of Mary Christianna Milne Lewis)

Death in High Heels

> Death in High Heels (G. B.)
> Marylebone/Exclusive Films, 1947

Green for Danger

> Green for Danger (G. B.)
> Independent Producers-Individual/General Film, 1946

Brande, Dorothea [Dorothea Thompson Brande Collins]

Wake Up and Live (NF)

>Wake Up and Live
>Twentieth Century-Fox Film Corp., 1937

Brandon, Dorothy

>**The Outsider** (P)

>>The Outsider (*)
>>Fox Film Corp., 1926

>>The Outsider
>>Metro-Goldwyn-Mayer, Inc., 1928

>>The Outsider (G. B.)
>>Cinema House/Metro-Goldwyn-Mayer, Inc., 1931

>>The Outsider (G. B.)
>>Associated British Picture Corp., 1939

>**Wild Heather** (P)

>>Wild Heather (*) (G. B.)
>>Hepworth, 1921

Bray, Isobel

>**The Shuttle of Life**

>>The Shuttle of Life (*) (G. B.)
>>British Actors/Phillips, 1920

"Brenda"
(pseud. of Mrs. G. Castle Smith)

>**Froggy's Little Brother**

>>Froggy's Little Brother (*) (G. B.)
>>Stoll/Equity British Film Prod., 1921

Brent, Joanna

>**A Few Days in Weasel Creek**

>>A Few Days in Weasel Creek (TVM)
>>Hummingbird Prod., Inc.-Warner Brothers Television/
>>Columbia Broadcasting System, 1981

Breuil, Beta

The Message of the Lilies (S)

> When a Woman Sins (*)
> Fox Film Corp., 1918

Breuer, Bessie

Memory of Love

> In Name Only
> RKO Radio Pictures, Inc., 1939

Bridgers, Ann Preston and George Abbott

Coquette: a Play in Three Acts (P)

> Coquette
> Pickford/United Artists Film Corp., 1929

Brightman, Virginia Hudson

Sonny

> Teeth (*) (also based on the short story "Teeth," by
> Clinton H. Stagg)
> Fox Film Corp., 1924

Brink, Carol R.

Caddie Woodlawn (RS/P)

> Caddie
> Hemdale, 1976

Stopover

> All I Desire
> Universal International Motion Pictures, 1953

Bristow, Gwen [Mrs. Bruce Manning] (see the entry below)

Jubilee Trail

> Jubilee Trail
> Republic Pictures Corp., 1954

Tomorrow is Forever

> Tomorrow is Forever

RKO Radio Pictures, Inc., 1946

Bristow, Gwen [Mrs. Bruce Manning] and Bruce Manning (see the
    entry above)

The Invisible Host

> The Ninth Guest (also based on the play The Ninth
> Guest, by Owen Davis)
> Columbia Pictures Corp., 1934

Bronder, Lucia

Rockabye (P)

> Rockabye
> RKO Radio Pictures, Inc., 1932

Bronson, Mrs. Owen

The Scorching Way (S)

> The Hidden Scar (*)
> Peerless/World Film Corp., 1916

Bronte, Charlotte

Jane Eyre

> Jane Eyre (*)
> Whitman Features Co./Blinkhorn Photoplays Corp., 1914
>
> Woman and Wife (*)
> Select Pictures Corp., 1918
>
> Jane Eyre (*)
> Hugo Ballin Prod./W. W. Hodkinson Corp., 1921
>
> Jane Eyre
> Monogram Pictures Corp., 1934
>
> I Walked with a Zombie
> RKO Radio Pictures Corp., 1943
> (Note: though uncredited, according to producer Val
> Lewton, this movie is loosely based on Bronte's novel.
> See Clarens, p. 113; Hardy, p. 82; and Stanley, p.
> 124.)
>
> Jane Eyre
> Twentieth Century-Fox Film Corp., 1944

Jane Eyre
Omnibus-Sagittarius Prod./British Lion, 1970

Shirley

Shirley (*) (G. B.)
Ideal, 1922

Bronte, Emily

Wuthering Heights

Wuthering Heights (*) (G. B.)
Ideal, 1920

Wuthering Heights
United Artists' Film Corp., 1939

Wuthering Heights (G. B.)
American International Pictures/Anglo-Electrical and
Musical Industries Film Dist., 1970

Brooke, Eleanor and Jean Kerr

The King of Hearts (P)

That Certain Feeling
Paramount Pictures Corp., 1956

Brooks, Virginia

Little Lost Sister

Little Lost Sister (*)
Selig Polyscope Co.-a Red Seal Play/K-E-S-E Service,
1917

Brown, Bernice and Elsie Janis, Sophie Kerr, Dorothy Parker, and
Carolyn Wells and Robert Gordon Anderson, Louis Bromfield,
George Agnew Chamberlain, Frank Craven, Rube Goldberg,
Wallace Irwin, George Barr McCutcheon, Meade Minnigerode,
Gerald Mygatt, George Palmer Putnam, Kermit Roosevelt,
Edward Streeter, John V. A. Weaver, H. C. Witwer, and
Alexander Woollcott

Bobbed Hair

Bobbed Hair (*)
Warner Brothers Pictures, Inc., 1925

Brown, Beth

    Applause

        <u>Applause</u>
        Paramount Famous Lasky Corp, 1929

    Ballyhoo

        <u>Ballyhoo</u>
        Metro-Goldwyn-Mayer, Inc., 1930

Brown, Grace Drew and Katherine Pinkerton

    Spring Fever (S)

        <u>Nancy</u> <u>From</u> <u>Nowhere</u> (*)
        Realart Pictures Corp./Paramount Pictures Corp., 1922

Brown, Helen Gurley

    Sex and the Single Girl (NF)

        <u>Sex</u> <u>and</u> <u>the</u> <u>Single</u> <u>Girl</u>
        Reynard Prod./Warner Brothers Pictures, Inc., 1964

Brown, Joan Winmill

    No Longer Alone (NF)

        <u>No</u> <u>Longer</u> <u>Alone</u>
        World Wide, 1978

Brown, Olga Hall

    The Slave Bracelet (S)

        <u>The</u> <u>Other</u> <u>Woman</u> (G. B.)
        Majestic/United Artists Film Corp., 1931

Brown, Vera

    Redhead

        <u>Redhead</u>
        Monogram Pictures Corp., 1933

        <u>Redhead</u>
        Monogram Pictures Corp., 1941

Browne, Eleanor

    Highway to Romance

        Cross Country Romance
        RKO Radio Pictures, Inc., 1940

Brush, Katharine

    Free Woman (S)

        My Love is Yours
        Paramount Pictures Corp., 1939

    Glitter (S)

        The Dropkick (*)
        First National, 1927

    Maid of Honor (S)

        Lady of Secrets
        Columbia Pictures Corp., 1936

    Mannequin (S)

        Mannequin
        Metro-Goldwyn-Mayer, Inc., 1937

    Night Club (S)

        Night Club
        Paramount Pictures Corp., 1929

    Red-Headed Woman

        Red Headed Woman
        Metro-Goldwyn-Mayer, Inc., 1932

    Young Man of Manhattan

        Young Man of Manhattan
        Paramount Pictures Corp., 1930

Bryan, Grace Lovell

    Class (S)

        You Never Can Tell (*) (also based on the short story
        "You Never Can Tell," by Bryan)
        Realart Pictures Corp., 1920

You Never Can Tell (S)

> You Never Can Tell (*) (also based on the short story
> "Class," by Bryan)
> Realart Pictures Corp., 1920

Bryant, Marguerite

Richard

> Railroaded (*)
> Universal Motion Pictures Co., 1923
>
> The Breathless Moment (*)
> Universal Motion Pictures Co., 1924

Buck, Pearl S.

The Big Wave

> The Big Wave (U. S./Jp.)
> Stratton Prod.-Toho Co./Allied Artists, 1962

China Sky

> China Sky
> RKO Radio Pictures, Inc., 1945

Dragon Seed

> Dragon Seed
> Metro-Goldwyn-Mayer, Inc., 1944

The Good Earth

> The Good Earth
> Metro-Goldwyn-Mayer, Inc., 1937

Satan Never Sleeps

> Satan Never Sleeps (U. S./G. B.)
> Twentieth Century-Fox Film Corp., 1962

Buffington, Stephanie

Three on a Date (NF)

> Three on a Date (TVM)
> American Broadcasting Co. Circle Films/American
> Broadcasting Co., 1978

Buhler, Kitty

    Time is a Memory (S)

        China Doll
        Romaina Prod., 1958

Bull, Lois

    Broadway Virgin

        Manhattan Butterfly
        Imperial, 1935

Burbridge, Betty

    Suicide Bridge (S)

        False Pretenses
        Chesterfield Motion Pictures/First Division Dist., 1935

Burkhardt, Eve (see Rob Eden)

Burnaby, Anne

    Mixed Company (S)

        Operation Bullshine (G. B.)
        Associated British Picture Corp./Seven Arts, Inc.-
        Manhattan Films International, 1963

Burnett, Frances Hodgson (also see the two entries below)

    The Dawn of a Tomorrow (N/P)

        The Dawn of a Tomorrow (*)
        Famous Players Film Co./Paramount Pictures Corp., 1915

        The Dawn of a Tomorrow (*)
        Famous Players-Lasky Corp./Paramount Pictures Corp.,
        1924

    Edith's Burglar, a Dramatic Sketch in One Act (P)

        The Family Secret (*) (also based on the short story
        "Edith's Burglar, a Story for Children," by Burnett,
        from which the play was derived)
        Universal Motion Pictures Co., 1924

    Edith's Burglar, a Story for Children (S)

The Family Secret (*) (also based on the play Edith's
Burglar, a Dramatic Sketch in One Act, by Burnett,
which was derived from her short story)
Universal Motion Pictures Co., 1924

Esmeralda (S)

Esmeralda (*) (also based on the same named play, by
Burnett and William Gillette)
Famous Players Film Co./Paramount Pictures Corp., 1915

A Fair Barbarian

The Fair Barbarian (*)
Pallas Pictures/Paramount Pictures Corp., 1917

A Lady of Quality

A Lady of Quality (*) (also based on the same named
play, by Burnett and Stephen Townsend)
Famous Players Film Co./State Rights, 1914

A Lady of Quality (*)
Universal Motion Pictures Co., 1924

Little Lord Fauntleroy

Little Lord Fauntleroy (*) (G. B.)
Natural Colour Kinematograph Co., 1914

Little Lord Fauntleroy (*)
Mary Pickford/United Artists Film Corp., 1921

Little Lord Fauntleroy
United Artists Film Corp., 1936

Little Lord Fauntleroy (TVM) (G. B.)
Norman Rosemont Prod./Gem-Toby Organisation, 1980

A Little Princess (P, based on the novel Sara Crewe, by
Burnett)

The Little Princess (*)
Mary Pickford/Artcraft Pictures Corp., 1917

The Little Princess
Twentieth Century-Fox Film Corp., 1939

A Little Princess (TVM)
Colin Shindler/WNET, 1987

Louisiana

Louisiana (*)

Famous Players-Lasky Corp./Famous Players-Lasky Corp.--Paramount Pictures Corp., 1919

The Pretty Sister of Jose (N/P)

Pretty Sister of Jose (*)
Famous Players Film Co./Paramount Pictures Corp., 1915

The Secret Garden

The Secret Garden (*)
Famous Players-Lasky Corp./Famous Players-Lasky Corp.;
Paramount Pictures Corp., 1919

The Secret Garden
Metro-Goldwyn-Mayer, Inc., 1949

The Secret Garden (TVM) (G. B.)
British Broadcasting Corp. TV--Dorothea
Brooking/Playhouse Video, 1975

The Secret Garden (TVM)
Norman Rosemont Prod./Columbia Broadcasting System,
1987

The Shuttle

The Shuttle (*)
Select Pictures Corp./Select Pictures Corp.-Select Star
Series, 1918

That Lass o' Lowries

Secret Love (*)
Bluebird Photoplays, Inc., 1916

Flame of Life (*)
Universal Motion Pictures Co., 1923

Burnett, Frances Hodgson and Stephen Townsend (also see the entry
above and the entry below)

A Lady of Quality (P)

A Lady of Quality (*) (also based on the same named
novel, by Burnett, from which the play was derived)
Famous Players Film Co./Paramount Pictures Corp., 1914

Burnett, Frances Hodgson and William Gillette (also see the two
entries above)

Esmeralda (P)

<u>Esmeralda</u> (*) (also based on the same named short
story, by Burnett, from which the play was derived)
Famous Players Film Co., 1915

Burnford, Sheila

    The Incredible Journey

        <u>The</u> <u>Incredible</u> <u>Journey</u>
        Walt Disney Prod.-Cangary, Ltd./Buena Vista Dist. Co.,
        1962

Burnham, Barbara and James Hilton

    Goodbye Mr. Chips   (P, based on the same named novel, by
    Hilton)

        <u>Goodbye</u> <u>Mr.</u> <u>Chips</u>
        Metro-Goldwyn-Mayer, Inc., 1939

        <u>Goodbye</u> <u>Mr.</u> <u>Chips</u>
        Metro-Goldwyn-Mayer, Inc., 1969

Burnham, Clara Louise

    Heart's Haven

        <u>Heart's</u> <u>Haven</u> (*)
        Benjamin B. Hampton Prod./W. W. Hodkinson Corp., 1922

    Jewel; A Chapter in Her Life

        <u>Jewel</u> (*)
        Universal Film Manufacturing Co./Universal Film
        Manufacturing Co.-a Broadway Universal Feature, 1915

        <u>A</u> <u>Chapter</u> <u>in</u> <u>Her</u> <u>Life</u> (*)
        Universal Motion Pictures Co., 1923

    The Open Shutters: a Novel

        <u>The</u> <u>Opened</u> <u>Shutters</u>
        Universal Film Manufacturing Co.-Gold Seal/Universal
        Film Manufacturing Co., 1914

Burr, Jane
    (pseud. of Rose Burr)

    I'll Tell My Husband (S)

        <u>The</u> <u>Arnelo</u> <u>Affair</u>

Metro-Goldwyn-Mayer, Inc., 1947

Burr, Rose (see Jane Burr)

Burt, Katharine Newlin

Body and Soul

Body and Soul (*)
Metro-Goldwyn-Mayer, Inc., 1927

The Branding Iron

The Branding Iron (*)
Goldwyn Pictures Corp.; Reginald Barker Prod./Goldwyn
Dist. Corp., 1920

The Red-Haired Husband (S)

The Silent Rider (*)
Universal International Motion Pictures, 1927

Snowblind

Snowblind (*)
Goldwyn Pictures Corp., 1921

Summoned (S)

The Way of a Girl (*)
Metro-Goldwyn-Mayer, Inc., 1925

Burton, Beatrice (maiden name of Mrs. Beatrice Burton Morgan)
(also see Beatrice Burton Morgan)

The Flapper Wife

His Jazz Bride (*)
Warner Brothers Pictures, Inc., 1926

Footloose

Footloose Widows (*)
Warner Brothers Pictures, Inc., 1926

Sally's Shoulders

Sally's Shoulders (*)
Film Booking Office Prod., Inc., 1928

Bushnell, Adelyn

Glory (P)

> Laughing at Trouble
> Twentieth Century-Fox Film Corp., 1936

Butler, Rachel Barton

Mamma's Affair: a Comedy in Three Acts (P)

> Mamma's Affair (*)
> Constance Talmadge Film Co./Associated First National,
> 1921

Byford, Joan Roy and Evadne Price

The Phantom Light (P, based on the novel The Haunted Light
by Evadne Price)

> The Phantom Light (G. B.)
> Gainsborough Prod./Gaumount, 1935

Byrne, Dorothea "Dolly" (see "Dorothea Donn-Byrne and Gilda
Varesi Archibald" entry)

Byrne, Muriel St. Clare and Dorothy Sayers

Busman's Honeymoon (P)

> Busman's Holiday (G. B.) (also based on the novel
> Busman's Honeymoon, by Dorothy Sayers, from which the
> play was derived)
> Metro-Goldwyn-Mayer British, 1940

Caddie
     (unidentified pseud.)

     Caddie, a Sydney Barmaid (NF)

               Caddie (Austr.)
               Atlantic, 1976

Cadieux, Pauline

     La Lampe dans La Fenetre [The Lamp in the Window]

               Cordelia (Fra./Can.)
               National Film board of Canada/Mutual Film Corp., 1980

Caine, Lynn

     Widow (NF)

               Widow (TVM)
               Lorimar Prod./National Broadcasting Co., 1976

Caldwell, Anne

     The Nest Egg (P)

               Marry Me (*)
               Famous Players-Lasky Corp./Paramount Pictures Corp.,
               1925

     Top O' the Mornin'; a Comedy in Three Acts (P)

               The Top O' the Morning (*)
               Universal Film Manufacturing Co., 1922

Calvan, Doris and E. B. "Zeke" Calvan (Note: sources differ
     about whether the last names are "Calvan" or "Culvan.")

     Hey Rookie (MP)

               Hey, Rookie
               Columbia Pictures Corp., 1944

Cameron, Anne

    Green Dice (S)

        Mr. Skitch
        Twentieth Century-Fox Film Corp., 1933

Cameron, George
    (pseud. of Gladys S. Rankin Drew)

    Agnes (P)

        A Million Bid (*)
        Vitagraph Co. of America-Broadway Star Features
        Co./General Film-Special Features Dept. by arrangement
        with Broadway Star Features Co., 1914

        A Million Bid (*)
        Warner Brothers Pictures, Inc., 1927

Cameron, (Lady) Mary

    Mr. Dayton, Darling

        Many Happy Returns
        Paramount Pictures Corp., 1934

Campbell, Alice

    Juggernaut

        Juggernaut (G. B.)
        J. H. Prod./Wardour, 1936

        The Temptress (G. B.)
        Bushey/Ambassador Film Prod., 1949

Campbell, Evelyn

    Barter (S)

        A Soul for Sale (*)
        Universal Film Manufacturing Co. (?)-Bluebird
        Photoplays, Inc. (?)/State Rights-Renowned Pictures
        Corp.-Jewel Prod., Inc. , 1917

    Empty Hearts (S)

        Empty Hearts (*)
        Banner Prod., 1924

Nobody's Bride (S)

>Which Woman (*)
>Bluebird Photoplays, Inc., 1918
>
>Nobody's Bride (*)
>Universal Film Manufacturing Co., 1923

Remorse (S)

>Masked Angel (*)
>Chadwick Pictures/First Division, 1928

Splurge (S)

>Early to Wed (*)
>Fox Film Corp., 1926

Yesterday's Wife (S)

>Yesterday's Wife (*)
>Columbia Pictures Corp./C. B. C. Film Sales, 1923

Campbell, Leslie (see R. A. Dick)

Campbell, Phyllis

The White Hen

>The White Hen (*) (G. B.)
>Zodiac/Walker, 1921

Canada, Lena

To Elvis with Love (NF)

>Touched by Love
>Columbia Pictures Corp., 1980

Canfield, Dorothy
(maiden name of Dorothea Frances Canfield Fisher)

The Eternal Masculine (S)

>Two Heads on a Pillow
>Liberty Pictures Corp., 1934

The Home-Maker

>The Home Maker (*)
>Universal Motion Pictures Co.-Jewel Prod., Inc., 1925

Carey, Enestine Gilbreath and Frank B. Gilbreath, Jr.

Belles on their Toes (NF)

Belles on their Toes
Twentieth Century-Fox Film Corp., 1952

Cheaper by the Dozen (NF)

Cheaper by the Dozen
Twentieth Century-Fox Film Corp., 1950

Carey, Gabrielle and Kathy Lette

Puberty Blues

Puberty Blues (Austr.)
Limelight/Universal Classics, 1983

Carleton, Marjorie Chalmers

Cry Wolf

Cry Wolf
Warner Brothers Pictures, Inc., 1947

Carlisle, Helen Grace

Mother's Cry

Mother's Cry
First National-Vitaphone Corp. of America, 1930

Carnegie, Margaret

Morgan the Bold Bushranger (NF)

Mad Dog Morgan (Austr.)
Motion Picture Co., 1976

Carpenter, Margaret

Experiment Perilous

Experiment Perilous
RKO Radio Pictures, Inc., 1944

Carpenter, Teresa

    Death of a Playmate (NF)

        Star 80
        Ladd/Warner Brothers Pictures, Inc., 1983

Carr, Mary Jane

    **Children of the Covered Wagon; a Story of the Old Oregon
    Trail**

        Westward Ho the Wagons!
        Buena Vista Dist. Co., 1956

Carrington, Elaine Sterne and John Wray and J. C. Nugent

    Nightstick (P)

        Alibi
        Feature Prod., Inc./United Artists Film Corp., 1929

Carroll, Gladys

    As the Earth Turns

        As the Earth Turns
        Warner Brothers Pictures, Inc., 1934

Carson, Rachel L.

    The Sea Around Us (NF)

        The Sea Around Us
        RKO Radio Pictures, Inc., 1953

Carter, Angela

    The Company of Wolves (RS)

        The Company of Wolves (G. B.)
        Inc. Television Co.-Palace Prod./Palace Prod., 1984

Carter, Mary

    Tell Me My Name: a Novel

        Tell Me My Name (TVM)
        Talent Associates, Ltd./Columbia Broadcasting System,

1977

Carter, Winifred

   Princess Fritz

      <u>Mrs.</u> <u>Fitzherbert</u> (G. B.)
      British National Films, Ltd./Pathe Exchange, Inc., 1947

Cartland, Barbara

   The Flame is Love

      <u>The</u> <u>Flame</u> <u>is</u> <u>Love</u> (TVM)
      Friendly-O'Herlihy, Ltd.--National Broadcasting Co.
      Entertainment/National Broadcasting Co., 1979

   A Hazard of Hearts

      <u>A</u> <u>Hazard</u> <u>of</u> <u>Hearts</u> (TVM) (G. B.)
      Albert Fennell-John Hough--Grade Co.--Gainsborough
      Pictures/Columbia Broadcasting System, 1987

Caruso, Dorothy

   Enrico Caruso, his Life and Death (NF)

      <u>The</u> <u>Great</u> <u>Caruso</u>
      Metro-Goldwyn-Mayer, Inc., 1951

Casey, Rosemary and Nancy Hamilton and James Shute

   Return Engagement (P)

      <u>Fools</u> <u>for</u> <u>Scandal</u>
      Warner Brothers Pictures, Inc., 1938

Caspary, Vera (also see the two entries below)

   Bedelia

      <u>Bedelia</u> (G. B.)
      John Corfield Prod./General Film, 1946

   Easy Living (P)

      <u>Easy</u> <u>Living</u>
      Paramount Pictures Corp., 1937

   Gardenia (Note: Emmens claims this is a published short

story, but we have found no confirmation.)

> The Blue Gardenia
> Warner Brothers Pictures, Inc., 1953

Laura

> Laura (also based on the play Laura, by Caspary and
> George Sklar, which was derived from Caspary's novel)
> Twentieth Century-Fox Film Corp., 1944

Odd Thursday (S)

> Such Women are Dangerous
> Twentieth Century Fox Film Corp., 1934

Suburbs (S)

> The Night of June 13th
> Paramount Pictures Corp., 1932

Caspary, Vera and George Sklar (also see the entry above and
    below)

Laura (P)

> Laura (also based on the same named novel, by Caspary,
> from which the play was derived)
> Twentieth Century-Fox Film Corp., 1944

Caspary, Vera and Winifred Lenihan (also see the two entries
    above)

Blind Mice (P)

> Working Girls
> Paramount Pictures Corp., 1931

Cassady, Carolyn

Heart Beat (NF)

> Heart Beat
> Warner Brothers Pictures, Inc., 1980

Castle, Agnes and Egerton Castle

The Bath Comedy

> Sweet Kitty Bellairs (also based on the play Sweet
> Kitty Bellairs, by David Belasco, which was derived

59

from the Castles' novel)
Warner Brothers Pictures, Inc., 1930

Rose of the World

Rose of the World (*)
Famous Players-Lasky Corp./Artcraft Pictures Corp.--
Famous Players-Lasky Corp., 1918

Secret Orchard

Secret Orchard (*) (also based on the play Secret
Orchard, by Channing Pollock)
Jesse L. Lasky Feature Play Co./Paramount Pictures
Corp., 1915

Castle, Irene

My Husband (NF)

The Story of Vernon and Irene Castle (also based on the
nonfiction book My Memories of Vernon Castle, by
Castle)
RKO Radio Pictures, Inc., 1939

My Memories of Vernon Castle (NF)

The Story of Vernon and Irene Castle (also based on the
nonfiction book My Husband, by Castle)
RKO Radio Pictures, Inc., 1939

Cathcart, Countess Vera

The Woman was Tempted

The Woman Tempted (*) (G. B.)
M.E. Prod./Wardour, 1926

Cather, Willa

A Lost Lady

A Lost Lady (*)
Warner Brothers Pictures, Inc., 1924

A Lost Lady
First National, 1934

Caylor, Rose and Ben Hecht

Man-Eating Tiger (P)

Spring Tonic
Twentieth Century-Fox Film Corp., 1935

Chais, Pamela

Six Weeks in August (P)

Guess Who's Sleeping in My Bed? (TVM)
American Broadcasting Co. Circle Films, 1973

Chamberlain, Lucia

Blackmail (S)

Blackmail (*)
Screen Classics, Inc.-a Metro Special Prod./Metro
Pictures Corp., 1920

The Other Side of the Door

The Other Side of the Door (*)
American Film/Mutual Film Corp.-Mutual Masterpictures
De Luxe Ed., 1916

Chambrun, Clara De Longworth (see Countess de Chambrun)

Chambrun, Countess de
(pseud. of Clara De Longworth Chambrun)

Playing With Souls: a Novel

Playing With Souls (*)
Thomas H. Ince/First National, 1925

Chapin, Anna Alice (also see the two entries below)

The Eagle's Mate

The Eagle's Mate (*)
Famous Players Film Co./Paramount Pictures Corp., 1914

Mountain Madness

Mountain Madness (*)
Lloyd Carleton Prod.-Clermont Photoplays Corp./Republic
Dist. Corp., 1920

Chapin, Anna Alice and Cleveland Moffatt (also see the entry

61

above and the entry below)

The Girl of Gold

> The <u>Girl</u> <u>of</u> <u>Gold</u> (*)
> Regal Pictures/Producers Dist. Corp., 1925

Chapin, Anna Alice and Robert Peyton Carter (also see the two
    entries above)

The Deserter (P)

> <u>Sacred</u> <u>Silence</u> (*)
> Fox Film Corp., 1919

Charles, Theresa
    (pseud. of Irene Maude Mossop Swatridge alone and in
    conjunction with Charles Swatridge)

Happy Now I Go

> The <u>Woman</u> <u>with</u> <u>No</u> <u>Name</u> (G. B.)
> Independent Film Producers/Associated British and Pathe
> Film Dist., 1950

Chase, Mary Coyle

Bernadine (P)

> <u>Bernadine</u>
> Twentieth Century Fox Film Corp., 1957

Sorority House (P)

> <u>Sorority</u> <u>House</u>
> RKO Radio Pictures, Inc., 1939

Harvey (P)

> <u>Harvey</u>
> General Film, 1950

Chauncy, Nan

They Found a Cave

> <u>They</u> <u>Found</u> <u>a</u> <u>Cave</u>
> Children's Film Foundation, 1962

Cheavans, Martha

Penny Serenade (S)

> Penny Serenade
> Columbia Pictures Corp., 1941

Chester, Lillian Eleanor and George Randolph Chester

The Enemy

> The Enemy (*)
> Vitagraph Co. of America-a Blue Ribbon Feature/Greater
> Vitagraph, 1916

Childress, Alice

A Hero Ain't Nothing but a Sandwich

> A Hero Ain't Nothing but a Sandwich
> Radnitz-Mattel/New World Cinema, 1977

Cholmondeley, Mary

Moth and Rust

> Moth and Rust (*) (G. B.)
> Progress/Butcher's Film Service, 1921

Red Pottage

> Red Pottage (*) (G. B.)
> Ideal, 1918

Chopin, Kate

The Awakening

> The End of August
> Enterprise Pictures, 1982

Chou, Elizabeth (see Suyin, Han)

Christian, Tina Chad

Baby Love

> Baby Love (G. B.)
> Avton Film Prod./Avco Embassy Pictures, 1968

Christie, Agatha (also see the entry below)

The ABC Murders

> The Alphabet Murders (G. B.)
> Metro-Goldwyn-Mayer British, 1965

Appointment with Death

> Appointment with Death
> Golan-Globus/Cannon Screen Entertainment, 1988

At Bertram's Hotel

> At Bertram's Hotel (TVM) (G. B./U. S./Austr.)
> British Broadcasting Corp. TV-Arts and Entertainment
> Network-The Seven network/British Broadcasting Corp.
> TV, 1986

Black Coffee (P)

> Black Coffee (G. B.)
> Twickenham/Woolf and Freedman Film Service, 1931

The Body in the Library

> The Body in the Library (TVM) (G. B.)
> British Broadcasting Corp. TV, 1984

A Caribbean Mystery

> Agatha Christie's "A Caribbean Mystery" (TVM)
> Stan Margulies Prod.-Warner Brothers Television/
> Columbia Broadcasting System, 1983

The Coming of Mr. Quin (S)

> The Passing of Mr. Quinn (*) (G. B.)
> Strand-Cecil Cattermoul/Argosy Prod., 1928

Dead Man's Folly

> Dead Man's Folly (TVM)
> Warner Brothers Television/Columbia Broadcasting
> System, 1986

Death on the Nile

> Death on the Nile (G. B.)
> Mersham/Electrical and Musical Industries, 1978

Endless Night

> Endless Night (G. B.)

Braywild-National Film Trustee-British Lion Film Corp.-
Electrical and Musical Industries/British Lion, 1972

Evil Under the Sun

Evil Under the Sun (G. B.)
Mersham-Titan/Columbia Pictures Corp.-Electrical and
Musical Industries-Warner Brothers Pictures, Inc., 1982

4:50 from Paddington

Murder She Said (G. B.)
Metro-Goldwyn-Mayer British, 1961

4:50 from Paddington (TVM) (G. B.)
British Broadcasting Corp., 1987

Funerals are Fatal

Murder at the Gallop (G. B.)
Metro-Goldwyn-Mayer British, 1963

Lord Edgware Dies

Lord Edgware Dies (G. B.)
Realart Pictures Corp./RKO Radio Pictures, Inc., 1934

Thirteen at Dinner (TVM)
Warner Brothers Television/Columbia Broadcasting
System, 1985

The Mirror Crack'd from Side to Side

The Mirror Crack'd (G. B.)
GW Films/Columbia Pictures Corp.-Electrical and Musical
Industries-Warner Brothers Pictures, Inc., 1981

The Moving Finger

The Moving Finger (TVM) (G. B.)
British Broadcasting Corp., 1985

Mrs. McGinty's Dead

Murder Most Foul (G. B.)
Metro-Goldwyn-Mayer British, 1964

The Murder at the Vicarage

Murder at the Vicarage (TVM) (G. B.)
British Broadcasting Corp., 1986

Murder in Three Acts

Agatha Christie's "Murder in Three Acts" (TVM)

Warner Brothers Television/Columbia Broadcasting system, 1986

A Murder is Announced

A Murder is Announced (TVM) (G. B.)
Guy Slater-British Broadcasting Corp.-Arts and
Entertainment, 1985

Murder is Easy

Agatha Christie's "Murder is Easy" (TVM)
David Wolper-Stan Margulies Prod.--Warner Brothers
Television/Columbia Broadcasting System, 1982

The Murder of Roger Ackroyd

Alibi (G. B.)
Twickenham, 1931

Murder on the Orient Express

Murder on the Orient Express (G. B.)
GW Films/Electrical and Musical Industries, 1974

Murder with Mirrors

Murder with Mirrors (TVM)
Hajeno Prod.-Warner Brothers Television/Columbia
Broadcasting System, 1985

Nemesis

Nemesis (TVM) (G. B.)
George Gallachio/British Broadcasting Corp. TV, 1987

Ordeal by Innocence

Ordeal by Innocence (G. B.)
London Cannon Screen Entertainment, 1985

Philomel Cottage (S)

Love from a Stranger (G. B.) (also based on the play
Love from a Stranger, by Frank Vesper, which was
derived from Christie's short story)
Trafalgar Film Prod./United Artists' Film Corp., 1937

Love From a Stranger (also based on the play Love from
a Stranger, by Frank Vesper, which was derived from
Christie's short story)
Eagle-Lion, 1947

A Pocket Full of Rye

A Pocket Full of Rye (TVM) (G. B.)
George Gallachio/British Broadcasting Corp. TV, 1985

The Secret Adversary

The Secret Adversary (TVM) (G. B.)
London Weekend Television, 1983

The Seven Dials Mystery

The Seven Dials Mystery (TVM) (G. B.)
London Weekend Television, 1981

The Sleeping Murder

The Sleeping Murder (TVM) (G. B./U. S./Austr.)
British Broadcasting Corp. TV-Arts and Entertainment
Network-The Seven Network/British Broadcasting Corp.
TV, 1986

Sparkling Cyanide

Agatha Christie's "Sparkling Cyanide" (TVM)
Stan Margulies Prod./Warner Brothers Television, 1983

The Spider's Web (P)

The Spider's Web (G. B.)
Danziger/United Artists' Film Corp., 1960

Ten Little Indians (N/P)

And Then There were None (G. B.)
Twentieth Century-Fox Film Corp., 1945

Ten Little Indians (G. B.)
Tenlit Films/WPD, 1965

Ten Little Indians (G. B.)
Filibuster/Electrical and Musical Industries, 1974

Why Didn't They Ask Evans?

Why Didn't They Ask Evans? (TVM) (G. B.) (Note: a
British miniseries, this was recut as a three hour film
for American TV.)
London Weekend Television, 1981

Witness for the Prosecution (S/P)

Witness for the Prosecution
United Artists Film Corp., 1957

Witness for the Prosecution (TVM)
Norman Rosemont Prod.-United Artists Television/

Columbia Broadcasting System, 1982

Christie, Agatha and Michael Morton (also see the entry above)

Alibi (P)

Alibi (G. B.)
Twickenham/Woolf and Freedman Film Service, 1931

Christie, Dorothy and Campbell Christie

Carrington, V. C. (P)

Carrington, V. C.
Remus/Independent Film Dist., 1954

Grand National Night (P)

Grand National Night (G. B.)
Talisman/Renown Pictures Corp., 1953

His Excellency (P)

His Excellency (G. B.,)
Ealing Studios, Ltd./General Film, 1952

Someone at the Door (P)

Someone at the Door (G. B.)
British International Pictures/Wardour, 1936

Someone at the Door (G. B.)
Hammer Films/Exclusive Films, 1950

Christman, Elizabeth

A Nice Italian Girl

Black Market Baby (TVM)
Brut Prod./American Broadcasting Co., 1978

Clark, Mabel Margaret (see Lesley Storm)

Clark, Mary Higgins

The Cradle Will Fall

The Cradle Will Fall (TVM)
Cates Films, Inc.-Procter and Gamble Prod./Columbia,
Broadcasting System, 1983

Stillwatch

>Stillwatch (TVM)
>Zev Braun-Lynda Carter/Columbia Broadcasting System,
>1987

A Stranger is Watching

>A Stranger is Watching
>Metro-Goldwyn-Mayer, Inc., 1982

Where are the Children?

>Where are the Children?
>Columbia Pictures Corp., 1986

Clatten, Lillian (see Margaret Mayo)

Clauser, Suzanne

A Girl Named Sooner

>A Girl Named Sooner (TVM)
>Frederick Brogger Associates--Twentieth Century-Fox
>Film Corp./National Broadcasting Co., 1975

Clay, Bertha M.
     (pseud. of Charlotte M. Braeme and others)

Dora Thorne

>Dora Thorne (*)
>Biograph Co./General Film, 1915

My Poor Wife

>His Wife (*)
>Thanhouser Film Corp., 1915

Thorns and Orange Blossoms

>Thorns and Orange Blossoms (*)
>Preferred Pictures/Al Lictman Corp., 1922

Cleaver, Vera and Bill Cleaver

Where the Lilies Bloom

>Where the Lilies Bloom
>United Artists' Film Corp., 1974

69

Clifford, Mrs. W. K.

    Eve's Lover (S)

        Eve's Lover (*)
        Warner Brothers Pictures, Inc., 1925

    The Likeness of the Night (P)

        The Likeness of the Night (*) (G. B.)
        Screen Plays/British Exhibitors' Films, 1921

Clifton, Ethel and Brenda Fowler

    The Doormat (P)

        The Honeymoon Express (*)
        Warner Brothers Pictures, Inc., 1926

Clooney, Rosemary and Raymond Strait

    This for Remembrance (NF)

        Rosie: The Rosemary Clooney Story (TVM)
        Charles Fries Prod.-Alan Sacks Prod./Columbia
        Broadcasting System, 1982

Clugston, Katherine Thatcher

    The Last Gentleman (P)

        The Last Gentleman
        Twentieth Century-Fox Film Corp., 1934

    These Days (P)

        Finishing School
        RKO Radio Pictures, Inc., 1934

Cobb, Elisabeth [Elisabeth Cobb Chapman]

    She Was a Lady

        She Was a Lady
        Twentieth Century-Fox Film Corp., 1934

Cockrell, Marian and Francis Marion

Dark Waters

> Dark Waters
> United Artists Film Corp., 1944

Coffee, Lenore J. (also see the entry below)

The Forbidden Woman

> The Forbidden Woman (*)
> Equity Pictures Corp., 1920

Weep No More

> Another Time, Another Place
> Paramount Pictures Corp., 1948

> Another Time, Another Place (G. B.)
> Kaydor/Paramount Pictures Corp., 1958

Coffee, Lenore J. and William Joyce (also see the entry above)

Miss Aesop Butters Her Bread (S)

> Good Girls Go to Paris
> Columbia Pictures Corp., 1939

Cole, Sophie

Money Isn't Everything

> Money Isn't Everything (*) (G. B.)
> Stoll, 1925

Colegate, Isabel

The Shooting Party

> The Shooting Party (G. B.)
> Edenflow-Geoff Reeve-Gavin-Premier/Curzon, 1985

Collier, Constance and Ivor Novello (also see David Lestrange and the entry below)

The Rat (P)

> The Rat (*) (G. B.)
> Gainsborough Prod./Woolf and Freeman Film Service, 1925

> The Rat (G. B.)

Imperator/RKO Radio Pictures, Inc., 1937

Collier, Constance and John Nathan Raphael and Edward Sheldon
(also see the two entries above)

Peter Ibbetson (P)

Forever (*) (also based on the novel Peter Ibbetson, by
George du Maurier)
Famous Players-Lasky Corp. for Paramount Pictures
Corp., 1921

Collins, Jackie

The Bitch

The Bitch (G. B.)
Spitebowl-Bitch/Brent Walker, 1979

The Stud

The Stud (G. B.)
Stud; Artoc Corp./Brent Walker, 1978

The World is Full of Married Men

The World is Full of Married Men (G. B.)
Married Men/New Realm Pictures, 1979

Colver, Alice Ross

The Dear Pretender

On Thin Ice(*)
Warner Brothers Pictures, Inc., 1925

Comaneci, Nadia

Nadia (NF)

Nadia (TVM) (U. S./G. B./Yugo.)
David Bell Prod.-Tribune Entertainment Co.-Jadran
Films-Hallet Street Prod./Channel 4 TV, 1984

Comden, Betty and Adolph Green

Bells are Ringing (MP)

Bells are Ringing
Metro-Goldwyn-Mayer Inc., 1960

On the Town (MP)

> On the Town
> Metro-Goldwyn-Mayer, Inc., 1949

Comstock, Harriet T.

Mam'selle Jo

> Silent Years (*)
> R-C Pictures, 1921

The Place Beyond the Winds

> The Place Beyond the Winds (*)
> Universal Film Manufacturing Co./Universal Film
> Manufacturing Co.-Red Feather Photoplays, 1916

A Son of the Hills

> A Son of the Hills (*)
> Vitagraph Co. of America/Greater Vitagraph, 1917

The Tenth Woman

> The Tenth Woman (*)
> Warner Brothers Pictures, Inc., 1924

Connell, Vivian

The Chinese Room

> In the Chinese Room
> Twentieth Century-Fox Film Corp., 1959

Connor, Marie and Robert Leighton

Convict 99 (NF)

> Convict 99 (*) (G. B.)
> G. B. Samuelson/Granger, 1919

Conran, Shirley

Lace

> Lace (TVM)
> Lorimar Prod./American Broadcasting Co., 1984

Constanduros, Mabel and Denis Constanduros

Acacia Avenue (P)

> 29 <u>Acacia</u> <u>Avenue</u>
> Columbia Pictures Corp., 1945

Here Come the Huggetts

> <u>Here</u> <u>Come</u> <u>the</u> <u>Huggetts</u>
> General Film, 1948

The Huggetts Abroad

> <u>The</u> <u>Huggetts</u> <u>Abroad</u>
> General Film, 1949

Cooke, (Mrs.) Grace MacGowan

The Power and the Glory

> <u>The</u> <u>Power</u> <u>and</u> <u>the</u> <u>Glory</u> (*)
> World Film Corp., 1918

Cooke, Marjorie Benton

Cinderella Jane

> <u>The</u> <u>Mad</u> <u>Marriage</u> (*)
> Universal Motion Pictures Co., 1921

The Girl Who Lived in the Woods

> <u>The</u> <u>Little</u> <u>'Fraid</u> <u>Lady</u> (*)
> Robertson-Cole, 1920

The Incubus

> <u>Her</u> <u>Husband's</u> <u>Friend</u> (*)
> Thomas H. Ince/Famous Players-Lasky Corp.--Paramount
> Pictures Corp., 1920

The Love Call (S)

> <u>The</u> <u>Love</u> <u>Call</u> (*)
> National Film Corp. of America/Robertson-Cole--
> Exhibitors Mutual Dist. Corp., 1919

Cookson, Catherine

Rooney

Rooney (G. B.)
J. Arthur Rank Film Prod./J. Arthur Rank Film Dist.,
Ltd., 1958

Cooper, Courtney Ryley

Christmas Eve in Pilot Butte (S)

Desperate Trails (*)
Universal Motion Pictures Co., 1921

Desperate Trails
Universal Motion Pictures Co., 1939

Cooper, Elizabeth

Drusilla with a Million

Drusilla with a Million (*)
Associated Arts Corp./Film Booking Office of America,
1925

Cooper, Susan and Hume Cronyn

Foxfire (P)

Foxfire (TVM)
Dorothea Petrie-Hallmark Hall of Fame
Presentation/Columbia Broadcasting System, 1987

Corelli, Marie

God's Good Man

God's Good Man (*) (G. B.)
Stoll, 1919

Holy Orders

Holy Orders (*) (G. B.)
I. B. Davidson/Ruffells, 1917

Innocent

Innocent (*) (G. B.)
Stoll, 1921

The Sorrows of Satan

The Sorrows of Satan (*) (G. B.)
G. B. Samuelson/Walker, 1917

The Sorrows of Satan (*)
Famous Players-Lasky Corp., 1926

Thelma, a Norwegian Princess

A Modern Thelma (*)
Fox Film Corp., 1916

Thelma (*) (G. B.)
I. B. Davidson/Russells, 1918

Thelma (*)
Chester Bennett Prod./Film Booking Offices of America,
1922

The Treasure of Heaven

The Treasure of Heaven (*) (G. B.)
I. B. Davidson-Tiger/Gaumont, 1916

Wormwood: A Drama of Paris

Wormwood (*)
Fox Film Corp., 1915

The Young Diana: an Experiment of the Future

Young Diana (*)
Cosmopolitan-Paramount, 1922

Corliss, Allene

Summer Lightning

I Met My Love Again
Walter Wanger, 1938

Cory, Vivian (see Victoria Cross)

Cosby, Vivian and Shirley Warde and Harry Wagstaff Gribble

Trick for Trick (P)

Trick for Trick
Fox Film Corp, 1933

Cottrell, Dorothy

Silent Reefs

76

The Secret of the Purple Reef
Twentieth Century-Fox Film Corp., 1960

Wild Orphan (S)

Wild Innocence
Herman J. Garfield, 1937

Coulson, Felicity Winifred Carter (see Emery Bonett)

Cousins, Margaret

The Life of Lucy Gallant

Lucy Gallant
Paramount Pictures Corp., 1955

Cowan, Sada

Playing the Game (P)

The Woman Under Cover (*)
Universal Film Manufacturing Co., 1919

Cowl, Jane and Jane Murfin

Daybreak (P)

Daybreak (*)
Metro Pictures Corp., 1918

Information Please (P)

A Temperamental Wife (*)
Constance Talmadge Film Co.--a John Emerson-Anita Loos
Prod./First National, 1919

Lilac Time (P)

Lilac Time (*)
John McCormick-First National, 1928

Smilin' Through (P)

Smilin' Through (*)
Warner Brothers Pictures, Inc., 1922

Smilin' Through
Metro-Goldwyn-Mayer, Inc., 1932

Smilin' Through

Metro-Goldwyn-Mayer, Inc., 1941

Cowles, Virginia Spencer

Looking for Trouble

<u>Ladies</u> <u>Courageous</u>
Universal Motion Pictures Co., 1944

Cowley, Joy

Nest in a Falling Tree

<u>The</u> <u>Night</u> <u>Digger</u>
Metro-Goldwyn-Mayer, Inc., 1971

Coxen, Muriel Hine

The Best in Life

<u>Fifth</u> <u>Avenue</u> <u>Models</u> (*)
Universal Motion Pictures Co., 1925

Coxhead, Elizabeth

The Friend in Need

<u>A</u> <u>Cry</u> <u>from</u> <u>the</u> <u>Streets</u> (G. B.)
Film Traders/Eros Films, 1958

Craig, Georgiana Ann Randolph (see Craig Rice and Gypsy Rose Lee)

Craik, Elizabeth

John Halifax, Gentleman

<u>John</u> <u>Halifax,</u> <u>Gentleman</u> (*) (G. B.)
G. B. Samuelson/Moss, 1915

<u>John</u> <u>Halifax,</u> <u>Gentleman</u> (G. B.)
George King/ Metro-Goldwyn-Mayer British, 1938

Cram, Mildred

The Beachcomber (S)

<u>Sinners</u> <u>in</u> <u>the</u> <u>Sun</u>
Paramount Pictures Corp., 1932

The Feeder (S)

> Behind the Make-Up
> Famous Players-Lasky Corp., 1930

Girls Together (S)

> This Modern Age
> Metro-Goldwyn-Mayer, Inc., 1931

Navy Born (S)

> Mariners of the Sky
> Republic Pictures Corp., 1936

Sadie of the Desert (S)

> Subway Sadie (*)
> Al Rockett Prod., 1926

Scotch Valley

> Amateur Daddy
> Fox Film Corp., 1932

Thin Air (S)

> Stars Over Broadway
> Warner Brothers Pictures, Inc., 1935

Tinfoil (S)

> Faithless
> Metro-Goldwyn-Mayer, Inc.,1932

Wings Over Honolulu (S)

> Wings Over Honolulu
> Universal International Motion Pictures, 1937

Crane, Caroline

Summer Girl

> Summer Girl (TVM)
> Bruce Lansbury Prod.-Roberta Haynes Prod.-Finnegan
> Associates-The Summer Girl Co./Columbia Broadcasting
> System, 1983

Craven, Margaret

I Heard the Owl Call My Name

I Heard the Owl Call My Name (TVM)
Tomorrow Entertainment, Inc./Columbia Broadcasting
System, 1973

Crawford, Christina

Mommie Dearest (NF)

Mommie Dearest
Paramount Pictures Corp., 1981

Crawford, Joanna

The Birch Interval

The Birch Interval
Delbert Mann/Gamma III, 1976

Creese, Irene (see Rene Ray)

Cresswell, Helen

The Secret World of Polly Flint

The Secret World of Polly Flint (TVM) (G. B.)
Central Independent Television Picture-Revocom
Television-Bayerische Rundfunk, 1986

Crockett, Lucy Herndon

The Magnificent Bastards

Proud and Profane
Paramount Pictures Corp., 1956

Crosney, Caroline B.

Rearview Mirror

Rearview Mirror (TVM)
Simon-Asher Entertainment Prod.--Schick Sunn Classics
Prod./National Broadcasting Co., 1984

Cross, Beverley

Half a Sixpence (MP, based on the novel Kipps, by H. G.
Wells)

Half a Sixpence (U. S./G. B.)
Ameran Films/Paramount Pictures Corp., 1967

Cross, Ruth

The Golden Cocoon

The Golden Cocoon (*)
Warner Brothers Pictures, Inc.,1926

A Question of Honor (S)

A Question of Honor (*)
Anita Stewart Prod., Inc./Associated First National,
1922

Cross, Victoria
(pseud. of Vivian Cory)

Five Nights

Five Nights (*) (G. B.)
Barker/Imperial, 1915

Five Nights (*)
State Rights; Classical Motion Picture Co., 1918
(Note: this may be only the American release of the
preceding British Film.)

Life's Shop Window

Life's Shop Window (*)
Box Office Attraction Co./Box Office Attraction Co.-a
Fox Special, 1914

Paula; a Sketch from Life

Paula (*) (G. B.)
Holmfirth/Initial, 1915

Crossley, Rosemary and Anne McDonald

Annie's Coming Out (NF)

Annie's Coming Out (Austr.)
Film Australia/Universal Motion Pictures Co., 1985

Crothers, Rachel (see entry below)

As Husbands Go (P)

As Husbands Go
Fox Film Corp., 1934

Let Us be Gay, a Comedy (P)

Let Us be Gay
Metro-Goldwyn-Mayer, Inc., 1930

A Little Journey, a Comedy in Three Acts (P)

A Little Journey (*)
Metro-Goldwyn-Mayer, Inc., 1927

A Man's World (P)

A Man's World (*)
Metro Pictures Corp., 1918

Mary the Third (P)

Wine of Youth (*)
Metro-Goldwyn Pictures, 1924

Nice People (P)

Nice People (*)
Famous Players Film Co./Paramount Pictures Corp., 1922

Old Lady 31   (P, based on the same named novel, by Mary Louise Foster)

Old Lady 31 (*)
Screen Classics, Inc./Metro Pictures Corp., 1920

The Captain is a Lady (also based on the novel Old Lady Number 31, by Louise Forsslund [pseud. of Mary Louise Foster], from which the play is derived)
Metro-Goldwyn-Mayer, Inc., 1940

Susan and God (P)

Susan and God
Metro-Goldwyn-Mayer, Inc., 1940

39 East (P)

39 East (*)
Realart Pictures Corp./Realart Pictures Corp.-a Star Prod., 1920

The Three of Us (P)

The Three of Us (*)
Rolfe Photoplays, Inc./Alco Film Corp., 1914

When Ladies Meet (P)

> When Ladies Meet
> RKO Radio Pictures, Inc., 1933

> When Ladies Meet
> Metro-Goldwyn-Mayer, Inc., 1941

Wine of Youth (P)

> Wine of Youth (*)
> Metro-Goldwyn-Mayer, Inc., 1924

Crothers, Rachel and Kate Douglas Wiggin (see entry above)

Mother Carey's Chickens (P)

> Mother Carey's Chickens (also based on the same named
> novel, by Wiggin, from which the play was derived)
> RKO Radio Pictures, Inc., 1938

Crozetti, Lora

The Widderburn Horror

> House of the Black Death
> Medallion-Taurus, 1965

Cummings, Marie Susana

The Lamplighter

> The Lamplighter (*)
> Fox Film Corp., 1921

Curie, Eve

Madame Curie (NF)

> Madame Curie
> Metro-Goldwyn-Mayer, Inc., 1943

Curran, Pearl Lenore

Rosa Alvaro, Entrante (S)

> What Happened to Rosa (*)
> Goldwyn Pictures Corp., 1920

Curtis, Peter (also see Nora Lofts)
    (pseud. of Nora Lofts)

    The Devil's Own

        The Witches (G. B.)
        Hammer Films-Seven Arts, Inc./WPD, 1966

    You're Best Alone

        Guilt is my Shadow (G. B.)
        Associated British Picture Corp./Associated British and
        Pathe Film Dist., 1950

Curtiss, Ursula

    The Forbidden Garden

        Whatever Happened to Aunt Alice?
        Associates & Aldrich Co./Cinerama, 1969

    Out of the Dark

        I Saw What You Did
        Universal Motion Pictures Co., 1965

Cushing, Catherine Chrisholm

    Jerry; a Comedy in Three Acts (P)

        Don't Call Me Little Girl (*)
        Realart Pictures Corp., 1921

    Kitty Mackay (P)

        Kitty Mackay (*)
        Vitagraph Co. of America/Greater Vitagraph, 1917

    Pollyanna (P)

        Pollyanna (*) (also based on the same named novel, by
        Eleanor H. Porter, from which the play was derived)
        Mary Pickford/United Artists Film Corp., 1920

    Topsy and Eva (P, based on the novel Uncle Tom's Cabin, by
    Harriet Beecher Stowe)

        Topsy and Eva (*)
        Feature Prod. Inc./United Artists Film Corp., 1927

    Widow by Proxy (P)

<u>Widow</u> <u>by</u> <u>Proxy</u> (*)
Famous Players-Lasky Corp./Famous Players-Lasky Corp.--
Paramount Pictures Corp.-Artcraft Pictures, 1919

Cushman, Clarissa

The Young Widow

<u>Young</u> <u>Widow</u>
United Artists' Film Corp., 1946

D'Agostino, Ruth

    The Revelations of a Woman's Heart

        A <u>Woman's</u> <u>Heart</u> (*)
        Sterling Pictures, 1926

Dalby, Liza

    Geisha (NF)

        <u>American</u> <u>Geisha</u> (TVM)
        Interscope Communications, Inc.-Stonehenge Prod./
        Columbia Broadcasting System, 1986

Dalrymple, Leona

    Dangerous Number (S)

        <u>Dangerous</u> <u>Number</u>
        Metro-Goldwyn-Mayer, Inc., 1937

    Diane of the Green Van

        <u>Diane</u> <u>of</u> <u>the</u> <u>Green</u> <u>Van</u> (*)
        Winsome Stars Corp./Robertson-Cole--Exhibitors Mutual
        Dist. Corp., 1919

Danby, Frank
    (pseud. of Mrs. Julia Davis Frankau)

    The Heart of a Child

        <u>The</u> <u>Heart</u> <u>of</u> <u>a</u> <u>Child</u> (*)
        The Nazimova Prod.-Metro Pictures Corp./Metro Pictures
        Corp., 1920

Dane, Clemence (also see entry below)
    (pseud. of Winifred Ashton)

    A Bill of Divorcement (P)

        A <u>Bill</u> <u>for</u> <u>Divorcement</u> (*) (G. B.)
        Ideal, 1922

A Bill of Divorcement
RKO Radio Pictures, Inc., 1933

A Bill of Divorcement
RKO Radio Pictures, Inc., 1940

St. Martin's Lane (S) (Note: Emmens claims this is a published short story, but other sources suggest it may be only a story treatment.)

Sidewalks of London
Paramount Pictures Corp., 1940

Dane, Clemence and Helen Simpson (also see entry above)

Enter Sir John (N/P)

Murder (G. B.)
British International Pictures/Wardour, 1930

Dart, Iris Rainer

Beaches

Beaches
Touchstone-Silver Screen Partners IV-Bruckheimer South-All Girl, 1988

Davees, Zelda

Wearing the Pants (P)

Those People Next Door (G. B.)
Film Studios Manchester/Eros Films, 1953

Davenport, Gwen

Belvedere

Sitting Pretty
Twentieth Century-Fox Film Corp., 1948

Davenport, Marcia

East Side, West Side

East Side, West Side
Metro-Goldwyn-Mayer, Inc., 1949

The Valley of Decision

87

The Valley of Decision
Metro-Goldwyn-Mayer, Inc., 1949

Davidson, Sara

   Loose Change: Three Women of the Sixties (NF)

      Those Restless Years (TVM) (Note: this is a retitled
      and recut film from the miniseries Loose Change.)
      Universal Motion Pictures Co./National Broadcasting
      Co., 1978

Daviess, Maria Thompson

   The Daredevil

      The Daredevil (*)
      Gail Kane Prod./Mutual Film Corp., 1918

   The Golden Bird

      Little Miss Hoover (*)
      Famous Players-Lasky Corp./Famous Players-Lasky Corp.;
      Paramount Pictures Corp., 1918

   Out of a Clear Sky

      Out of a Clear Sky (*)
      Famous Players-Lasky Corp./Famous Players-Lasky Corp.--
      Paramount Pictures Corp., 1918

Davis, Dorothy Salisbury

   Where Dark Streets Go

      Broken Vows (TVM)
      Columbia Broadcasting System, 1987

Davis, Elizabeth
      (pseud. of Lou Ellen Davis)

   There was an Old Woman

      Revenge (TVM)
      Mark Carliner Prod./American Broadcasting System, 1971

Davis, Lavinia

   Come Be My Love

        Once More, My Darling
        Universal Motion Pictures Co., 1949

Davis, Lou Ellen (see Elizabeth Davis)

Davis, Maisie Sharman (see Stratford Davis)

Davis, Mary Evelyn Moore [Mary Evelyn Moore]

    The Little Chevalier

        The Little Chevalier (*)
        Thomas A. Edison, Inc./K-E-S-E Service--Conquest
        Program, 1917

Davis, Meredith

    When Smith Meets Smith (S)

        When Smith Meets Smith (*)
        Rogstrom Prod., 1925

Davis, Nora

    The Other Woman

        The Other Woman (*)
        J. L. Frothingham Prod./W. W. Hodkinson Corp., 1921

Davis, Ruth Helen and Charles Klein

    The Guilty Man (P, based on the foreign language play Le
    Coupable, by Francois Coppee)

        The Guilty Man (*)
        Thomas H. Ince/Paramount Pictures Corp.--Famous
        Players-Lasky Corp., 1918

Davis, Stratford
        (pseud. of Maisie Sharman Davis [maiden name: Maisie
        Sharman])

    Death in Seven Hours

        Death Goes to School (G. B.)
        Independent Artists/Eros Films, 1953

Dawson, Cleo

She Came to the Valley

> She Came to the Valley
> R. G. V. Pictures, 1981

Day, Beth and Helen Kalaben

Hey, I'm Alive (NF)

> Hey, I'm Alive (TVM)
> Charles Fries Prod.-Worldvision Enterprises/American
> Broadcasting Co., 1975

Day, Dorothy

The Eleventh Virgin

> The Woman Hater (*)
> Warner Brothers Pictures, Inc., 1925

Day, Ester Lynd

Beggars in Ermine

> Beggars in Ermine
> Monogram Pictures Corp., 1934

Day, Lillian (also see entry below)

Living Up to Lizzie (S)

> Personal Maid's Secret
> Warner Brothers Pictures, Inc., 1935

The Youngest Profession

> The Youngest Profession
> Metro-Goldwyn-Mayer, Inc., 1943

Day, Lillian and Lyon Mearson (also see entry above)

Our Wife (P)

> Our Wife
> Columbia Pictures Corp., 1941

Dayton, Katharine and George S. Kaufman

> **First Lady** (P)
>
>> First Lady
>> Warner Brothers Pictures, Inc., 1937

Deal, Babs H.

> **The Walls Came Tumbling Down**
>
>> Friendships, Secrets, and Lies (TVM)
>> Whittman-Riche Prod.--Warner Brothers Television/
>> National Broadcasting Co., 1979

de Beaumont, Madame Leprince

> **Beauty and the Beast**
>
>> Beauty and the Beast
>> United Artists Film Corp., 1963
>>
>> Beauty and the Beast
>> Golan-Globus/Cannon Screen Entertainment, 1987

De Beauvoir, Simone

> **The Blood of Others**
>
>> The Blood of Others (TVM)
>> International Cinema Corp.--Kemeny-Heroux Prod.--Cine-
>> Simone, Inc.--Filmex--Antenne 2--Home Box Office Prod./
>> Home Box Office, 1984
>
> **The Mandarins**
>
>> The Mandarins
>> Twentieth Century-Fox Film Corp., 1969

Decaux, Lucile
> (pseud. of Princess Marthe Bibesco)
>
> **Katia**
>
>> Katia
>> Joseph Burstyn Inc., 1939

de Crespigny, (Mrs.) Champion [Rose Champion de Crespigny]

> **Tangled Evidence**

Tangled Evidence (G. B.)
Realart Pictures Corp./RKO Radio Pictures, Inc., 1934

De Forest, Marian

Erstwhile Susan (P)

Erstwhile Susan (*) (also based on the novel
Barnabetta, by Helen R. Martin, from which De Forest's
play was derived)
Realart Pictures Corp., 1919

De Frece, Lady Matilda Alice

Recollections of Besta Tilly (NF)

After the Ball (G. B.) (also based on a TV play, by
Hubert Gregg)
Beaconsfield/Independent Film Dist., 1957

De Gresac, Mme. Fred and F. De Croisset

La Passerelle (P)

Afraid to Love (*) (also based on the adapted play The
Marriage of Kitty, by C. Bordon Lennox)
Paramount Famous Lasky Corp., 1927

DeJaffa, Kathleen H. B.

Sadko (P, based on the same named foreign language play, by
Rimsky Korsakoff)

Sadko
Artkino Pictures, Inc., 1953

De Jagers, Dorothy

The Average Woman (S)

The Average Woman (*)
C. C. Burr Pictures, 1924

DeJeans, Elizabeth

If a Woman Will (S)

Crashin' Thru (*)

92

Robertson-Cole/Film Booking Office of America, 1923

Romance of a Million Dollars

> The Romance of a Million Dollars (*)
> J. G. Bachman/Preferred Pictures, 1926

The Tiger's Coat

> The Tiger's Coat (*)
> Dial Film Co./W. W. Hodkinson Corp.-Pathe Exchange,
> Inc., 1920

Deland, Margaret

The Awakening of Helena Richie

> The Awakening of Helena Richie (*)
> Rolfe Photoplays, Inc./Metro Pictures Corp.--a Metro
> Wonderplay Supreme, 1916

The Iron Woman

> The Iron Woman (*)
> Popular Plays and Players, Inc./Metro Pictures Corp.,
> 1916

Delaney, Shelagh

A Taste of Honey (P)

> A Taste of Honey
> Woodfall Film Prod./Bryanston Films, 1961

The White Bus (S)

> The White Bus (G. B.)
> Holly/United Artists Film Corp., 1967

Delano, Edith Barnard

Flaming Ramparts (S)

> The Prodigal Wife (*)
> Screencraft Pictures Corp., 1918

When Carey Came to Town

> All Woman (*)
> Goldwyn Pictures Corp., 1918

de la Pasture, Mrs. Henry (Elizabeth Bonham)

    The Lonely Lady of Grosvenor Square

        The Lonely Lady of Grosvenor Square (*) (G. B.)
        Ideal, 1922

de la Ramee, Marie Louise (see "Ouida")

Delay, Mme. Claude

    Chanel Solitaire (NF)

        Chanel Solitaire
        United Film, 1981

Dell, Ethel M.

    Bars of Iron

        Bars of Iron (*) (G. B.)
        Stoll, 1920

    A Debt of Honour

        A Debt of Honour (*) (G. B.)
        Stoll, 1922

    The Eleventh Hour

        The Eleventh Hour (*) (G. B.)
        Stoll, 1922

    Greatheart

        Greatheart (*) (G. B.)
        Stoll, 1921

    Her Own Free Will (S)

        Her Own Free Will (*)
        Eastern Prod./W. W. Hodkinson Corp., 1924

    The Hundredth Chance

        The Hundredth Chance (*) (G. B.)
        Stoll, 1920

    Keeper of the Door

        Keeper of the Door (*) (G. B.)
        Stoll, 1919

The Knave of Diamonds

    The Knave of Diamonds (*) (G. B.)
    Stoll, 1921

The Knight Errant

    The Knight Errant (*) (G. B.)
    Stoll, 1922

Lamp in the Desert

    Lamp in the Desert (*) (G. B.)
    Stoll, 1922

The Place of Honour

    The Place of Honour (*) (G. B.)
    Stoll, 1921

The Prey of the Dragon

    The Prey of the Dragon (*) (G. B.)
    Stoll, 1921

A Question of Trust

    A Question of Trust (*) (G. B.)
    Stoll, 1920

The Rocks of Valpre

    The Rocks of Valpre (*) (G. B.)
    Stoll, 1919

    The Rocks of Valpre (G. B.)
    Realart Pictures Corp./RKO Radio Pictures, Inc., 1935

The Safety Curtain (S)

    The Safety Curtain (*)
    Norma Talmadge/Select Pictures Corp., 1918

The Swindler (S)

    The Swindler (*) (G. B.)
    Stoll, 1919

The Tidal Wave

    The Tidal Wave (*) (G. B.)
    Stoll, 1920

The Top of the World

The Top of the World (*)
Famous Players-Lasky Corp./Paramount Pictures Corp.,
1925

The Way of an Eagle

The Way of an Eagle (*) (G. B.)
G. B. Samuelson/Sun, 1918

The Woman of his Dream

The Woman of his Dream (*) (G. B.)
Stoll, 1921

Delmar, Vina (also see the two entries below)

About Mrs. Leslie

About Mrs. Leslie
Paramount Pictures Corp., 1954

Angie (S)

Uptown New York
E. W. Hammons, 1932

Bad Boy (S)

Bad Boy
Twentieth Century-Fox Film Corp., 1936

Bad Girl

Bad Girl (also based on the same named play, by Delmar
and Brian Marlow, which was derived from Delmar's
novel)
Fox Film Corp., 1931

Manhattan Heartbeat (also based on the play Bad Girl,
by Delmar and Brian Marlow, which was derived from
Delmar's novel)
Twentieth Century-Fox Film Corp., 1940

Bracelets (S)

Hands Across the Table
Paramount Pictures Corp., 1935

Dance Hall (S)

Dance Hall
RKO Radio Pictures, Inc., 1929

        King of Burlesque
        Twentieth Century-Fox Film Corp., 1936

The Human Side (S)

        The Great Man's Lady
        Paramount Pictures Corp., 1942

Playing Dead (S)

        Restless Soul (*)
        Vitaphone Corp., 1922

Pretty Sadie McKee (S)

        Sadie McKee
        Metro-Goldwyn-Mayer, Inc., 1934

The Rich Full Life (P)

        Cynthia
         Metro-Goldwyn-Mayer, Inc., 1947

Sheba (S)

        Playing Around (also from the play Playing Around, by
        Francis Nordstrom, which was adapted from the story by
        Delmar)
        Warner Brothers Pictures, Inc.-First National, 1930

Delmar, Vina and Brian Marlow (also see the entry above and the
    entry below)

Bad Girl (P)

        Bad Girl (also based on the novel Bad Girl, by Vina
        Delmar, from which the play was derived)
        Fox Film Corp., 1931

        Manhattan Heartbeat (also based on the novel Bad Girl,
        by Vina Delmar, from which the play was derived)
        Twentieth Century-Fox Film Corp., 1940

Delmar, Vina and Gertrude Atherton, Vicki Baum, Sophie Kerr, and
    Ursula Parrott and Polan Banks, Irvin S. Cobb, Zane Grey,
    Rupert Hughes, and J. P. Mc Evoy (also see the two entries
    above)

Woman Accused

        Woman Accused
        Paramount Pictures Corp., 1933

                            97

Del Rivo, Laura

> **The Furnished Room**
>
> > <u>West</u> <u>11</u> (G. B.)
> > Dial Film Co./WPD, 1963

De Meyer, Baroness and Erich von Stroheim

> **Clothes and Treachery** (S)
>
> > <u>The</u> <u>Devil's</u> <u>Passkey</u> (*)
> > Universal Motion Pictures Co., 1920

Dempsey, Barbara Piattelli and Jack Dempsey

> **Dempsey** (NF)
>
> > <u>Dempsey</u> (TVM)
> > Charles Fries Prod./Columbia Broadcasting System, 1983

Denison, Muriel

> **Susannah; a Little Girl with the Mounties** [Susannah de la Police Montee]
>
> > <u>Susannah</u> <u>of</u> <u>the</u> <u>Mounties</u>
> > Twentieth Century-Fox Film Corp., 1939

De Savallo, Dona Teresa
(pseud. of Alice Muriel Williamson)

> **The House of the Lost Court**
>
> > <u>The</u> <u>House</u> <u>of</u> <u>the</u> <u>Lost</u> <u>Court</u> (*)
> > Thomas A. Edison, Inc./Paramount Pictures Corp., 1915

des Ligneris, Francoise

> **Psyche 58**
>
> > <u>Psyche</u> <u>59</u> (G. B.)
> > Troy-Schenck Prod./Columbia Pictures Corp., 1963

De S. Wentworth James, Gertrude

> **The Girl Who Wouldn't Work**

The Girl Who Wouldn't Work (*)
B. P. Schulberg Prod., 1925

The Scarlet Kiss

The Scarlet Kiss (*) (G. B.)
Martin's Photoplays/Faulkner, 1920

The Wife Who Wasn't Wanted

The Wife Who Wasn't Wanted (*)
Warner Brothers Pictures, Inc., 1925

Dew, Joan and Tammy Wynette

Stand by Your Man (NF)

Stand by Your Man (TVM)
Robert Papazian Prod.--JNP Associates--Peter Gruber-Jon
Peters Prod./Columbia Broadcasting System, 1981

Dick, R. A.
(pseud. of Josephine Leslie)

The Ghost and Mrs. Muir

The Ghost and Mrs. Muir
Twentieth Century-Fox Film Corp., 1947

Stranger in the Night
Twentieth Century-Fox Film Corp., 1955

Dickens, Monica

One Pair of Feet

The Lamp Still Burns (G. B.)
Two Cities Films, Ltd./General Film, 1943

Didion, Joan

Play it as it Lays

Play it as it Lays
Universal Motion Pictures Co., 1972

Dikty, Judy (see Julian May)

Dinesen, Isak
    (pseud. of Karen Blixen)

    Out of Africa (NF)

        <u>Out</u> <u>of</u> <u>Africa</u> (also based on the nonfiction books <u>The</u>
        <u>Life</u> <u>of</u> <u>a</u> <u>Storyteller</u>, by Judith Thurman, and <u>Silence</u>
        <u>Will</u> <u>Speak</u>, by Errol Trzebinski)
        Universal Motion Pictures Co., 1985

Disney, Doris Miles

    Family Skeleton

        <u>Stella</u>
        Twentieth Century-Fox Film Corp., 1950

    Fugitive Lady

        <u>Fugitive</u> <u>Lady</u>
        Republic Pictures Corp., 1951

    Night of Clear Choice

        <u>Yesterday's</u> <u>Child</u> (TVM)
        William Kayden Prod.-Paramount Television/National
        Broadcasting Co., 1977

    Only Couples Need Apply

        <u>Betrayal</u> (TVM)
        Metromedia Producers Corp./American Broadcasting Co.,
        1974

    The Straw Man

        <u>The</u> <u>Straw</u> <u>Man</u> (G. B.)
        Hedgerley/United Artists' Film Corp., 1953

Dix, Beulah Marie (also see the two entries below)

    The Fighting Blade

        <u>The</u> <u>Fighting</u> <u>Blade</u> (*)
        Inspirational Pictures/First National, 1923

    Friends in the End

        <u>The</u> <u>Heart</u> <u>of</u> <u>Youth</u> (*)
        Famous Players-Lasky Corp./Famous Players-Lasky Corp.--
        Paramount Pictures Corp., 1919

Dix, Beulah Marie and Bertram Milhauser (also see the entry above and the entry below)

The Sucker (P)

> The Life of Jimmy Dolan
> Warner Brothers Pictures, Inc., 1933

> They Made me a Criminal
> Warner Brothers Pictures, Inc., 1939

Dix, Beulah Marie and Evelyn Greenleaf Sutherland (also see the two entries above)

The Breed of the Treshams (P)

> The Breed of the Treshams (*) (G. B.)
> Astra Films, 1920

The Road to Yesterday (P)

> The Road to Yesterday (*)
> De Mille Prod./Producers Dist. Corp., 1925

Dixon, Rosie

Confessions of a Night Nurse (NF)

> Rosie Dixon -- Night Nurse (G. B.)
> Multiscope/Columbia Pictures Corp., 1978

Dodge, Mary Mapes

Hans Brinker; or the Silver Skates

> Hans Brinker; or the Silver Skates (TVM)
> Walt Disney Prod./National Broadcasting Co., 1961

Doerr, Harriett

Stones for Ibarra (NF)

> Stones for Ibarra (TVM)
> Herbert Brodkin-Robert Berger--Hallmark Hall of Fame
> Presentation/Columbia Broadcasting System, 1988

Donisthorpe, (Gladys) Sheila

First Night (P)

       First Night (G. B.)
       Crusade/Paramount Pictures Corp., 1937

Donn-Byrne, Dorothea (also see the entry below)

   Irish and Proud of It (S)

       Irish and Proud of It (G. B.)
       Crusade/Paramount Pictures Corp., 1936

Donn-Byrne, Dorothea and Gilda Varesi Archibald (also see the entry above)

   Enter Madame; a Play in Three Acts (P)

       Enter Madame (*)
       Samuel Zierler Photoplay Corp./Metro Pictures Corp.,
       1922

       Enter Madame
       Paramount Pictures Corp., 1935

Donnelly, Dorothy (also see both entries below)

   Poppy (MP)

       Sally of the Sawdust (*)
       Famous Players-Lasky Corp., 1925

       Poppy
       Paramount Pictures Corp., 1936

Donnelly, Dorothy and Charlotte E. Wells (also see the entry above and the entry below)

   The Riddle: Woman (P, based on the foreign language play, by Carl Jacobi)

       The Riddle: Woman (*)
       Associated Exhibitors, Inc./Pathe Exchange, Inc., 1920

Donnelly, Dorothy and Sigmund Romberg (also see the two entries above)

   The Student Prince (O)

       The Student Prince in Old Heidelberg (*) (also based on
       the book Karl Heinrich and the play Alt Heidelberg
       Schauspiel in funf Aufzugen, both by Wilhelm Meyer-
       Foerster)

Metro-Goldwyn-Mayer, Inc., 1927

The Student Prince (also based on the novel Karl
Heinrich and the play Alt Heidelberg Schauspiel in funf
Aufzugen, both by Wilhelm Meyer-Foerster)
Metro-Goldwyn-Mayer, Inc., 1954

Doremus, Mrs. Charles A.

Nell Gwyne (P, based on the novel Mistress Nell Gwyne, by
Marjorie Bowen)

Nell Gwynne (*)
Sawyer, Inc., 1914

Nell Gwynne (*) (G. B.) (also based on the novel
Mistress Nell Gwyne, by Marjorie Bowen)
W. M. Prod.-British National Films, Ltd./First
National, 1926

Dorrance, Ethel and James Dorrance

His Robe of Honor

His Robe of Honor (*)
Paralta Plays, Inc./W. W. Hodkinson Corp., 1918

Whitewashed Walls (S)

Whitewashed Walls (*)
Jesse D. Hampton Prod./Robertson-Cole--Exhibitors
Mutual Dist. Corp., 1919

Who Knows? (S)

Who Knows? (*)
Bernstein Film Prod./State Rights, 1917

Doss, Helen

The Family Nobody Wanted (NF)

The Family Nobody Wanted (TVM)
Groverton Prod.-Universal Motion Pictures Co./American
Broadcasting Co., 1975

Douglas, Felicity

It's Never too Late (P)

It's Never too Late (G. B.)

103

Park Lane Films/Associated British and Pathe Film
Dist., 1956

Downing, Sybil and W. F. Downing

Lady Tetley's Decree (P)

Lady <u>Tetley's</u> <u>Decree</u> (*) (G. B.)
London Films/Jury Imperial Pictures, 1920

Drabble, Margaret

The Millstone

<u>A</u> <u>Touch</u> <u>of</u> <u>Love</u> (G. B.)
Amicus Prod.-Palomar Pictures International/British
Lion, 1969

Drexler, Rosalyn

To Smithereens

<u>Below</u> <u>the</u> <u>Belt</u>
Aberdeen--RLF--Tom-Mi/Atlantic, 1980

Drew, Gladys S. Rankin (see George Cameron)

Duckett, Eleanor Shipley

Alfred the Great (NF)

<u>Alfred</u> <u>the</u> <u>Great</u> (G. B.)
Bernard Smith Films--Metro-Goldwyn-Mayer British/Metro-
Goldwyn-Mayer British, 1969

(Mme.) Dudevant: Amandine-Aurore Lucille Dupin (see George Sand)

Duer, Caroline and Harriet Ford

A Lady in Love (P)

<u>A</u> <u>Lady</u> <u>in</u> <u>Love</u> (*)
Famous Players-Lasky Corp./Famous Players-Lasky Corp.--
Paramount Pictures-Artcraft Pictures Corp., 1920

Duganne, Phyllis

Nice Girl (P)

> Nice Girl
> Universal Motion Picture Co., 1941

Du Maurier, Daphne

The Birds (S)

> The Birds
> Alfred J. Hitchcock Prod./Universal Motion Pictures
> Co., 1963

Don't Look Now (S)

> Don't Look Now (G. B./Ita.)
> Casey-Elderado/British Lion, 1973

Frenchman's Creek

> Frenchman's Creek
> Paramount Pictures Corp., 1944

Hungry Hill

> Hungry Hill (G. B.)
> Two Cities Films, Ltd./General Film, 1947

Jamaica Inn

> Jamaica Inn (G. B.)
> Mayflower Photoplay Corp./Associated British Picture
> Corp., 1939

> Jamaica Inn (TVM) (G. B.)
> HTV Prod.-Metromedia Producers Corp., 1983

My Cousin Rachel

> My Cousin Rachel
> Twentieth Century-Fox Film Corp., 1952

> My Cousin Rachel (TVM) (G. B.)
> British Broadcasting Corp. TV--Twentieth Century-Fox
> Television/Public Broadcasting System, 1985

Rebecca

> Rebecca
> United Artists' Film Corp., 1940

The Scapegoat

> The Scapegoat (G. B.)

Du Maurier-Guiness/Metro-Goldwyn-Mayer British, 1959

The Years Between (P)

The Years Between (G. B.)
Sydney Box/General Film, 1946

Dunbar, Andrea

The Arbor (P)

Rita, Sue and Bob Too! (G. B.) (also based on the play
Rita, Sue, and Bob Too, by Dunbar)
Film Four International-Umbrella-British Screen
Service/Orion, 1987

Rita, Sue and Bob Too! (P)

Rita, Sue and Bob Too! (G. B.) (also based on the play
The Arbor, by Dunbar)
Film Four International-Umbrella-British Screen
Service/Orion, 1987

Duncan, Isadora

My Life (NF)

Isadora (G. B.) (also based on the nonfiction book
Isadora Duncan, an Intimate Portrait, by Sewell Stokes)
Universal International Motion Pictures/J. Arthur Rank
Film Dist., Ltd., 1969

Duncan, Jane

Camerons on the Train

The Camerons (G. B.)
Cherrill/Children's Film and Television Foundation,
1974

Duncan, Lois [Lois Duncan Arquette]

Summer of Fear

Stranger in Our House
Brent Walker, 1978

Duncan, Sara J.

The Gold Cure

The Gold Cure (*) (G. B.)
Stoll, 1925

Dunn, Elizabeth

Candy Takes a Job (S)

Meet the Stewarts
Columbia Pictures Corp., 1942

Dunn, Nell

Poor Cow

Poor Cow (G. B.)
Fenchurch Films-Vic Films/Anglo-Amalgamated, 1967

Steaming (P)

Steaming (G. B.)
World Film/Columbia Pictures Corp.-Electrical and
Musical Industries-Warner Brothers Pictures, Inc., 1985

Up the Junction

Up the Junction (G. B.)
British Home Entertainments-Collinson-Crasto
Prod./Paramount Pictures Corp., 1967

Dunning, Frances and Philip Dunning

Night Hostess (P)

The Woman Racket
Metro-Goldwyn-Mayer, Inc., 1929

Dupre, Anne and Etta Shiber and Paul Dupre and Oscar Ray

Paris-Underground (NF)

Paris-Underground
United Artists Film Corp., 1945

Duras, Marguerite

Entire Days in the Trees (P)

Entire Days in the Trees
Theatre D'Orsay, 1976

107

The Sailor from Gibraltar [Le Marin de Gilbraltar]

> The Sailor from Gilbraltar (G. B.)
> Woodfall Film Prod./United Artists' Film Corp., 1967

10:30 P.M. on a Summer Night [Dix Heures et Deme du Soir en Ete]

> 10:30 P.M. Summer (U. S./Spa.)
> Jorilie Prod.-Argos Films/Lopert Pictures, 1965

Durber, Rose and Douglas Durber

Me and My Girl (P)

> The Lambeth Walk
> Pinebrook Prod., 1940

Durham, Marilyn

The Man Who Loved Cat Dancing

> The Man Who Loved Cat Dancing
> Metro-Goldwyn-Mayer, Inc., 1973

During, Stella

The Temptation of Carlton Earle

> The Temptation of Carlton Earle (*) (G. B.)
> British Actors; C. Aubrey Smith Theatres/Phillips, 1923

Durrant, Theo
(group pseud. of Eunice Mays Boyd, Florence Ostern Faulkner, Dana Lyon, Lenore Glen Offord, and Virginia Rath and Terry Adler, Anthony Boucher, Allen Hymson, Carry Lucas, Richard Shattuck, Darwin L. Teilhet, and William Worley)

The Marble Forest

> Macabre
> Allied Artists, 1958

Eagan, Alberta Stedman [Alberta Stedman]

    They Call It Sin

        They Call It Sin
        First National-Warner Brothers Pictures, Inc., 1932

Eareckson, Joni

    Joni (NF)

        Joni
        World Wide, 1980

Eastman, Rebecca Lane Hooper

    The Big Little Person

        The Big Little Person (*)
        Universal Film Manufacturing Co., 1917

Eberhart, Mignon G.

    Dead Yesterday (S)

        The Great Hospital Mystery
        Twentieth Century-Fox Film Corp., 1937

    From This Dark Stairway

        The Murder of Dr. Harrigan
        First National/Warner Brothers Pictures, Inc., 1936

        The Dark Stairway (G. B.)
        Warner Brothers Pictures, Inc.-First National/Warner
        Brothers Pictures, Inc., 1938

    Hasty Wedding

        Three's a Crowd
        Republic Pictures Corp., 1945

    Murder by an Aristocrat

        Murder by an Aristocrat

First National/Warner Brothers Pictures, Inc., 1936

The Mystery of Hunting's End

Mystery House
First National/Warner Brothers Pictures, Inc., 1938

The Patient in Room 18

While the Patient Slept
First National-Warner Brothers Pictures, Inc., 1935

The Patient in Room 18
Warner Brothers Pictures, Inc., 1938

The White Cockatoo

The White Cockatoo
Warner Brothers Pictures, Inc., 1935

Eby, Lois Christine and John C. Fleming

The Velvet Fleece

Larceny
Universal Motion Pictures Co., 1948

Echard, Margaret

A Man Without Friends

Lightning Strikes Twice
Warner Brothers Pictures, Inc., 1951

Eden, Rob
(joint pseud. of Eve Burkhardt and Robert Ferdinand
Burkhardt)

Dancing Feet

Dancing Feet
Republic Pictures Corp., 1936

I Demand Payment

I Demand Payment
Imperial, 1938

Jenifer Hale

Jenifer Hale (G. B.)
Fox Film Co. British, 1937

Edens, Olive

    Hearts and Hands (S)

        A House Divided
        Universal Film Manufacturing Co., 1932

Edginton, May (also see the entry below)
    (pseud. of Helen Marion Edginton Bailey)

    A Child in their Midst

        Man of Mayfair (G.B.)
        Paramount Pictures Corp. British, 1931

    The Heart is Young (S)

        The False Madonna
        Paramount Pictures Corp., 1932

    The Joy Girl

        The Joy Girl (*)
        Fox Film Corp., 1927

    Judgment (S)

        Her Husband's Secret (*)
        Frank Lloyd Prod./First National, 1925

    The Man Who Dared

        Creation (*) (G. B.)
        Raleigh King, 1922

    Purple and Fine Linen (S)

        Three Hours (*)
        Corinne Griffith Prod./First National, 1927

        Adventure in Manhattan (also based on the play Purple
        and Fine Linen, by Anita Fairgrieve and Helena Miller,
        which was derived from Edginton's short story)
        Columbia Pictures Corp., 1936

    Triumph

        Triumph (*)
        Famous Players-Lasky Corp./Paramount Pictures Corp.,
        1924

    The Woman Who Squandered Men (P)

<u>Crossroad</u> <u>of</u> <u>Love</u>
Superlative Pictures/Hi Mark Release, 1928

Edginton, May and Rudolph Besier (also see the entry above)
  (May Edginton: pseud. of Helen Marion Edginton Bailey)

The Prude's Fall (P)

   <u>The</u> <u>Prude's</u> <u>Fall</u> (*) (G. B.)
   Gainsborough Prod./Woolf & Freedman Film Service, 1924

Secrets, a Play in a Prologue, Three Acts and an Epilogue
(P)

   <u>Secrets</u> (*)
   Joseph M. Schrenk Prod./Associated First National, 1924

   <u>Secrets</u>
   United Artists Film Corp., 1933

Edington, Carmen and Arlo C. Edington

The Studio Murder Mystery

   <u>The</u> <u>Studio</u> <u>Murder</u> <u>Mystery</u>
   Paramount Famous Lasky Corp., 1929

Edler, Sarah and Rob Eloder

Crash (NF)

   <u>Crash</u> (TVM)
   Charles Fries Prod./American Broadcasting Co., 1978

Eisinger, Jo

The Walls Came Tumbling Down

   <u>The</u> <u>Walls</u> <u>Came</u> <u>Tumbling</u> <u>Down</u>
   Columbia Pictures Corp., 1946

Elder, Lauren and Shirley Streshinsky

And I Alone Survived (NF)

   <u>And</u> <u>I</u> <u>Alone</u> <u>Survived</u> (TVM)
   Jerry Leider/OJL Prod., 1978

Elfman, Blossom

The Girls of Huntington House

The Girls of Huntington House (TVM)
Lorimar Prod./American Broadcasting Co., 1973

Eliot, George
(pseud. of Mary Ann Evans)

Adam Bede

Adam Bede (*) (G. B.)
International Exclusives, 1918

Daniel Deronda

Daniel Deronda (*) (G. B.)
Master Films/Butcher's Film Service, 1921

The Mill on the Floss

The Mill on the Floss (*)
Thanhouser Film Corp./Mutual Film Corp.-a Mutual
Masterpicture, 1915

The Mill on the Floss (G. B.)
Morgan/National Provincial Film Dist., 1937

Romola

Romola (*)
Inspiration Pictures/Metro-Goldwyn Dist. Corp., 1925

Scenes of Clerical Life

Mr. Gilfil's Love Story (*) (G. B.)
Ideal, 1920

Silas Marner

Silas Marner (*)
Thanhouser Film Corp./Mutual Film Corp.-Mutual Master
De Luxe Ed., 1916

The Little Outcast (*)
Chopin Features/State Rights-Industrial Film Co., 1920
[Note: same as Are Children to Blame?, 1922]

Silas Marner (TVM) (G. B.)
Louis Marks-British Broadcasting Corp. TV-the Arts and
Entertainment Network, 1985

113

"Elizabeth"
    (pseud. of Mary Annette Beauchamp Russell)

    Enchanted April

        Enchanted April (also based on the same named play, by
        Kane Campbell, which was derived from Elizabeth's
        novel)
        RKO Radio Pictures, Inc., 1935

    Mr. Skeffington

        Mr. Skeffington
        Warner Brothers Pictures, Inc./First National, 1944

Elliott, Janice

    The Buttercup Chain

        The Buttercup Chain (G. B.)
        Columbia British, 1970

    Secret Places

        Secret Places (G. B.)
        Rediffusion--Skreba Films-Virgin/ J. Arthur Rank Film
        Dist., Ltd., 1984

Ellis, Edith (maiden name of Edith Ellis Furness) (also see the
    two entries below)

    Mary Jane's Pa (P, based on the novel Mary Jane's Pa, by
    Norman Way)

        Mary Jane's Pa (*)
        Vitagraph Co. of America-a Blue Ribbon Feature/Great
        Vitagraph, 1917

        Mary Jane's Pa (also based on the same named novel, by
        Norman Way)
        First National/Warner Brothers Pictures, Inc., 1935

    The Point of View (P)

        The Point of View (*)
        Selznick Pictures Corp., 1920

    Seven Sisters (P, based on the foreign Language play, by
    Ferencz Herczeg)

        Seven Sisters (*)
        Famous Players Film Co./Paramount Pictures Corp., 1915

White Collars; a Comedy in Three Acts (P)

> The Idle Rich
> Metro-Goldwyn-Mayer, Inc., 1929

> Rich Man, Poor Girl
> Metro-Goldwyn-Mayer, Inc., 1938

Ellis, Edith and Edward Ellis (also see the entry above and the entry below)

Women in His Life (P)

> Affairs of a Gentleman
> Universal Motion Pictures Co., 1934

Ellis, Edith and Forrest Halsey (also see the two entries above)

My Man (P)

> The Triumph of the Weak (*)
> Vitagraph Co. of America-a Blue Ribbon Feature/Greater
> Vitagraph, 1918

Ellis, Elizabeth

Barbara Winslow -- Rebel

> The Dangerous Maid (*)
> Joseph M. Schenck Prod./Associated First National, 1923

Elwen, Eva

Mary Latimer, Nun

> Mary Latimer, Nun (*) (G. B.) (also based on the play
> Mary Latimer, Nun, by Will H. Glaze)
> Famous Pictures Film Co., 1920

Emmons, Della Gould

Sacajawea of the Shoshones

> The Far Horizons
> Paramount Pictures Corp., 1955

Endicott, Ruth Belmore

Carolyn of the Corners

Carolyn of the Corners (*)
Anderson-Brunton Co./Pathe Exchange, Inc., 1919

Enters, Angna

Tenth Avenue Angel (S)

Tenth Avenue Angel (also based on a radio play, by Craig Rice)
Metro-Goldwyn-Mayer, Inc., 1948

Ephron, Phoebe and Henry Ephron

Take Her, She's Mine (P)

Take Her, She's Mine
Twentieth Century-Fox Film Corp., 1963

Three is a Family (P)

Three is a Family
United Artists' Film Corp., 1944

Ertz, Susan

In the Cool of the Day

In the Cool of the Day (G. B.)
Metro-Goldwyn-Mayer British, 1963

Etons, Ursula

Angel Dusted (NF)

Angel Dusted (TVM)
NRW Features/National Broadcasting Co., 1981

Eunson, Katherine

The Day They Gave Babies Away (A)

All Mine to Give
Universal Motion Pictures Co., 1957

Eustis, Helen

The Fool Killer

The Fool Killer
Landau/Allied Artists, 1965

Evans, August J. (maiden name of Augusta Jane Evans Wilson) (also
    see Augusta Jane Evans Wilson)

St. Elmo

St. Elmo (*)
Balboa Amusement Prod. Co./State Rights-Box Office
Attraction Co., 1914

St. Elmo (*) (G. B.)
R. W. Syndicate/Capitol Film Exchange, 1923

Evans, Ida M.

Limousine Life (S)

Limousine Life (*)
Triangle Film Corp./Triangle Dist. Corp., 1918

The Way of a Maid with a Man (S)

The Way of a Maid with a Man (*)
Famous Players-Lasky Corp./Famous Players-Lasky Corp.--
Paramount Pictures Corp., 1918

Evans, Marguerite Florence Helene Jarvis (see Countess Helene
    Barcynska)

Evans, Mary Ann (see George Eliott)

Ewer, Monica

Not for Sale

Not for Sale (*) (G. B.)
Stoll, 1924

Ring O' Roses

He Found a Star (G. B.)
John Corfield Prod./General Film, 1941

- F -

F., Christiane (as edited by Kai Hermann and Horst Rieck)

    Christiane F **(NF)**

        <u>Christiane F</u>
        Twentieth Century-Fox Film Corp., 1982

Fabricus, Jean

    Insult (P)

        <u>Insult</u> (G. B.)
        Paramount Pictures Corp. British, 1932

Fairfield, Cecily Isabel (see Rebecca West)

Fairgrieve, Anita and Helena Miller

    Purple and Fine Linen (P)

        <u>Adventure in Manhattan</u> (also based on the short story
        "Purple and Fine Linen," by May Edginton, from which
        the play was derived)
        Columbia Pictures Corp., 1936

Farmer, Frances

    Will There Really Be a Morning? (NF)

        <u>Will There Really Be a Morning?</u> (TVM)
        Jaffe-Blakely Films--Sama Prod.--Orion TV/Columbia
        Broadcasting System, 1983

Farnham, Matee Howe

    Wild Beauty

        <u>Wayward</u>
        Paramount Pictures Corp., 1932

Farre, Rowena

Seal Morning

> Seal Morning (TVM) (G. B.)
> Independent Television Corp., 1986

Farrell, M. J. (also see the entry below)
    (pseud. of Mary Nester Shrine Keane)

Treasure Hunt (P)

> Treasure Hunt (G. B.)
> Romulus Films/Independent Film Dist., 1952

Farrell, M. J. and John Perry (also see the entry above)
    (M. J. Farrell: pseud. of Mary Nester Shrine Keane)

Spring Meeting (P)

> Three Wise Brides
> Monogram Pictures Corp., 1942

Faulkner, Florence Ostern (see Theo Durrant)

Feiner, Ruth

Three Cups of Coffee

> The Woman's Angle (G. B.)
> Bow Bells/ Associated British and Pathe Film Dist.,
> 1952

Fenelon, Fania

Playing for Time (NF)

> Playing for Time (TVM)
> Szyszy Prod./Columbia Broadcasting System, 1980

Fenollosa, Mary McNeil
    (also see Sidney McCall)

The Dragon Painter

> The Dragon Painter (*)
> Haworth Pictures Corp./Robertson-Cole--Exhibitors
> Mutual Dist. Corp., 1919

Ferber, Edna (also see the two entries below)

Cimarron

> Cimarron
> RKO Radio Pictures, Inc., 1931
>
> Cimarron
> Metro-Goldwyn-Mayer, Inc., 1960

Classified (S)

> Classified (*)
> Corinne Griffith Prod./First National, 1925
>
> Hard to Get
> First National, 1929
>
> Hard to Get
> Warner Brothers Pictures, Inc., 1938

Come and Get It

> Come and Get It
> Samuel Goldwyn Prod./United Artists Film Corp., 1936

Emma McChesney & Co. (RS)

> Our Mrs. McChesney (*) (also based on the related
> stories Roast Beef Medium: The Business Adventures of
> Emma McChesney, by Ferber, and the play Our Mrs.
> McChesney, by Ferber and George V. Hobart, which was
> derived from Ferber's stories)
> Metro Pictures Corp./Metro Pictures Corp.--Metro All-
> Star Series, 1918

Fanny Herself

> No Woman Knows (*)
> Universal Film Manufacturing Co., 1921

The Gay Old Dog (S)

> The Gay Old Dog (*)
> Hobart Henley Prod., Inc./Pathe Exchange, Inc.-a Pathe
> Special, 1919

Giant

> Giant
> Warner Brothers Pictures, Inc., 1956

Gigolo (S)

> Gigolo (*)
> De Mille/Producers Dist. Corp., 1926

Glamour (S)

> Glamour
> Universal International Motion Pictures, 1934

Ice Palace

> Ice Palace
> Warner Brothers Pictures, Inc., 1960

Mother Knows Best (S)

> Mother Knows Best
> Fox Film Corp., 1928

Not a Day Over Twenty-One (S)

> Summer Resort
> World Wide, 1932

Old Man Minick (S)

> Welcome Home (*) (also based on the play Minick; a Play
> Based on the Short Story "Old Man Minick", by Ferber
> and George S. Kaufman, which was derived from Ferber's
> short story)
> Famous Players-Lasky Corp./Paramount Pictures Corp.,
> 1925

> The Expert (also based on the play Minick; a Play Based
> on the Short Story "Old Man Minick", by Ferber and
> George S. Kaufman, which was derived from Ferber's
> short story)
> Warner Brothers Pictures, Inc., 1932

Roast Beef Medium: The Business Adventures of Emma McChesney (RS)

> Our Mrs. McChesney (*) (also based on the related
> stories Emma McChesney & Co., by Ferber, and the play
> Our Mrs. McChesney, by Ferber and George V. Hobart,
> which was derived from Ferber's stories)
> Metro Pictures Corp./Metro Pictures Corp.--Metro All-
> Star Series, 1918

Saratoga Trunk

> Saratoga Trunk
> Warner Brothers Pictures, Inc., 1943

Showboat

> Showboat (also based on the Flo Ziegfield stage
> production of Ferber's novel)

Universal Motion Pictures Co., 1929

Showboat (also based on the musical play Showboat, by
Oscar Hammerstein, which was derived from Ferber's
novel)
Universal Motion Pictures Co., 1936

Showboat
Metro-Goldwyn-Mayer, Inc., 1951

So Big

So Big (*)
First National, 1924

So Big
Warner Brothers Pictures, Inc., 1932

So Big
Warner Brothers Pictures, Inc., 1953

Ferber, Edna and George S. Kaufman (also see the entry above and
the entry below)

Dinner at Eight (P)

Dinner at Eight
Metro-Goldwyn-Mayer, Inc., 1933

Minick; a Play Based on the Short Story "Old Man Minick" (P)

Welcome Home (*) (also based on the short story "Old
Man Minick," by Ferber, from which the play was
derived)
Famous Players-Lasky Corp./Paramount Pictures Corp.,
1925

The Expert (also based on the short story "Old Man
Minick," by Ferber, from which the play was derived)
Warner Brothers Pictures, Inc., 1932

No Place to Go
First National/Warner Brothers Pictures, Inc., 1939

The Royal Family (P)

Royal Family of Broadway
Paramount Pictures Corp., 1930

Stage Door (P)

Stage Door
RKO Radio Pictures, Inc., 1937

Ferber, Edna and George V. Hobart (also see the two entries above)

 Our Mrs. McChesney (P, based on Ferber's McChesney stories)

  Our Mrs. McChesney (*) (also based on Ferber's two books of related stories Emma McChesney & Co. and Roast Beef Medium: The Business Adventures of Emma McChesney, from which the play was derived)
  Metro Pictures Corp./Metro Pictures Corp.--Metro All-Star Series, 1918

Ferguson, Margaret

 The Sign of the Ram

  The Sign of the Ram
  Columbia Pictures Corp., 1948

Fergusson, (Lady) Hannay (see Doris Leslie)

Fetter, Elizabeth Head (see "Hanna Lees and Laurence P. Bachmann" entry)

Fidler, Kathleen

 Flash the Sheepdog

  Flash the Sheepdog (G. B.)
  International Film Associates/Children's Film Foundation, 1967

Field, Medora

 Blood on her Shoe

  The Girl Who Dared
  Republic Pictures Corp., 1944

 Who Killed Aunt Maggie?

  Who Killed Aunt Maggie?
  Republic Pictures Corp., 1940

Field, Rachel

 All This and Heaven Too

All This and Heaven Too
Warner Brothers Pictures, Inc., 1940

And Now Tomorrow

And Now Tomorrow
Paramount Pictures Corp., 1944

The Londonderry Air (P)

The Londonderry Air (G. B.)
Fox Film Co. British, 1938

Time Out of Mind

Time Out of Mind
Universal Motion Pictures Co., 1947

Fields, Dorothy and Herbert Fields (also see the two entries
   below)

Annie Get Your Gun (MP, for which Irving Berlin wrote the
music and lyrics)

Annie Get Your Gun
Metro-Goldwyn-Mayer, Inc./Loew's, Inc., 1950

Let's Face It (MP, based on the play Cradle Snatchers by
Russell Medcraft and Norma Mitchell [q. v.])

Let's Face It
Paramount Pictures Corp., 1943

Mexican Hayride (MP)

Mexican Hayride
Universal Motion Picture Co., 1948

Something for the Boys (MP, for which Cole Porter wrote the
music and lyrics)

Something for the Boys
Twentieth Century-Fox Film Corp., 1944

Up in Central Park (MP)

Up in Central Park
Universal Motion Pictures Co., 1948

Fields, Dorothy (lyrics) and Neil Simon (book) (also see the
   entry above and the entry below)

Sweet Charity (P, based on the screenplay Notti Di Cabiria, by Federico Fellini)

> Sweet Charity
> Universal Motion Pictures Co., 1969

Fields, Dorothy and Otto Harbach (also see Alice Duer Miller and
the two entries above)

> Roberta (MP, based on the novel Gowns by Roberta, by Alice
> Duer Miller)

>> Lovely to Look at
>> Metro-Goldwyn Mayer, Inc., 1952

Figes, Eva

> **The Walking**

>> Nelly's Version (G. B.)
>> Mithras/Channel 4 TV, 1983

Finklestein, Eva (see "Eva Kay Flint and Martha madison" entry)

Fiore, Evelyn and Mary Glatzle

> **Muggable Mary** (NF)

>> Muggable Mary: Street Cop (TVM)
>> Columbia Broadcasting System Entertainment/Columbia
>> Broadcasting System, 1982

Fisher, Dorothea Frances Canfield Fisher (see Dorothy Canfield)

Fitzgerald, Edith (also see the entry below)

> **Compromised** (P)

>> Compromising Daphe (G. B.)
>> British International Pictures/Wardour, 1930

>> Compromised
>> First National, 1931

Fitzgerald, Edith and Robert Riskin (also see the entry above)

> **Many a Slip** (P)

>> Illicit

Warner Brothers Pictures, Inc., 1931

Many a Slip
Universal Motion Pictures Co., 1931

Ex-Lady
Warner Brothers Pictures, Inc., 1933

Fleming, Joan M.

The Deeds of Dr. Deadcert

Family Doctor (G. B.)
Templar Prod., Ltd./Twentieth Century-Fox Film Corp.,
1958

Fletcher, Lucille [Lucille Fletcher Wallop]

Blindfold

Blindfold
Universal International Motion Pictures, 1966

$80 to Stamford

Revenge Squad
Comworld,. 1983

Night Watch (P)

Night Watch (G. B.)
Brut-Night Watch/Avco Embassy Pictures, 1973

Flexner, Anne Crawford (also see Alice Hegan Rice)

All Souls' Eve (P)

All Soul's Eve (*)
Realart Pictures Corp., 1921

The Blue Pearl (P)

The Blue Pearl (*)
L. Lawrence Weber Photo Dramas, Inc./Republic Dist.
Corp., 1920

Mrs. Wiggs of the Cabbage Patch (P, based on the same named
novel, by Alice Hegan Rice)

Mrs. Wiggs of the Cabbage Patch (*) (also based on the
novel Lovey Mary, by Alice Hegan Rice, and the novel
Mrs. Wiggs of the Cabbage Patch, by Rice, from which

126

the play was derived)
California Motion Pictures Corp.-Liebler Co./World
Film, 1914

Mrs. Wiggs of the Cabbage Patch (*) (also based on the
same named novel, by Alice Hegan Rice, from which the
play was derived)
Famous Players-Lasky Corp./Famous Players-Lasky Corp.--
Paramount Pictures Corp., 1919

Mrs. Wiggs of the Cabbage Patch (also based on the same
named novel, by Alice Hegan Rice, from which the play
was derived)
Paramount Pictures Corp., 1934

Mrs. Wiggs of the Cabbage Patch (also based on the same
named novel, by Alice Hegan Rice, from which the play
was derived)
Paramount Pictures Corp., 1942

Flint, Eva Kay and Martha Madison
    (Eva Kay Flint: pseud. of Eva Finklestein; Martha Madison:
    pseud. of Martha O'Dwyer)

    Subway Express (P)

        Subway Express
        Columbia Pictures Corp., 1931

    The Up and Up (P)

        Reckless Living (Note: Nass and Ross claim the picture
        was also based on the story "Twenty Grand," which the
        authors derived from their play. We find no
        verification it is a short story and not just a story
        treatment.)
        Universal Motion Pictures Co., 1931

Foldes, Yolanda

    Golden Earrings

        Golden Earrings
        Paramount Pictures Corp., 1947

    Make You a Good Wife

        My Own True Love
        Paramount Pictures Corp., 1948

Forbes, Esther

Johnny Tremain, a Novel for Old and Young

> Johnny Tremain
> Walt Disney Prod./Buena Vista Dist. Co., 1957

The Running of the Tide

> The Running of the Tide
> Metro-Goldwyn-Mayer, Inc., 1949

Forbes, Kathryn
  (pseud. of Kathryn Anderson McLean)

Mama's Bank Account (RS)

> I Remember Mama (also based on the play I Remember
> Mama, by John Van Druten, which was derived from
> Forbes' book)
> RKO Radio Pictures, Inc., 1948

Forbes, (Joan) Rosita

If the Gods Laugh

> Fighting Love (*)
> De Mille/Producers Dist. Corp., 1927

King's Mate

> The White Sheik (*) (G. B.)
> British International Pictures/Wardour, 1928

Forbes-Dennis, Phillis (see Phyllis Bottome)

Ford, Betty and Chris Chase

The Times of My Life (NF)

> The Betty Ford Story (TVM)
> Robert Papazian Prod.-David Wolper/American
> Broadcasting Co., 1987

Ford, Harriet and Alma Tell (also see the five entries below)

Main Street (P)

> Main Street (*) (also based on the same named novel, by
> Sinclair Lewis, from which the play was derived)
> Warner Brothers Pictures, Inc., 1923

Ford, Harriet and Caroline Duer (also see the entry above and the four entries below)

A Lady in Love (P)

> A Lady in Love (*)
> Famous Players-Lasky Corp./Famous Players-Lasky Corp.--
> Paramount Pictures Corp.-Artcraft Pictures Corp., 1920

Ford, Harriet and Eleanor Robson Belmont (also see the two entries above and the three entries below)

In the Next Room (P, based on the novel The Mystery of the Boule Cabinet; a Detective Story, by Burton Egbert Stevenson)

> In the Next Room (also based on the novel The Mystery of the Boule Cabinet; a Detective Story, by Burton E. Stevenson, from which the play was derived)
> First National, 1930

> The Case of the Black Parrot (also based on the novel The Mystery of the Boule Cabinet; a Detective Story, by Burton E. Stevenson, from which the play was derived)
> First National/Warner Brothers Pictures, Inc., 1941

Ford, Harriet and Harvey J. O'Higgins (also see the three entries above and the two entries below)

The Dummy; a Detective Comedy in Four Acts (P)

> The Dummy (*)
> Famous Players Film Co./Paramount Pictures Corp., 1917

> The Dummy
> Paramount Famous Lasky Corp., 1929

On the Hiring Line (P)

> Make Your Own Bed
> Warner Brothers Pictures, Inc., 1944

Ford, Harriet and Joseph Medill Patterson (also see the four entries above and the entry below)

The Fourth Estate (P)

> The Fourth Estate (*)
> Fox Film Corp., 1916

Ford, Harriet and William J. Burns and Harvey J. O'Higgins (also
    see the five entries above)

   The Argyle Case (P)

        The <u>Argyle</u> <u>Case</u> (*)
        Robert Warwick Film Corp./Lewis J. Selznick
        Enterprises, Inc.--Selznick Pictures Corp., 1917

        The <u>Argyle</u> <u>Case</u>
        Warner Brothers Pictures, Inc., 1929

Ford, Ruth

   Requiem for a Nun (P)

        <u>Sanctuary</u> (also based on the novel <u>Sanctuary</u>, by
        William Faulkner, from which the play was derived)
        Darryl F. Zanuck Prod./Twentieth Century-Fox Film
        Corp., 1961

Forney, Pauline and Dudley Murphy

   Boarding House Blues (S)

        <u>Jazz</u> <u>Heaven</u>
        RKO Radio Pictures, Inc., 1929

Forrester, Izola

   A Cafe in Cairo

        <u>A</u> <u>Cafe</u> <u>in</u> <u>Cairo</u> (*)
        Hunt Stromberg Prod./Producers Dist. Corp., 1924

   **The Dangerous Inheritance; or, the Mystery of the Tittani
   Rubies**

        <u>How</u> <u>Women</u> <u>Love</u> (*)
        B. B. Prod., 1922

   The Gray Path (S)

        <u>Youth</u> <u>for</u> <u>Sale</u> (*)
        C. C. Burr Pictures, 1924

   Restless Wives (S)

        <u>Restless</u> <u>Wives</u> (*)
        C. C. Burr Pictures, 1924

   Salvage (S)

        Wreckage (*)
        Banner Prod./Henry Ginsberg Dist. Corp., 1925

Forsslund, Louise (see Mary Louise Foster)

Forster, Margaret

    Georgy Girl

            Georgy Girl (G. B.)
            Everglades/Columbia Pictures Corp., 1966

Foster, Mary Louise (also see Rachel Crothers)
    (pseud. of Louise Forsslund)

    Old Lady Number 31

            The Captain is a Lady (also based on the play Old Lady
            31, by Rachel Crothers, which was derived from the
            novel by Forsslund)
            Metro-Goldwyn-Mayer, Inc., 1940

Fowler, Brenda and Ethel Clifton

    The Doormat (P)

            The Honeymoon Express (*)
            Warner Brothers Pictures, Inc., 1926

Fowler, Helen Marjorie

    Shades will not Vanish

            Strange Intruder
            Allied Artists, 1956

Fox, Paula

    Desperate Characters

            Desperate Characters
            Inc. Television Co./Paramount Pictures Corp., 1971

Foxman, Sherri

    Classified Love: a Guide to the Personals (NF)

Classified Love (TVM)
Columbia Broadcasting System Entertainment/Columbia
Broadcasting System, 1986

Francos, Ania

Sauve-Toi, Lola

Sauve-Toi, Lola (Fra./Can.)
Onyx-Cinepix-Films A2-Telefilm Canada-CNC-Sofimage-
Sofica Conseil-Gestimage, 1986

Frank, Anne (also see "Frances Goodrich and Albert Hackett"
    entry)

The Diary of Anne Frank (D)

The Diary of Anne Frank (also based on the play The
Diary of Anne Frank, by Frances Goodrich and Albert
Hackett, which was derived from Frank's diary)
Twentieth Century-Fox Film Corp., 1959

Frankau, Mrs. Julia Davis (see Frank Danby)

Frankau, Pamela

Jezebel

Jezebel
Warner Brothers Pictures, Inc., 1938

Franke, Caroline and Mack Crane

Bombshell (P)

Bombshell
Metro-Goldwyn-Mayer, Inc., 1933

Franken, Rose

Another Language (P)

Another Language
Metro-Goldwyn-Mayer, Inc., 1933

Claudia (P)

Claudia (also based on several unidentified short
stories in Redbook, by the same author, from which the

play was derived)
Twentieth Century-Fox Film Corp., 1943

Claudia and David

Claudia and David
Twentieth Century-Fox Film Corp., 1946

Holiday (P)

The Secret Heart (also based on the short story
"Twenty-Two," by Franken, from which the play was
derived)
Metro-Goldwyn-Mayer, Inc., 1946

Twenty-Two (S)

The Secret Heart (also based on the play Holiday, by
Franken, which was derived from the short story)
Metro-Goldwyn-Mayer, Inc., 1946

Franklin, J. E.

Black Girl (P)

Black Girl
Cinerama, 1972

Franklin, Pearl

Thunder, or Howdy Folks (P, based on an unidentified short
story, by Elia W. Peattie)

Thunder Mountain (*)
Fox Film Corp., 1925

Fraser-Smith, Cecily

A Honeymoon Adventure

A Honeymoon Adventure (G. B.)
Associated Talking Pictures/RKO Radio Pictures, Inc.,
1931

Frazer-Simpson, Cicely

The Clock

The Fatal Hour (G. B.)
British and Dominions Film Corp./Paramount Pictures
Corp. British, 1937

Fredrickson, Olive and Ben East

   Silence of the North (NF)

        <u>Silence</u> <u>of</u> <u>the</u> <u>North</u> (Can.)
        Universal Motion Pictures Co., 1981

Freedman, Nancy Mars and Benedict Freedman

   Mrs. Mike

        <u>Mrs.</u> <u>Mike</u>
        Regal Films International/United Artists Film Corp.,
        1949

Freeman, Lucy and Julie Roy

   **Betrayal: the True Story of the First Woman to Successfully
   Sue her Psychiatrist for Using Sex in the Guise of Therapy**
   (NF)

        <u>Betrayal</u> (TVM)
        Roger Gimbel Prod./Electrical and Musical Industries
        Television/National Broadcasting Co., 1978

Freeman, Mary Wilkins (also see the entry below)

   Madelon

        <u>False</u> <u>Evidence</u> (*)
        Metro Pictures Corp., 1919

Freeman, Mary Wilkins and Florence Morse Kingsley (also see the
   entry above)

   An Alabaster Box

        <u>An</u> <u>Alabaster</u> <u>Box</u> (*)
        Vitagraph Co. of America-a Blue Ribbon Feature/Greater
        Vitagraph, 1917

French, Marilyn

   The Woman's Room

        <u>The</u> <u>Women's</u> <u>Room</u> (TVM)
        Philip Mandelker Prod.-Warner Brothers
        Televison/American Broadcasting Co., 1980

Frings, Ketti
    (pseud. of Catherine Hartley)

    Hold Back the Dawn

        Hold <u>Back</u> <u>the</u> <u>Dawn</u>
        Paramount Pictures Corp., 1941

    Mr. Sycamore (P, based on the same named novelette, by Robert Ayres)

        Mr. <u>Sycamore</u>
        Capricorn/Film Venture, 1975

Fuller, Sarita
    (unidentified pseud.)

    Their Own Desire

        <u>Their</u> <u>Own</u> <u>Desire</u>
        Metro-Goldwyn-Mayer, Inc., 1929

Fulton, Maude

    The Brat (P)

        <u>The</u> <u>Brat</u> (*)
        The Nazimova Prod./Metro Pictures Corp.-Screen Classics, Inc., 1919

        <u>Brat</u>
        Fox Film Corp., 1931

        <u>Girl</u> <u>from</u> <u>Avenue</u> <u>A</u>
        Twentieth Century-Fox Film Corp., 1940

    The Humming Bird (P)

        <u>The</u> <u>Humming</u> <u>Bird</u> (*)
        Famous Players-Lasky Corp./Paramount Pictures Corp., 1924

Furness, Edith Ellis   (see Edith Ellis)

Furniss, Grace Livingston (also see the entry below)

    Gretna Green (P)

        <u>Gretna</u> <u>Green</u> (*)

Famous Players Film Co./Paramount Pictures Corp., 1915

Furniss, Grace Livingston and Abby Sage Richardson (also the see entry above)

The Pride of Jennico (P)

The Pride of Jennico (*)
Famous Players Film Co./State Rights, 1914

Futrelle, May Peel

Secretary of Frivolous Affairs

Secretary of Frivolous Affairs (*)
American Film/Mutual Film Corp.-A Mutual Masterpiece, 1915

- G -

Gaddis, Peggy

The Part-Time Wife (S)

The Part-Time Wife (*)
Gotham/Lumas Film Corp., 1925

Gale, Zona

Faint Perfume

Faint Perfume (*)
B. P. Schulberg Prod., 1925

Miss Lulu Bett (N/P)

Miss Lulu Bett (*)
Famous Players-Lasky Corp./Paramount Pictures Corp.,
1921

The Way (S)

When Strangers Meet
Liberty, 1934

Galland, Victoria

The Golden Gallows (S)

The Golden Gallows (*)
Universal Motion Pictures Co., 1922

Gallico, Pauline and Paul Gallico

Trial by Terror

Assignment Paris
Columbia Pictures Corp., 1952

Gannet, Lotta

Her Decision (S)

Her Decision (*)

137

Triangle Film Corp./Triangle Dist. Corp., 1918

Gare, Nene

The Fringe Dwellers

The Fringe Dwellers (Austr.)
Fringe Dwellers-Ozfilm/Atlantic, 1986

Garland, June

Widows are Dangerous (P)

Trouble with Eve (G. B.)
Blakeley's Films/Butcher's Film Service, 1960

Garner, Helen

Monkey Grip

Monkey Grip (Austr.)
Pavilion Films-Cinecom-Mainline, 1982

Garnier, Christine

The Heroes are Tired (S)

Heroes and Sinners
Janus Films, 1959

Gaskell, Jane

All Neat in Black Stockings

All Neat in Black Stockings (G. B.)
Miron/Anglo-Amalgamated Film, 1968

Gaskell, (Mrs.) Elizabeth

A Manchester Marriage

Heartstrings (*) (G. B.)
British and Colonial Kinematograph, Co., 1923

Gates, Eleanor

Cupid: The Cow-Punch

Cupid, the Cowpuncher (*)
Goldwyn Pictures Corp./Goldwyn Dist. Corp., 1920

Doc (S)

Doc (*)
Bosburn Photoplay Co./Sawyer, Inc., 1914

The Plow Woman

The Plow Woman (*)
Universal Film Manufacturing Co.-a Butterfly
Picture/Universal Film Manufacturing Co., 1917

The Poor Little Rich Girl (N/P)

The Poor Little Rich Girl (*)
Artcraft Pictures Corp., 1917

Poor Little Rich Girl
Twentieth Century-Fox Film Corp., 1936

Search for the Spring

Once to Every Bachelor
M. H. Hoffman/Liberty, 1934

Gehrig, Eleanor and Joseph Durso

My Luke and I (NF)

A Love Affair: The Eleanor and Lou Gehrig Story (TVM)
Charles Fries Prod.-Stonehenge Prod./National
Broadcasting Co., 1978

Geoffreys, Oliver W.
(Pseud. of Eve M. Unsell)

The Marionettes (P)

The Ransom (*)
Triumph Film Corp./Equitable Motion Picture Corp.-World
Film, 1916

George, Jean Craighead

My Side of the Mountain

My Side of the Mountain (U. S./Can.)
Robert Radnitz Prod./Paramount Pictures Corp., 1969

139

George, Kathleen B. and Robert A. Granger

    Ten Against Caeser

        <u>Gun</u> <u>Fury</u>
        Columbia Pictures Corp., 1953

Gerald, Florence

    The Woman Pays (P)

        <u>The</u> <u>Woman</u> <u>Pays</u> (*)
        Columbia Pictures Corp./Metro Pictures Corp., 1915

Gerard, Louise

    A Son of the Sahara

        <u>A</u> <u>Son</u> <u>of</u> <u>the</u> <u>Sahara</u> (*)
        Edwin Carewe Prod./Associated First National, 1924

Gerould, Katherine F.

    Conquistador

        <u>The</u> <u>Yankee</u> <u>Senor</u> (*)
        Fox Film Corp., 1926

        <u>Romance</u> <u>of</u> <u>the</u> <u>Rio</u> <u>Grande</u>
        Fox Film Corp., 1929

        <u>Romance</u> <u>of</u> <u>the</u> <u>Rio</u> <u>Grande</u>
        Twentieth Century-Fox Film Corp., 1941

Giancana, Antoinette and Thomas C. Renner

    Mafia Princess (NF)

        <u>Mafia</u> <u>Princess</u> (TVM)
        Jack Farren Prod.-Group W. Prod./National Broadcasting
        Co., 1986

Gibson, Margaret

    Making It (S)

        <u>Outrageous!</u> (Can.)
        Film Consortium of Canada-Canadian Film
        Development/Cinema 5, 1977

Gies, Miep and Alison Leslie Gold

    Anne Frank Remembered (NF)

        Attic: The Hiding of Anne Frank (TVM) (U. S./G. B.)
        Telecom Entertainment-Yorkshire Television/Columbia
        Broadcasting System, 1988

Gilbert, Anthony
    (pseud. of Lucy Beatrice Malleson)

    The Mouse Who Wouldn't Play Ball

        Candles at Nine (G. B.)
        British National Films, Ltd./Anglo, 1944

    The Vanished Corpse

        They Met in the Dark (G. B.)
        I. P.-Excelsior Feature Film Co./General Film, 1943

    The Woman in Red

        My Name is Julia Ross
        Columbia Pictures Corp., 1945

Gilden, Katya (see K. B. Gilden)

Gilden, K. B.
    (joint pseud. of Katya Gilden and Bert Gilden)

    Hurry Sundown

        Hurry Sundown
        Sigma Prod./Paramount Pictures Corp., 1966

Gilman, Dorothy [Dorothy Gilman Butters]

    The Unexpected Mrs. Pollifax

        Mrs. Pollifox -- Spy
        United Artists Film Corp., 1971

Gilman, Mildred

    Sob Sister

        Sob Sister

Fox Film Corp., 1931

Gittelson, Celia

   Saving Grace

      Saving Grace
      Embassy Pictures Corp./Columbia Pictures Corp., 1986

Glasgow, Ellen

   In This our Life

      In This our Life
      Warner Brothers Pictures, Inc., 1942

Glaspell, Susan

   Brook Evans

      The Right to Love
      Paramount Pictures Corp., 1930

Glass, Franckina

   Marvin and Tige

      Marvin and Tige
      Marvin Film Partners/Major Films, 1983

Glatzle, Mary and Evelyn Fiore

   Muggable Mary (NF)

      Muggable Mary: Street Cop (TVM)
      Columbia Broadcasting System Entertainment/Columbia
      Broadcasting System, 1982

Glyn, Elinor

   Beyond the Rocks; a Love Story

      Beyond the Rocks (*)
      Paramount Pictures Corp., 1922

   The Career of Katherine Bush

      The Career of Catherine Bush (*)
      Famous Players-Lasky Corp./Famous Players-Lasky Corp.--

a Paramount-Artcraft Special, 1919

The Great Moment

The Great Moment (*)
Famous Players-Lasky Corp., 1921

His Hour

His Hour (*)
Louis B. Mayer Prod./Metro-Goldwyn Pictures, 1924

It (S)

It (*)
Famous Players Film Co./Paramount Pictures Corp., 1927

Knowing Men

Knowing Men (G. B.)
Talkicolor/United Artists Film Corp., 1930

Love's Blindness

Love's Blindness (*)
Metro-Goldwyn-Mayer, Inc., 1926

Man and Maid

Man and Maid (*)
Metro-Goldwyn-Mayer, Inc., 1925

The Man and the Moment

The Man and the Moment (*) (G. B.)
Windsor Pictures Corp./Walturdaw, 1918

Mad Hour (*)
First National-Warner Brothers Pictures, Inc., 1928

Man and the Moment
First National, 1929

One Day: a Sequel to Three Weeks

One Day (*)
Moss/M. H. Hoffman-Foursquare Pictures, 1916

One Hour

One Hour (*)
Moss, 1917

The Price of Things

The Price of Things
Elinor Glyn/United Artists Film Corp., 1930

The Reason Why

The Reason Why (*)
C. K. Y. Film Corp./Select Picturess Corp.-Select Star
Series, 1918

Soul Mates (*)
Metro-Goldwyn-Mayer, Inc., 1925

Six Days

Six Days (*)
Goldwyn Pictures Corp./Goldwyn Dist. Corp.-
Cosmopolitan, 1923

Such Men are Dangerous (S)

Such Men are Dangerous
Fox Film Corp., 1930

Three Weeks

Three Weeks (*)
Reliable Feature Film Corp./State Rights, 1914

Three Weeks (*)
Goldwyn Pictures Corp./Goldwyn Dist. Corp.-
Cosmopolitan, 1924

The Vicissitudes of Evangeline

Red Hair (*)
Paramount Famous Lasky Corp., 1928

Godden, (Margaret) Rumer

The Battle of the Villa Fiorita

The Affair at the Villa Fiorita (G. B.)
Warner Brothers Pictures, Inc., 1964

Black Narcissus

Black Narcissus (G. B.)
Independent Producers-Archers Film Prod./General Film
Dist., 1947

An Episode of Sparrows

Innocent Sinners (G. B.)
J. Arthur Rank Film Prod./J. Arthur Rank Film Dist.,

Ltd., 1957

Fugue in Time

> Enchantment
> RKO Radio Pictures Corp., 1949

The Greengage Summer

> The Greengage Summer (G. B.)
> PKL Pictures/Columbia Pictures Corp., 1960

In This House of Brede

> In This House of Brede (TVM)
> Tomorrow Entertainment, Inc./Columbia Broadcasting
> System, 1975

The River

> The River
> United Artists Film Corp., 1951

Gold, Alison Leslie and Miep Gies

Anne Frank Remembered (NF)

> Attic: The Hiding of Anne Frank (TVM) (U. S./G. B.)
> Telecom Entertainment-Yorkshire Television/Columbia
> Broadcasting System, 1988

Goldman, Wendy and Judy Toll

Casual Sex? (P)

> Casual Sex?
> Jascat/Universal Motion Pictures Co., 1988

Goldsmith, Barbara

Little Gloria . . . Happy at Last (NF)

> Little Gloria . . . Happy at Last (TVM)
> Edgar J. Scherick--Metromedia Producers Corp.--London
> Films Prod.--Cine-Gloria Prod/National Broadcasting
> Co., 1982

Goldstein, Marilyn

Always a Victim (A)

        Murder: By Reason of Insanity (TVM)
        LS Entertainment, Inc./ Columbia Broadcasting System,
        1985

Goode, Ruth and Sol Horok

        Impressario

                Tonight We Sing
                Twentieth Century-Fox Film Corp., 1953

Goodfellow, Dorothy

        The Street of the Flying Dragon (S)

                Five Days to Live (*)
                R-C Pictures, 1922

Goodin, Peggy

        Clementine

                Mickey
                Eagle-Lion, 1948

        Take Care of My Little Girl

                Take Care of My Little Girl
                Twentieth Century-Fox Film Corp., 1951

Goodman, Ruth [Ruth Goodman Goetz] and Augustus Goetz

        The Heiress (P, based on the novel Washington Square by
        Henry James)

                The Heiress
                Paramount Pictures Corp., 1949

Goodrich, Frances and Albert Hackett

        The Diary of Anne Frank (P, based on The Diary of Anne Frank,
        by Frank)

                The Diary of Anne Frank (also based on the nonfiction
                book The Diary of Anne Frank, by Frank, from which the
                play was derived)
                Twentieth Century-Fox Film Corp., 1959

                The Diary of Anne Frank (TVM)
                Katz-Gallin/Half Pint Prod.--Twentieth Century-Fox

                                146

Television/National Broadcasting Co., 1980

Up Pops the Devil (P)

Up Pops the Devil
Paramount Pictures Corp., 1931

Thanks for the Memory
Paramount Pictures Corp., 1938

Goose, Elizabeth Foster

Polly Put the Kettle On (So)

Polly Put the Kettle On (*)
Universal Film Manufacturing Co./Universal Film
Manufacturing Co.-Red Feather Photoplays, 1917

Gordon, Barbara

I'm Dancing as Fast as I Can (NF)

I'm Dancing as Fast as I Can
Paramount Pictures Corp., 1982

Gordon, Mildred and Gordon Gordon

Case File: FBI

Down Three Dark Streets
Edward Small Prod./United Artists Film Corp., 1954

Make Haste to Live

Make Haste to Live
Republic Pictures Corp., 1954

Operation Terror

Experiment in Terror
Geoffrey-Kate Prod./Columbia Pictures Corp., 1962

Undercover Cat

That Darn Cat
Walt Disney Prod./Buena Vista Dist. Co., 1965

Gordon, Ruth (also see the entry below)

Over 21 (P)

Over 21
Columbia Pictures Corp., 1945

A Very Rich Woman (P, based on the foreign language play Les Joies de Famille, by Phillippe Heriat)

Rosie!
Ross Hunter Prod./Universal Motion Pictures Co., 1967

Years Ago (P)

The Actress
Metro-Goldwyn-Mayer, Inc./Loew's, Inc., 1953

Gordon, Ruth and Garson Kanin (also see the entry above)

Adam's Rib (P)

Adam's Rib
Metro-Goldwyn-Mayer, Inc., 1949

Gosling, Paula

Fair Game

Cobra
Cannon Screen Entertainment/Warner Brothers Pictures, Inc., 1986

Gottlieb, Linda and Joan Silver

Limbo

Limbo
Universal Motion Pictures Co., 1972

Goudge, Elizabeth

Green Dolphin Street

Green Dolphin Street
Metro-Goldwyn-Mayer, Inc., 1947

Gould, Amy Kennedy (also see the entry below)

The Love Outcast

Checkmate (G. B.)
British and Dominions Film Corp.-Parmount Pictures Corp. British, 1935

Gould, Amy Kennedy and Ralph Neale (also see the entry above)

Wayward Youth (P)

> The Way of Youth (G. B.)
> British and Dominions Film Corp./Paramount Pictures
> Corp. British, 1934

Gould, Lois

Such Good Friends

> Such Good Friends
> Sigma Prod./Paramount Pictures Corp., 1972

Goyder, Margot (see Margot Neville)

Grafton, Sue

Lolly-Madonna XXX

> The Lolly-Madonna War
> Metro-Goldwyn-Mayer, Inc., 1973

Graham, Sheilah and Gerald Frank

Beloved Infidel (NF)

> Beloved Infidel
> Twentieth Century Fox Film Corp., 1960

Graham, (Matilda) Winifred

The Love Story of a Mormon

> Trapped by the Mormons (*) (G. B.)
> Master Films/White, 1922

Gray, Maxwell
(pseud. of Mary Gleed Tuttiett)

The Last Sentence

> The Last Sentence (*)
> Thomas A. Edison, Inc./Greater Vitagraph, 1917

The Silence of Dean Maitland: a Novel by Maxwell Gray

Sealed Lips (*)
Equitable Motion Pictures Corp./World Film, 1915

Green, Anna Katherine (married name of Anna Katherine Rohlfs)

The Leavenworth Case

The Leavenworth Case (*)
Whitman Bennett Prod./Vitagraph Co. of America, 1923

The Leavenworth Case
Republic Pictures Corp., 1936

The Mayor's Wife

His Wife's Husband (*)
Pyramid Pictures/American Releasing Corp, 1922

The Millionaire Baby

The Millionaire Baby (*)
Selig Polyscope Co.-a Red Seal Play/Greater Vitagraph,
1915

Green, Hannah (also see Joanne Greenberg)
(pseud. of Joanne Greenberg)

I Never Promised You a Rose Garden

I Never Promised You a Rose Garden
Imorh/New World Cinema, 1977

Green, Janet
(pseud. of Victoria McCormick)

Mathilda Shouted Fire (P)

Midnight Lace
Ross Hunter Prod.-Arwin Prod., Inc.,/Universal Motion
Pictures Co., 1960

Midnight Lace (TVM)
Four R Prod./Universal Television/National Broadcasting
Co., 1981

Murder Mistaken (P)

Cast a Dark Shadow (G. B.)
Frobisher/Eros Films, 1955

Greenberg, Joanne (see Hannah Green)

    In This Sign

        Love is Never Silent (TVM)
        Marian Rees Associates/National Broadcasting Co., 1985

Greene, Bette

    Summer of My German Soldier

        Summer of My German Soldier (TVM)
        Highgate Prod./National Broadcasting Co., 1978

Greene, Frances Nimmo

    The Devil to Pay

        The Devil to Pay (*)
        Robert Brunton Prod./Pathe Exchange, Inc., 1920

    One Clear Call

        One Clear Call (*)
        Louis B. Mayer/Associated First National, 1922

Greene, Sarah P. McLean [Sarah P. McLean]

    Cape Cod Folks

        Women Who Give (*)
        Louis B. Mayer Prod./Metro-Goldwyn Dist. Corp., 1924

Gregory, Lady

    1921 (P)

        The Rising of the Moon (G. B.) (AF, the other two
        segments of the movie are based on the plays The
        Majesty of the Law, by Frank O'Connor and A Minute's
        Wait by Martin McHugh)
        Four Provinces/Warner Brothers Pictures, Inc., 1957

Greig, Maysie

    Peggy of Beacon Hill

        The Love Gamble (*)
        Banner Prod./Henry Ginsberg Dist. Corp., 1925

Satin Straps

> Satin Straps
> Tiffany Prod., 1929

Griffin, Eleanore

Class Prophecy (S)

> When Love is Young
> Universal International Motion Pictures, 1937

Griffith, Corine

Papa's Delicate Condition

> Papa's Delicate Condition
> Amro/Paramount Pictures Corp., 1962

Grimshaw, Beatrice

My Lady of the Island

> Thunder Island (*)
> Universal Film Manufacturing Co., 1921

Gross, (Mrs.) Alexander

Break the Walls Down (P)

> Walls of Prejudice (*) (G. B.)
> Gaumont/British Screencraft, 1920

> Serving Two Masters (*)
> Lee-Bradford Corp., 1921

Gross, Cordelia Baird

It's Hard to Find Mecca in Flushing (S)

> This Could be the Night (also based on the short story
> "Protection for a Tough Racket," by Gross)
> Metro-Goldwyn-Mayer, Inc., 1957

Protection for a Tough Racket (S)

> This Could be the Night (also based on the short story
> "It's Hard to Find Mecca in Flushing," by Gross)
> Metro-Goldwyn-Mayer, Inc., 1957

Grundy, Mabel Barnes

Candytuft, I Mean Veronica

Candytuft, I Mean Veronica (*) (G. B.)
Zodiac/Cosmograph, 1921

The Mating of Marcus

The Mating of Marcus (*) (G. B.)
Stoll, 1924

Guest, Judith

Ordinary People

Ordinary People
Wildwood/Paramount Pictures Corp., 1981

Gundy, Elizabeth

Bliss

The Seduction of Miss Leona (TVM)
Edgar J. Scherick/Columbia Broadcasting System, 1980

Gunn, (Mrs.) Aeneas (Jeannie)

We of the Never Never (NF)

We of the Never Never (Austr.)
Adams-Packer-Mainline/Triumph Film Corp., 1982

Gutcheon, Beth

Still Missing

Without a Trace
Twentieth Century-Fox Film Corp., 1983

Haber, Joyce

The Users

> The Users (TVM)
> Aaron Spelling Prod./American Broadcasting Co., 1978

Halbert, Sandra and Frederic Halbert

Bitter Harvest (NF)

> Bitter Harvest (TVM)
> Charles Fries Prod./National Broadcasting Co., 1981

Hall, Jane

These Glamour Girls (S)

> These Glamour Girls
> Metro-Goldwyn-Mayer, Inc., 1939

Hall, Jenni

Ask Agamemnon

> Goodbye Gemini (G. B.)
> Josef Shaftel/Cinerama, 1970

Halvorson, Marilyn

Cowboys Don't Cry

> Cowboys Don't Cry (Can.)
> Atlantis-Canadian Broadcasting Co.-Beacon/Cineplex
> Odeon, 1988

Hambledon, Phyllis
(pseud. of Phyllis MacVean)

No Difference to Me

> No Place for Jennifer (G. B.)
> Associated British Picture Corp./Associated British and
> Pathe Film Dist., 1950

Hamilton, Cicely

    Diana of Dobson's (P)

        Diana of Dobson's (*) (G. B.)
        Reginald Barker Prod./Ideal, 1917

Hamilton, Nancy and Rosemary Casey and James Shute

    Return Engagement (P)

        Fools for Scandal
        Warner Brothers Pictures, Inc., 1938

Hamlin, Mary and George Arliss

    Alexander Hamilton (P)

        Alexander Hamilton
        Warner Brothers Pictures, Inc., 1931

Handcock, Mary A.

    Menace of the Mountain

        Menace on the Mountain (TVM)
        Walt Disney Prod./National Broadcasting Co., 1970

Handley, Dorothy Curnow

    Room for Two (S)

        Rosie the Riveter
        Republic Pictures Corp., 1944

Hanff, Helene

    84 Charing Cross Road (NF/P)

        84 Charing Cross Road
        Brooksfilms/Columbia Pictures Corp., 1987

Hanlon, Brooke

    Delicatessen (S)

        It Must be Love (*)

John McCormick Prod./First National, 1926

Hannum, Alberta

Roseanna McCoy

Roseanna Mc Coy
Samuel Goldwyn Prod./RKO Radio Pictures, Inc., 1949

Hansberry, Lorraine

A Raisin in the Sun (P)

A Raisin in the Sun
Paman-Doris/Columbia Pictures Corp., 1961

Hansford-Johnson, Pamela

The Trojan Brothers

The Trojan Brothers (G. B.)
British National Films, Ltd./Anglo-Amalgamated Film,
1946

Harding, Bertita

Magic Fire

Magic Fire
Republic Pictures Corp., 1956

**Phantom Crown: The Story of Maximilian and Carlotta of
Mexico**

Juarez (also based on the play Juarez and Maximilian,
by Franz Werfel)
Warner Brothers Pictures, Inc.., 1939

Hardy, Jocelyn Lee

Everything is Thunder

Everything is Thunder (G. B.)
Gaumont, 1936

Hardy, Rene
(pseud. of Amere Victoire)

Bitter Victory

Bitter Victory (Fra./G. B.)
Transcontinental-Robert Laffont/Columbia Pictures
Corp., 1957

Harmon, Leola Mae

Why Me? (NF)

Why Me? (TVM)
Lorimar Prod./American Broadcasting Co., 1984

Harper, Barbara

Safe Harbour (S)

Port of Escape (G. B.)
Wellington/ Renown Pictures Corp., 1956

Harragan, Betty Lehan

Games Mother Never Taught You: Corporate Gamesmanship for
Women (NF)

Games Mother Never Taught You (TVM)
Columbia Broadcasting System Entertainment/Columbia
Broadcasting System, 1982

Harrington, Cicely

Lady Noggs-Peeress (P)

Lady Noggs-Peeress (*) (G. B.) (also based on the same
named novel, by Selwyn Jepson, from which the play was
derived)
Progress/Butcher's Film Service, 1920

Harris, Barbara S.

Who is Julia?

Who is Julia? (TVM)
Columbia Broadcasting System Entertainment/Columbia
Broadcasting System, 1986

Harris, Corra

Circuit Rider's Wife

> I'd Climb the Highest Mountain
> Twentieth Century-Fox Film Corp., 1951

Making Her His Wife

> Husbands and Wives (*)
> Gaumont Co./State Rights, 1920

Harris, Marilyn [Marilyn Harris Springer]

Hatter Fox

> The Girl Called Hatter Fox (TVM)
> Roger Gimbel Prod./Electrical and Musical Industries
> Television/Columbia Broadcasting System, 1977

Harris, Theodosia

Martyrs of the Alamo (N, which may not have been published)

> The Martyrs of the Alamo (*)
> Fine Arts Film Co./Triangle Film Corp., 1915

Harrison, (Mrs.) Burton (Constance Cary)

The Unwelcome Mrs. Hatch (P)

> The Unwelcome Mrs. Hatch (*)
> Famous Players Film Co., 1914

Hart, Frances Noyes

The Bellamy Trial

> The Bellamy Trial
> Metro-Goldwyn-Mayer, Inc., 1929

Hartley, Catherine (see Ketti Frings)

Harvey, Lola and Syd Courtenay

The Idol of Moolah (P)

> Kiss Me Sergeant (G. B.)
> British International Pictures/Wardour, 1930

Haskin, Louise

The Man at the Gate (Po)

>   The Man at the Gate (G. B.)
>   Gregory, Hake and Walker Prod./General Film, 1941

Hastings, Charlotte

Bonaventure (P)

>   Thunder on the Hill
>   Universal Motion Pictures Co., 1951

Uncertain Joy (P)

>   The Scamp (G. B.)
>   Lawrie/Grand National Pictures, 1957

Hastings, Phyllis

Rapture in my Rags

>   Rapture (U. S./Fra.)
>   Panoramic Prod./Twentieth Century-Fox Film Corp., 1965

Hatton, Fanny and Frederic Hatton (also see the entry below)

The Azure Shore (S)

>   The Rush Hour (*)
>   De Mille/Pathe Exchange, Inc., 1927

Dancing Partner (P, based on a play by, Alexander Engel and Alfred Grunwald)

>   Just a Gigolo
>   Metro-Goldwyn-Mayer, Inc., 1931

The Indestructible Wife (P)

>   The Indestructible Wife (*)
>   Select Pictures Corp., 1919

Lombardi, Ltd. (P)

>   Lombardi, Ltd. (*)
>   Screen Classics, Inc./Metro Pictures Corp., 1919

Synthetic Sin (P)

>   Synthetic Sin (*)
>   First National, 1929

159

The Waning Sex (P)

>The Waning Sex (*)
>Metro-Goldwyn-Mayer, Inc., 1926

Upstairs and Down (P)

>Upstairs and Down (*)
>Selznick Pictures Corp./Select Pictures Corp.-a Star
>Series Attraction, 1919

The Walk-Offs (P)

>The Walk-Offs (*)
>Screen Classics, Inc./Metro Pictures Corp., 1920

With the Tide (S)

>South Sea Love (*)
>Fox Film Corp., 1923

Hatton, Fanny and Frederic Hatton and Leo Ditrichstein (also see
the entry above)

The Great Lover (P)

>The Great Lover (*)
>Goldwyn Pictures Corp.-Frank Lloyd Prod./Goldwyn Dist.
>Corp., 1920

>The Great Lover
>Metro-Goldwyn-Mayer, Inc., 1931

Hatvany, Lily

Tonight or Never (P)

>Tonight or Never
>Samuel Goldwyn Prod./United Artists Film Corp., 1931

Hayden, Torey

Murphy's Boy (NF)

>Trapped in Silence (TVM)
>Reader's Digest Entertainment, Inc./Columbia
>Broadcasting System, 1986

Hayes, Marrijane and Joseph Hayes

Bonvoyage

<u>Bonvoyage</u>
Walt Disney Prod./Buena Vista Dist. Co., 1962

Hayward, Brooke

Haywire

<u>Haywire</u> (TVM)
Pando Prod.-Warner Brothers Television/Columbia
Broadcasting System, 1980

Hayward, Grace and Howard McKent Barnes and Melville Burke

Her Unborn Child (P)

<u>Her</u> <u>Unborn</u> <u>Child</u>
Windsor Pictures Corp., 1929

Head, Ann
(pseud. of Anne Christensen Morse)

Mr. and Mrs. Bo Jo Jones

<u>Mr.</u> <u>and</u> <u>Mrs.</u> <u>Bo</u> <u>Jo</u> <u>Jones</u> (TVM)
Twentieth Century-Fox Television/American Broadcasting
Co., 1971

Hearst, Patty and Alvin Moscow

Every Secret Thing (NF)

<u>Patty</u> <u>Hearst</u>
Atlantic-Zenith, 1988

Hebert, Anne

Kamouraska

<u>Kamouraska</u> (Can./Fra.)
France Film-Carle-Lamy-Pare-SDICC/New Line Cinema, 1973

Les Four de Bassan

<u>Les</u> <u>Fous</u> <u>de</u> <u>Bassan</u> [The Crazy People of Bassan]
(Can./Fra.)
Vivafilms International, 1987

Heidish, Marcy

161

A Woman Called Moses: A Novel Based on the Life of Harriet Tubman

> A <u>Woman</u> <u>Called</u> <u>Moses</u> (TVM)
> Jaffe Prod./I K E Prod./Jaffe Enterprises/National
> Broadcasting Co., 1978

Hellman, Lillian Florence

Another Part of the Forest (P)

> <u>Another</u> <u>Part</u> <u>of</u> <u>the</u> <u>Forest</u>
> Universal Motion Pictures Co., 1948

The Children's Hour (P)

> <u>These</u> <u>Three</u>
> Samuel Goldwyn Prod./United Artists Film Corp., 1936

> <u>The</u> <u>Children's</u> <u>Hour</u>
> Mirsch Corp.-World Wide/United Artists Film Corp., 1961

The Little Foxes (P)

> <u>The</u> <u>Little</u> <u>Foxes</u>
> RKO Radio Pictures, Inc., 1941

North Star

> <u>The</u> <u>North</u> <u>Star</u>
> Crescent Prod./RKO Radio Pictures, Inc., 1943

Pentimento (NF)

> <u>Julia</u>
> Twentieth Century-Fox Film Corp., 1977

The Searching Wind (P)

> <u>The</u> <u>Searching</u> <u>Wind</u>
> Paramount Pictures Corp., 1946

Toys in the Attic (P)

> <u>Toys</u> <u>in</u> <u>the</u> <u>Attic</u>
> Mirsch Corp.-Claude Prod./United Artists Film Corp.,
> 1963

Watch on the Rhine (P)

> <u>Watch</u> <u>on</u> <u>the</u> <u>Rhine</u>
> Warner Brothers Pictures, Inc., 1943

162

Hemmingway, Joan and Paul Bonnecarrere

    Rosebud

        <u>Rosebud</u>
        Otto Preminger/United Artists Film Corp., 1975

Henderson, Sylvia (see Sylvia Ashton-Warner)

Henderson, Zenna

    Ararat (S)

        <u>The People</u> (TVM)
        Metromedia Producers Corp.-American Zoetrope/American
        Broadcasting Co., 1972

Henley, Beth

    Crimes of the Heart (P)

        <u>Crimes of the Heart</u>
        Fields-Sugarman/DD Entertainment, 1986

Henry, Clarissa and Marc Hillel

    Au Nom de la Race [Of the Name of the Race] (NF)

        <u>Of Pure Blood</u>
        K-M Prod.--Joseph Sargent Prod.--Warner Brothers
        Televison/Columbia Broadcasting System, 1986

Henry, Harriet

    Jackdaws Strut

        <u>Bought</u>
        Warner Brothers Pictures, Inc., 1931

    Lady with a Past

        <u>Lady With a Past</u>
        RKO Radio Pictures, Inc., 1932

Henry, Joan
    (unidentified pseud.)

    Who Lie in Gaol

The Weak and the Wicked (G. B.)
Marble Arch/Associated British and Pathe Film Dist.,
1954

Yield to the Night

Yield to the Night (G. B.)
Kenwood/Associated British and Pathe Film Dist., 1956

Henry, Marguerite

Brighty of the Grand Canyon

Brighty of the Grand Canyon
Stephen F. Booth Prod./Feature Film Corp., 1966

Misty of Chincoteague

Misty
Twentieth Century-Fox Film Corp., 1961

San Domingo, the Medicine Hat Stallion

Peter Lundy and the Medicine Hat Stallion (TVM)
Ed Friendly Prod., 1977

Henry, Noelle

Je ne Suis Pas une Heroine

So Little Time (G. B.)
Mayflower Photoplay Corp./Associated British and Pathe
Film Dist., 1952

Henstell, Diana

Friend

Deadly Friend
Pan Arts Co.-Layton/Warner Brothers Pictures, Inc.,
1986

Herkes, Maibelle

Hope Rides with Me (S)

The End of the Trail (*)
Fox Film Corp., 1916

Herman, Muriel and Arthur Herzog, Jr. and Al Rosen

Mary Had a Little (P)

Mary Had a Little (G. B.)
Caralan and Dador/United Artists Film Corp., 1961

Herne, Julie

The Outsider (P)

The Misfit Wife (*)
Metro Pictures Corp., 1920

Herron, Stella

Shoes (S)

Shoes (*)
Bluebird Photoplays, Inc., 1916

Heyer, Georgette

The Reluctant Widow

The Reluctant Widow (G. B.)
Two Cities Films, Ltd./General Film, 1950

Heyland, Alexine

"Oh, Annice!" (S)

The Gold Cure (*)
Metro Pictures Corp., 1919

Heyward, Dorothy and Dubose Heyward

Porgy (P)

Porgy and Bess (also based on the operetta Porgy and
Bess, by Dubose Heyward and George Gershwin, which was
derived from the play by the Heywards, and on the novel
Porgy, by Dubose Heyward, from which the play was
derived)
Samuel Goldwyn Prod./Columbia Pictures Corp., 1959

Highsmith, (Mary) Patricia

Strangers on a Train

        Strangers on a Train
        Warner Brothers Pictures, Inc., 1951

        Once You Kiss a Stranger
        Warner Brothers Pictures, Inc.-Seven Arts, Inc., 1969

Hill, Betty and Barney Hill and John G. Fuller

    The Interrupted Journey (NF)

        The UFO Incident (TVM)
        Universal Television/National Broadcasting Co., 1975

Hill, Katherine

    The Shuttle Soul

        Dusk to Dawn (*)
        Florence Vidor Prod./Associated Exhibitors, Inc., 1922

Hill, Ruth Beebe

    Hanta Yo

        The Mystic Warrior (TVM)
        David Wolper-Stan Margulies Prod.--Warner Brothers
        Television/American Broadcasting Co., 1984

Hinton, Jane

    The Devil was Sick (P)

        God's Gift to Women
        Warner Brothers Pictures, Inc., 1931

Hinton, S. E.

    The Outsiders

        The Outsiders
        American Zoetrope/Warner Brothers Pictures, Inc., 1983

    Rumblefish

        Rumble Fish
        American Zoetrope/Universal Motion Pictures Co., 1983

    Tex

Tex
Walt Disney Prod./Buena Vista Dist. Co., 1982

That was Then . . . This is Now

That was Then . . . This is Now
Media Ventures-Alan Belkin/Paramount Pictures Corp.,
1985

Hintze, Naomi A.

Aloha Means Goodbye

Aloha Means Goodbye (TVM)
Universal Televison/Columbia Broadcasting System, 1974

You'll Like my Mother

You'll Like my Mother
BCP/Universal Motion Pictures Co., 1972

Hobart, Alice Tisdale

The Cup and the Sword

This Earth is Mine
Vintage Prod./Universal Motion Pictures Co., 1959

Oil for the Lamps of China

Oil for the Lamps of China
Cosmopolitan Films/Warner Brothers Pictures, Inc.-
First National, 1935

Law of the Tropics
Warner Brothers Pictures, Inc., 1941

Hobart, Vera

Ring Around the Moon

Ring Around the Moon
Chesterfield Motion Pictures, 1936

Hobson, Laura Z.

Consenting Adult

Consenting Adult (TVM)
Starger Co. Presentations--Lawrence-Aghayan Prod./
American Broadcasting Co., 1985

Gentlemen's Agreement

Gentlemen's Agreement
Twentieth Century-Fox Film Corp., 1947

The Tenth Month

The Tenth Month (TVM)
Joe Hamilton Prod./Columbia Broadcasting System, 1979

Hocken, Sheila

Emma and I (NF)

Second Sight: A Love Story (TVM)
Entheos Unlimited Prod.-TTC Enterprises/Columbia
Broadcasting System, 1984

Hocking, Anne
(pseud. of Mona Messer)

The Wicked Flee

The Surgeon's Knife (G. B.)
Gibraltar/Grand National Pictures, 1957

Holden, Anne

The Witnesses

The Bedroom Window
DeLaurentiis Entertainment Group, 1987

Holding, Elizabeth Saxnay

The Blank Wall

The Reckless Moment
Columbia Pictures Corp., 1949

The Bride Comes Home (S)

The Bride Comes Home
Paramount Pictures Corp., 1935

Holdsworth, Mrs. E. (Ethel Carnie)

Helen of Four Gates, by an Ex-Mill-Girl

Helen of Four Gates (*) (G. B.)
Hepworth, 1920

Poison

The Pleydell Mystery (*) (G. B.)
British Empire, 1916

Holiday, Billie and William Dufty

Lady Sings the Blues (NF)

Lady Sings the Blues
Motown-Weston-Furie/Paramount Pictures Corp., 1972

Holland, Hester

The Scream (S)

Three's Company (G. B.) ("The Scream" segment of AF
which was compiled from three episodes of the "Douglas
Fairbanks Presents" TV series, and released
theatrically in Great Britain)
British Lion, 1953

Holland, Katherine

Talk about Jacqueline

Talk about Jacqueline (G. B.)
Excelsior Feature Film Co./Metro-Goldwyn-Mayer British,
1942

Hollander, Xaviera

The Happy Hooker (NF)

The Happy Hooker
Cannon Screen Entertainment, 1975

Holmes, Mary Jane [Mary Jane Hawes]

Lena Rivers

Lena Rivers (*) (also based on the same named play, by
Beulah Poynter, which is derived from Holmes' novel)
Cosmos Feature Film Corp./Cosmos Feature Film Corp.-
State Rights, 1914

<pre>
          Lena Rivers (*)
          Whitman Features Co./Blinkhorn Photoplays Corp.-State
          Rights, 1914

          Lena Rivers (*)
          Chord Pictures/Arrow Pictures, 1925

          Lena Rivers
          Tiffany Pictures, 1932
</pre>

Tempest and Sunshine

<pre>
          Tempest and Sunshine (*)
          Dixie Film Co./State Rights, 1916
</pre>

Holtby, Winifred

South Riding

<pre>
          South Riding (G. B.)
          London Films/United Artists' Film Corp., 1938
</pre>

Hooke, Nina Warner

Darkness I Leave You

<pre>
          The Gypsy and the Gentleman (G. B.)
          J. Arthur Rank Film Prod./J. Arthur Rank Film Dist.,
          Ltd., 1958
</pre>

Deadly Record

<pre>
          Deadly Record (G. B.)
          Independent Artists/Anglo-Amalgamated Film, 1959
</pre>

Horton, Sue

The Billionaire Boys Club (NF)

<pre>
          Billionaire Boys Club (TVM)
          Donald March--Gross-Weston Prod.--Inc. Televison Co.
          Prod./Columbia Broadcasting System, 1987
</pre>

Hovick, (Rose) Louise (also see Gypsy Rose Lee)
     (pseud. of Rose Louise Hovick)

The Naked Genius (P)

<pre>
          Doll Face
          Twentieth Century-Fox Film Corp., 1946
</pre>

Hovick, Rose Louise (see Louise Hovick and Gypsy Rose Lee)

Howard, Jennifer

    The Wager (S)

        <u>Gentleman's Agreement</u> (G. B.)
        British and Dominions Film Corp./Paramount Pictures
        Corp. British, 1935

Howell, Dorothy

    Black Sheep (S)

        <u>Guilty?</u>
        Columbia Pictures Corp., 1930

    The Spice of Life (S)

        <u>The Quitter</u>
        Columbia Pictures Corp., 1929

Howker, Janni

    The Nature of the Beast

        <u>The Nature of the Beast</u> (G. B.)
        Rosso/Film Four International, 1988

Huckaby, Elizabeth P.

    Crisis at Central High, Little Rock, 1957-58 (NF)

        <u>Crisis at Central High</u> (TVM)
        Time-Life Prod., Inc./Columbia Broadcasting System,
        1981

Hughes, Dorothy Belle

    The Expendable Man

        <u>The Hanged Man</u> (TVM)
        Universal Televison/National Broadcasting Co., 1964

    The Fallen Sparrow

        <u>The Fallen Sparrow</u>
        RKO Radio Pictures, Inc., 1943

In a Lonely Place

> In a Lonely Place
> Santana Pictures/Columbia Pictures Corp., 1950

Ride the Pink Horse

> Ride the Pink Horse
> Universal International Motion Pictures, 1947

Hull, Edith Maude

The Desert Healer

> Old Loves and New (*)
> Sam E. Rork Prod./First National, 1926

The Shadow of the East

> The Shadow of the East (*)
> Fox Film Corp., 1924

The Sheik

> The Sheik (*)
> Famous Players-Lasky Corp., 1921

The Sons of the Sheik

> The Son of the Sheik (*)
> Feature Prod., Inc./United Artists Film Corp., 1926

Hull, Helen Rose

Heat Lightning

> Heat Lightning
> Warner Brothers Pictures, Inc., 1934

Hulme, Kathryn

The Nun's Story

> The Nun's Story
> Warner Brothers Pictures, Inc., 1959

Hume, Doris (maiden name of Doris Hume Kilburn) (also see Doris Hume Kilburn)

The Sin of Susan Slade

172

Susan Slade
Warner Brothers Pictures, Inc., 1961

Humphreys, Eliza Margaret J. Gollan (see "Rita")

Hungerford, (Mrs.)

Molly Bawn

Molly Bawn (*) (G. B.)
Hepworth, 1916

Hunter, Kristin

The Landlord

The Landlord
Mirsch Corp.-Cartier Prod./United Artists Film Corp.,
1970

Hurlbut, Gladys and Emma B. C. Wells (also see the entry below)

By Your Leave (P)

By Your Leave
RKO Radio Pictures, Inc., 1934

Hurlbut, Gladys and Joshua Logan (also see the entry above)

Higher and Higher (MP)

Higher and Higher
RKO Radio Pictures, Inc., 1943

Hurst, Fannie

Anatomy of Me

Imitation of Life
Universal Motion Pictures Co., 1934

Imitation of Life
Universal Motion Pictures Co., 1959

Back Pay (S/P)

Back Pay (*)
Cosmopolitan Films, 1922

173

Back Pay
First National/ Warner Brothers Pictures, Inc., 1930

Back Street

Back Street
Universal Motion Pictures Co., 1931

Back Street
Universal Motion Pictures Co., 1941

Back Street
Ross Hunter Prod.-Carrollton, Inc./Universal Motion
Pictures Co., 1961

Five and Ten

Five and Ten
Cosmopolitan Films/Metro-Goldwyn-Mayer, Inc., 1931

Give This Little Girl a Hand (S)

The Painted Angel
First National/Warner Brothers Pictures, Inc., 1929

Golden Fleece (S)

Her Great Chance (*)
Select Pictures Corp., 1918

The Good Provider

The Good Provider (*)
Cosmopolitan Prod./Paramount Pictures Corp., 1922

Humoresque (S)

Humoresque (*)
Cosmopolitan Prod.-International Film Service/Famous
Players-Lasky Corp--Paramount Pictures Corp.-Artcraft
Pictures Corp., 1920

Humoresque
Warner Brothers Pictures, Inc., 1947

It Is to Laugh (P)

Younger Generation
Columbia Pictures Corp., 1929

Just Around the Corner (S)

Just Around the Corner (*)
Cosmopolitan Prod./Paramount Pictures Corp., 1921

Lummox

Lummox
Feature Prod., Inc./United Artists Film Corp., 1930

Mannequin (S)

Mannequin (*)
Famous Players-Lasky Corp./Paramount Pictures Corp.,
1926

The Nth Commandment (S)

The Nth Commandment (*)
First National, 1923

Oats for the Woman (S)

The Day She Paid (*)
Universal Film Manufacturing Co., 1919

The Petal on the Current (S)

The Petal on the Current (*)
Universal Film Manufacturing Co./Universal Film
Manufacturing Co.-a Universal Special Attraction, 1919

Roulette (S)

Wheel of Chance (*)
First National, 1928

Sister Act

Four Daughters
Warner Brothers Pictures, Inc., 1938

Four Wives
Warner Brothers Pictures, Inc., 1939

Four Mothers
Warner Brothers Pictures, Inc., 1941

Young at Heart
Arwin Prod., Inc./Warner Brothers Pictures, Inc., 1954

Stardust

Stardust (*)
Hobart Henley Prod./Associated First National, 1921

The Untamed Lady (S)

The Untamed Lady (*)

Famous Players-Lasky Corp./Paramount Pictures Corp.,
1926

Hurst, Vida

Blind Date

Blind Date
Columbia Pictures Corp., 1934

Tango

Tango
Chesterfield Motion Pictures-Invincible Films, 1936

Hutson, Sandy

Eff Off

The Class of Miss McMichael (G. B./U. S.)
Brut, 1978

Ingram, Eleanor M.

   The House of Little Shoes (N, which may not have been published)

      Little Shoes (*)
      Essanay Film Manufacturing Co./K-E-S-E Service, 1917

   The Unafraid

      The Unafraid (*)
      Jesse L. Lasky Feature Play Co./Paramount Pictures
      Corp., 1915

Irvine, Lucy

   Castaway (NF)

      Castaway (also based on the nonfiction book The
      Islander, by Gerald Kinsland) (G. B.)
      Cannon Screen Entertainment-United British
      Artists/Cannon Screen Entertainment, 1986

Irwin, Margaret

   Young Bess

      Young Bess
      Metro-Goldwyn-Mayer, Inc., 1953

Irwin, Violet

   Human Desire

      Human Desire (*)
      Louis   B.   Mayer   Prod.-Anita   Stewart   Prod.,
      Inc./Associated First national, 1919

Isaacs, Susan

   Compromising Positions

      Compromising Positions
      Blackhawk Enterprises-C. P. Films/Paramount Pictures

Corp., 1985

Jackson, Helen Hunt

    Ramona: a Story

        <u>Ramona</u> (*)
        Clune Film Prod. Co./State Rights, 1916

        <u>Ramona</u> (*)
        Inspirational Pictures/United Artists Film Corp., 1928

        <u>Ramona</u>
        Twentieth Century-Fox Film Corp., 1936

Jackson, Shirley

    The Bird's Nest

        <u>Lizzie</u>
        Bryna Prod./Metro-Goldwyn-Mayer, Inc., 1957

    The Haunting of Hill House

        <u>The Haunting</u> (G. B.)
        Argyle Enterprises/Metro-Goldwyn-Mayer, Inc., 1963

Jacobs, Naomi

    Under New Management

        <u>Under New Management</u> (G. B.)
        Mancuniam/Butcher's Film Service, 1946

Jacobs, Sally and Denis Cannan, Peter Brook, Albert Hunt, Michael
    Kustow, Adrian Mitchell, and Richard Peaslee

    US (P)

        <u>Tell Me Lies</u>
        Ronorus/Continental Dist., 1968

Jaffe, Rona

    The Best of Everything

<u>The</u> <u>Best</u> <u>of</u> <u>Everything</u>
Twentieth Century-Fox Film Corp., 1962

Mazes and Monsters

<u>Rona</u> <u>Jaffe's</u> "<u>Mazes</u> <u>and</u> <u>Monsters</u>" (TVM) (Can.)
McDermott Prod.-Procter and Gamble Prod./Columbia
Broadcasting System, 1982

James, Florence Alice Price (see Florence Warden)

James, P. D.

The Black Tower

<u>The</u> <u>Black</u> <u>Tower</u> (TVM) (G. B.)
Anglia TV, 1985

Death of an Expert Witness

<u>Death</u> <u>of</u> <u>an</u> <u>Expert</u> <u>Witness</u> (TVM) (G. B.)
Anglia TV, 1982

An Unsuitable Job for a Woman

<u>An</u> <u>Unsuitable</u> <u>Job</u> <u>for</u> <u>a</u> <u>Woman</u> (G. B.)
Boyd's Co./Goldcrest Films and Televison, Ltd., 1982

Jamison, Mrs. C. V. (Cecilia Viets)

Toinett's Philip

<u>Rainbow</u> <u>On</u> <u>the</u> <u>River</u>
RKO Radio Pictures, Inc., 1936

Janeway, Elizabeth

Daisy Kenyon

<u>Daisy</u> <u>Kenyon</u>
Twentieth Century-Fox Film Corp., 1947

Janis, Elsie and Bernice Brown, Sophie Kerr, Dorothy Parker, and
   Carolyn Wells and Robert Gordon Anderson, Louis Bromfield,
   George Agnew Chamberlain, Frank Craven, Rube Goldberg,
   Wallace Irwin, George Barr McCutcheon, Meade Minnigerode,
   Gerald Mygatt, George Palmer Putnam, Kermit Roosevelt,
   Edward Streeter, John V. A. Weaver, H. C. Witwer, and
   Alexander Woollcott (also see the entry below)

Bobbed Hair

> Bobbed Hair (*)
> Warner Brothers Pictures, Inc., 1925

Janis, Elsie and Gene Markey (also see the entry above)

Close Harmony

> Close Harmony
> Paramount Pictures Corp., 1928

Listen Baby (S)

> Listen Baby
> Pathe Exchange, Inc., 1928

Jay, Harriet and Robert Buchanan

Alone in London (P)

> Alone in London (*) (G. B.)
> Turner Films/Ideal, 1915

Jaynes, Clare
(pseud. of Jane Rothschild Mayer)

My Reputation

> My Reputation
> Warner Brothers Pictures, Inc., 1946

Jellicoe, Ann

The Knack -- and How to Get It (P)

> The Knack -- and How to Get It (G. B.)
> Woodfall Film Prod./United Artists Film Corp., 1965

Jennings, Gertrude

The Young Person in Pink (P)

> The Girl Who Forgot (G. B.)
> Daniel Birt/Butcher's Film Service, 1939

Jerome, Helen

Pride and Prejudice (P, based on the same named novel, by

Jane Austen)

>Pride and Prejudice (also based on the same named
>novel, by Jane Austen)
>Metro-Goldwyn-Mayer, Inc., 1940

Jesse, F. (Fryniwyd) Tennyson (also see the entry below)

Quarantine (P)

>Lovers in Quarantine (*)
>Famous Players-Lasky Corp./Famous Players-Lasky Corp.--
>Paramount Pictures Corp.-Artcraft Pictures Corp., 1925

Jesse, F. (Fryniwyd) Tennyson and Harold M. Harwood (also see the
entry above)

Billeted (P)

>The Misleading Widow (*)
>Famous Players-Lasky Corp./Paramount Pictures Corp.,
>1919

The Pelican (P)

>'Marriage License? (*)
>Fox Film Corp., 1926

>Sacrifice (*) (G. B.)
>British Instructional Films/Fox Film Corp., 1929

Jhabvala, Ruth Prawer

The Householder

>The Householder (U. S./Ind.)
>Merchant-Ivory Prod./Royal Pictures International, 1963

Heat and Dust

>Heat and Dust (G. B.)
>Merchant-Ivory Prod./Curzon-Universal Motion Pictures
>Co., 1983

Johns, Florence and Wilton Lackaye, Jr.

Miss Benton, R. N. (P)

>Registered Nurse
>First National-Vitaphone Corp., 1934

Johnson, Dorothy M.

   The Hanging Tree (S)

      The Hanging Tree
      Baroda Prod./Warner Brothers Pictures, Inc., 1959

   A Man Called Horse (S)

      A Man Called Horse
      Sandy Howard Prod.-Cinema Center Films/National General
      Picture, 1970

   The Man Who Shot Liberty Valance (S)

      The Man Who Shot Liberty Valance
      Paramount Pictures Corp.-John Ford Prod./Paramount
      Pictures Corp., 1962

Johnson, Emille

   Blind Hearts (S)

      Blind Hearts (*)
      Associated Producers, Inc., 1921

Johnson, Gladys E.

   Two-Bit Seats (S)

      Two-Bit Seats (*)
      Essanay Film Manufacturing Co.-Perfection Pictures/
      George Kiline System, 1917

Johnson, Laurie and Bernard Miles and Lionel Bart

   Lock Up Your Daughters (P)

      Lock Up Your Daughters (G. B.) (also based on the play,
      Rape Upon Rape, by Henry Fielding)
      Domino/Columbia Pictures Corp., 1969

Johnson, Margurite (see Maya Angelou)

Johnson, Nora

   The World of Henry Orient: a Novel

      The World of Henry Orient
      Pan Arts Co./United Artists Film Corp., 1964

Johnson, Osa and Martin Johnson

I Married Adventure (NF)

I <u>Married</u> <u>Adventure</u>
Columbia Pictures Corp., 1940

Johnston, Annie

Little Colonel

The <u>Little</u> <u>Colonel</u>
Twentieth Century-Fox Film Corp., 1935

Johnston, Jennifer

The Old Jest

The <u>Dawning</u> (G. B.)
TVS-Vista, 1988

Johnston, Mary

Audrey

<u>Audrey</u> (*)
Famous Players Film Co./Paramount Pictures Corp., 1916

Pioneers of the Old South; A Chronicle of English Colonial Beginnings (NF)

<u>Jamestown</u> (*)
Chronicles of America/Pathe Exchange, Inc., 1923

To Have and to Hold

<u>To</u> <u>Have</u> <u>and</u> <u>to</u> <u>Hold</u> (*)
James L. Lasky Feature Play Co./Paramount Pictures Corp., 1916

<u>To</u> <u>Have</u> <u>and</u> <u>to</u> <u>Hold</u> (*)
Famous Players-Lasky Corp./Paramount Pictures Corp., 1922

Johnston, Velda

A Howling in the Woods

<u>A</u> <u>Howling</u> <u>in</u> <u>the</u> <u>Woods</u> (TVM)

184

Universal Television/National Broadcasting Co., 1971

Jones, Constance and Guy Jones

   Peabody's Mermaid

     Mr. Peabody and the Mermaid
     Universal Motion Pictures Co., 1948

   There Was a Little Man

     Luck of the Irish
     Twentieth Century-Fox Film Corp., 1948

Jones, Joanna

   Nurse is a Neighbour

     Nurse on Wheels (G. B.)
     Gregory, Hake and Walker Prod./Anglo-Amalgamated Film,
     1963

Jones, Rachel and Trudy Baker

   Coffee, Tea or Me? (NF)

     Coffee, Tea or Me? (TVM)
     Columbia Broadcasting System Entertainment/Columbia
     Broadcasting System, 1973

Jope-Slade, Christine and Sewell Stokes

   Britannia of Billingsgate (P)

     Britannia of Billingsgate (G. B.)
     Gaumont/Ideal, 1933

Jordan, Anne

   Kitchen Privileges (S)

     Luckiest Girl in the World
     Universal Motion Pictures Co., 1936

Jordan, Elizabeth

   Black Butterflies

     Black Butterflies (*)

Quality Dist. Corp., 1928

Daddy and I

Make Way for a Lady
RKO Radio Pictures, Inc., 1936

The Girl in the Mirror

The Girl in Number 29 (*)
Universal Film Manufacturing Co., 1920

Jordan, Kate
(pseud. of Mrs. F. M. Vermilye)

A City Sparrow (S)

A City Sparrow (*)
Famous Players-Lasky Corp./Famous Players-Lasky Corp--
Paramount Pictures Corp., 1920

The Creeping Tides: a Romance of an Old Neighborhood (S)

Tides of Fate (*)
Equitable Motion Pictures Corp./World Film, 1917

The Next Corner

The Next Corner (*)
Paramount Pictures Corp., 1924

Transgression
RKO Radio Pictures, Inc., 1931

Orchestra D-2 (S)

Castles in the Air (*)
Metro Pictures Corp., 1919

Secret Strings (P, based on a short story, by Jordan)

Secret Strings (*)
Metro Pictures Corp., 1918

The Spirit of the Road (S)

In Search of a Thrill (*)
Metro Pictures Corp., 1923

Time, the Comedian

Time, the Comedian (*)
Metro-Goldwyn-Mayer, Inc., 1925

186

Jorgensen, Christine

    Christine Jorgensen: a Personal Autobiography (NF)

        The <u>Christine Jorgensen Story</u>
        Edprod Pictures/United Artists Film Corp., 1970

Joske, Anne Neville Goyder (see Margot Neville)

Joudry, Patricia

    Teach Me How to Cry (P)

        The <u>Restless Years</u>
        Universal Motion Pictures Co., 1958

Judson, Jeanne

    The Call of Life

        <u>Beckoning Roads</u> (*)
        B. B. Features, Inc./Robertson-Cole--Superior Pictures,
        1919

- K -

Kanin, Fay (also see the entry below)

> **Goodbye My Fancy** (P)
>
>> Goodbye My Fancy
>> Warner Brothers Pictures, Inc., 1951

Kanin, Fay and Michael Kanin (also see the entry above)

> **Rashomon** (P, based on the screenplay for Rashomon, which was itself derived from two short stories by Akira Kurosawa)
>
>> Outrage
>> KHF Prod./Metro-Goldwyn-Mayer, Inc., 1964

Kark, Nina Mary Mabel (see Nina Bawden)

Kata, Elizabeth

> **Be Ready with Bells and Drums**
>
>> A Patch of Blue
>> Pandro S. Berman Prod./Metro-Goldwyn-Mayer, Inc., 1965
>
> **Witches' Friday** (S)
>
>> The Night Walker
>> Castle Co./Universal Motion Pictures Co., 1964

Kaufman, Bel

> **Up the Down Staircase**
>
>> Up the Down Staircase
>> Park Place Prod./Warner Brothers Pictures, Inc., 1967

Kaufman, Sue

> **Diary of a Mad Housewife**
>
>> Diary of a Mad Housewife
>> Frank Perry Films/Universal Motion Pictures Co., 1970

Kaus, Gina (also see the two entries above)

    Dark Angel

        Her <u>Sister's</u> <u>Secret</u>
        Producers Releasing Corp., 1946

    Luxury Liner

        <u>Luxury</u> <u>Liner</u>
        Paramount Pictures Corp., 1933

Kaus, Gina and Hilde Koveloff, E. Eis, and O. Eis (also see the
    entry above and the entry below)

    Prison Sans Barreaux (P)

        <u>Prison</u> <u>Without</u> <u>Bars</u> (G. B.)
        London Films/United Artists Film Corp., 1938

Kaus, Gina and Ladislaus Fodor (also see the two entries above)

    City in Darkness (P)

        <u>Charlie</u> <u>Chan</u> <u>in</u> <u>the</u> <u>City</u> <u>in</u> <u>Darkness</u>
        Twentieth Century-Fox Film Corp., 1938

    The Night Before the Divorce

        <u>The</u> <u>Night</u> <u>Before</u> <u>the</u> <u>Divorce</u>
        Twentieth Century-Fox Film Corp., 1942

    White Lady (P)

        <u>Isle</u> <u>of</u> <u>the</u> <u>Missing</u> <u>Men</u>
        Monogram Pictures Corp., 1942

Kavanagh, Hermine Templeton

    Darby O'Gill and the Good People (RS)

        <u>Darby</u> <u>O'Gill</u> <u>and</u> <u>the</u> <u>Little</u> <u>People</u>
        Walt Disney Prod./Buena Vista Dist. Co., 1959

Kavanaugh, Katharine

    Adam's Enemy (P)

        <u>His</u> <u>Exciting</u> <u>Night</u>
        Universal Motion Pictures Co., 1938

Let's Get Together (P)

>> Every Saturday Night
>> Twentieth Century-Fox Film Corp., 1936

Kaye-Smith, Sheila (see Sheila Kaye Smith)

Keane, Mary Nester Shine (see M. J. Farrell)

Keane, Molly

> **Time After Time**

>> Time After Time (TVM) (G. B./U. S./Austr.)
>> British Broadcasting Corp.-TV--Arts and Entertainment--
>> Australian Broadcasting Corp., 1985

Keene, Carolyn
> (house pseud. controlled by Harriet Stratemeyer Adams, the
> author of the two following books)

> **The Hidden Staircase**

>> Nancy Drew and the Hidden Staircase
>> Warner Brothers Pictures, Inc., 1939

> **Password to Larkspur Lane**

>> Nancy Drew, Detective
>> Warner Brothers Pictures, Inc., 1938

Keir, Ursula

> **The Vintage**

>> The Vintage
>> Metro-Goldwyn-Mayer, Inc., 1957

Keith, Agnes Newton

> **Three Came Home** (NF)

>> Three Came Home
>> Twentieth Century-Fox Film Corp., 1950

Keller, Helen

The Story of My Life (NF)

>The Miracle Worker (also based on the play The Miracle
>Worker, by William Gibson)
>Playfilms Prod./United Artists Film Corp., 1962

Kelley, Audrey (see Kelly Roos)

Kelley, Ethel May

Turn About, Eleanor

>The Deciding Kiss (*)
>Bluebird Photoplays, Inc., 1918

Kellino, Pamela

Del Palma, a Novel

>A Lady Possessed
>Portland Pictures Prod./Republic Pictures Corp., 1951

Kellogg, Marjorie

Tell me that you Love me, Junie Moon

>Tell Me That you Love me, Junie Moon
>Sigma Prod./Paramount Pictures Corp., 1970

Kellogg, Virginia

Mary Stevens, M. D.

>Mary Stevens, M. D.
>Warner Brothers Pictures, Inc., 1933

The Road to Reno (S)

>The Road to Reno
>Paramount Pictures Corp., 1931

Kelly, Eleanor Mercein (married name of Eleanor Mercein) (also
see Eleanor Mercein)

Kildare of Storm

>Kildare of Storm (*)
>Metro Pictures Corp./Metro Pictures Corp.--All-Star
>Series, 1918

191

Kelly, Florence Finch

With Hoops of Steel

> With Hoops of Steel (*)
> Paralta Plays, Inc./W. W. Hodkinson Corp.-General Film,
> 1918

Kelly, Judith

Marriage is a Private Affair

> Marriage is a Private Affair
> Metro-Goldwyn-Mayer, Inc., 1944

Kelly, Myra

Little Aliens

> Little Miss Smiles (*)
> Fox Film Corp., 1922

Kennedy, Margaret (also see the two entries below)

The Constant Nymph (also see the same named play, by Kennedy and Basil Dean)

> The Constant Nymph (*) (G. B.)
> Gainsborough Prod./Woolf and Freedman Film Service,
> 1928

Escape Me Never (P)

> Escape Me Never (G. B.)
> British and Dominions Films Corp./United Artists Film
> Corp., 1935

> Escape Me Never (also based on the novel The Fool of
> the Family, by Kennedy, from which the play was
> derived)
> Warner Brothers Pictures, Inc., 1947

The Fool of the Family

> Escape Me Never (also based on the play Escape Me
> Never, by Kennedy, which was derived from her novel)
> Warner Brothers Pictures, Inc., 1947

The Midas Touch

The <u>Midas Touch</u> (G. B.)
Warner Brothers Pictures, Inc.-First National/Warner
Brothers Pictures, Inc., 1939

Kennedy, Margaret and Basil Dean (also see the entry above and
   below)

   The Constant Nymph   (P, based on the same named novel, by
   Kennedy)

      The <u>Constant</u> <u>Nymph</u> (G. B.)
      Gaumont, 1933

      The <u>Constant</u> <u>Nymph</u>
      Warner Brothers Pictures, Inc., 1943

Kennedy, Margaret and Ilya Surgutchoff (also see the two entries
   above)

   Autumn (P)

      <u>That</u> <u>Dangerous</u> <u>Age</u> (G. B.)
      London Films/British Lion, 1949

Kenny, Elizabeth and Martha Ostenso

   And They Shall Walk (NF)

      <u>Sister</u> <u>Kenny</u>
      RKO Radio Pictures, Inc., 1946

Kerr, Jean (also see the entry below)

   Mary, Mary (P)

      <u>Mary,</u> <u>Mary</u>
      Warner Brothers Pictures, Inc., 1963

   Please Don't Eat the Daisies

      <u>Please</u> <u>Don't</u> <u>Eat</u> <u>the</u> <u>Daisies</u>
      Metro-Goldwyn-Mayer, Inc., 1960

Kerr, Jean and Eleanor Brooke (also see the entry above)

   The King of Hearts (P)

      <u>That</u> <u>Certain</u> <u>Feeling</u>
      Paramount Pictures Corp., 1956

Kerr, Sophie (maiden name of Sophie Kerr Underwood) (also see the three entries below)

Beauty's Worth (S)

> Beauty's Worth (*)
> Cosmopolitan Prod./Paramount Pictures Corp., 1922

The Blue Envelope

> The Blue Envelope Mystery (*)
> Vitagraph Co. of America/Greater Vitagraph, 1916

Kayo, Oke (S)

> People Will Talk (also based on the short story "Such a Lovely Couple," by F. Hugh Herbert)
> Paramount Pictures Corp., 1935

Mareea Maria

> Mareea Maria
> Tiffany Pictures, 1930

Relative Values (S)

> Young Ideas (*)
> Universal Motion Pictures Co., 1924

The See-Saw: a Story of Today (S)

> The Invisible Bond (*)
> Famous Players-Lasky Corp./Famous Players-Lasky Corp.--
> Paramount Pictures Corp.-Artcraft Pictures Corp., 1919

Sitting on the World (S)

> Fickle Women (*)
> D. N. Schwab Prod., Inc./State Rights, 1920

Sweetie Peach (S)

> The House That Jazz Built (*)
> Realart Pictures Corp., 1921

Worldly Goods

> Worldly Goods (*)
> Paramount Pictures Corp., 1924

Kerr, Sophie and Bernice Brown, Elsie Janis, Dorothy Parker, and Carolyn Wells and Robert Gordon Anderson, Louis Bromfield, George Agnew Chamberlain, Frank Craven, Rube Goldberg,

194

Wallace Irwin, George Barr McCutcheon, Meade Minnigerode, Gerald Mygatt, George Palmer Putnam, Kermit Roosevelt, Edward Streeter, John V. A. Waver, H. C. Witwer, and Alexander Woollcott (also see the entry above and the two entries below)

Bobbed Hair

> Bobbed Hair (*)
> Warner Brothers Pictures, Inc., 1925

Kerr, Sophie and Anna S. Richardson   (also see the two entries above and the entry below)

Big Hearted Herbert (P)

> Big Hearted Herbert
> Warner Brothers Pictures, Inc., 1934

> Father is a Prince
> First National/Warner Brothers Pictures, Inc., 1940

Kerr, Sophie and Gertrude Atherton, Vicki Baum, Vina Delmar, and Ursula Parrott and Polan Banks, Irvin S. Cobb, Zane Grey, Rupert Hughes, and J. P. Mc Evoy (also see the three entries above)

Woman Accused

> Woman Accused
> Paramount Pictures Corp., 1933

Kerruish, Jessie Douglas

Miss Haroun al Raschid

> A Romance of Old Bagdad (*) (G. B.)
> Astra Films, 1922

The Undying Monster

> The Undying Monster
> Twentieth Century-Fox Film Corp., 1942

Kesson, Jessie

Another Time, Another Place

> Another Time, Another Place
> Umbrella-Rediffusion, 1984

Key, Mrs. E. J.

A Daughter of Love

A Daughter of Love (*) (G. B.)
Stoll, 1925

Kilbourne, Fannie

The Girl who was the Life of the Party (S)

Girls Men Forget (*)
Principal Pictures, 1924

Sunny Goes Home (S)

The Major and the Minor (also based on the play Connie
Goes Home, by Edward Childs Carpenter, which was
derived from Kilbourne's short story)
Paramount Pictures Corp., 1942

You're Never Too Young
Paramount Pictures Corp., 1955

Kilburn, Doris Hume (married name of Doris Hume) (also see Doris
Hume)

Dark Purpose

Dark Purpose (Fra./Ita./U. S.)
Universal Motion Pictures Co., 1964

Kilpatrick, Florence

Virginia's Husband (P)

Virginia's Husband (*) (G. B.)
Nettlefold/Butcher's Film Service, 1928

Virginia's Husband (G. B.)
George Albert Smith Films/Fox Film Corp., 1934

Wildcat Hetty (P)

The Hellcat (*) (G. B.)
Nettlefold/Butcher's Film Service, 1928

Kimbrough, Emily and Cornelia Otis Skinner

Our Hearts Were Young and Gay (NF)

    Our Hearts Were Young and Gay
    Paramount Pictures Corp., 1944

King-Hall, Magdalen

    The Life and Death of the Wicked Lady Skelton

        The Wicked Lady (G. B.)
        Gainsborough Prod./Eagle Lion, 1946

        The Wicked Lady (G. B.)
        London Cannon Screen Entertainment/Columbia Pictures
        Corp.-Electrical and Musical Industries-Warner Brothers
        Pictures, Inc., 1982

Kingsley, Florence Morse (also see the entry below)

    Hurrying Fate and Geraldine

        Cupid Forecloses (*)
        Vitagraph Co. of America, 1919

    Sloth (?) (S)

        Sloth (*)
        McClure Pictures, Inc./Triangle Dist. Corp.-
        Superpictures, Inc., 1917

    To the Highest Bidder

        To the Highest Bidder (*)
        Vitagraph Co. of America-a Blue Ribbon Feature/Greater
        Vitagraph, 1918

Kingsley, Florence Kingsley and Mary Wilkins Freeman (also see
    the entry above)

    An Alabaster Box

        An Alabaster Box (*)
        Vitagraph Co. of America, 1917

Klaben, Helen and Beth Day

    Hey, I'm Alive (NF)

        Hey, I'm Alive (TVM)
        Charles Fries Prod.-Worldvision Enterprises/American
        Broadcasting Co., 1975

Klausen, Gina

    Confessions of a Kept Woman

        <u>Let's Get Married</u> (G. B.)
        Viceroy/Eros Films, 1960

Klein, Norma

    Mom, the Wolfman, and Me

        <u>Mom, the Wolfman, and Me</u> (TVM)
        Operation Prime Time--Time-Life Television, 1980

Knapp, Penelope

    Marcene (N, which may not have been published)

        <u>The Broken Butterfly</u> (*)
        Maurice Tourneur Prod., Inc./Robertson-Cole, 1919

Kohn, Rose Simon

    Pillar to Post (P)

        <u>Pillar to Post</u>
        Warner Brothers Pictures, Inc.-First National, 1945

Konigsburg, E. L.

    From the Mixed-Up Files of Mrs. Basil E. Frankweiler

        <u>From the Mixed-Up Files of Mrs. Basil E. Frankweiler</u>
        Cinema 5, 1973

Koveloff, Hilde and Gina Kaus and E. Eis, and O. Eis

    Prison Sans Barreaux (P)

        <u>Prison Without Bars</u> (G. B.)
        London Films/United Artists Film Corp., 1938

Krantz, Judith

    Princess Daisy

        <u>Princess Daisy</u> (TVM)
        Steve Krantz Prod.-National Broadcasting Co.

Entertainment/National Broadcasting Co., 1983

Kroeber, Theodora

    Ishi, Last of His Tribe (NF)

        <u>Ishi</u>: <u>The</u> <u>Last</u> <u>of</u> <u>His</u> <u>Tribe</u> (TVM)
        Edward and Mildred Lewis Prod./National Broadcasting
        Co., 1978

Kuchler-Silberman, Lena

    My Hundred Children (NF)

        <u>Lena</u>: <u>My</u> <u>100</u> <u>Children</u>
        National Broadcasting Co., 1987

Kummer, Clare

    Good Gracious Annabelle (P)

        <u>Good</u> <u>Gracious,</u> <u>Annabelle</u> (*)
        Famous Players-Lasky Corp./Famous Players-Lasky Corp.--
        Paramount Pictures Corp., 1919

        <u>Annabelle's</u> <u>Affairs</u>
        Twentieth Century-Fox Film Corp., 1931

    Her Master's Voice (P)

        <u>Her</u> <u>Master's</u> <u>Voice</u>
        Paramount Pictures Corp., 1936

    The Rescuing Angel (P)

        <u>The</u> <u>Rescuing</u> <u>Angel</u> (*)
        Famous Players-Lasky Corp./Famous Players-Lasky Corp--
        Paramount Pictures Corp., 1919

    A Successful Calamity (P)

        <u>A</u> <u>Successful</u> <u>Calamity</u>
        Warner Brothers Pictures, Inc., 1932

Kurth, Ann

    Prescription Murder (NF)

        <u>Murder</u> <u>in</u> <u>Texas</u> (TVM)
        Dick Clark Cinema Prod.-Billy Hale Films/National
        Broadcasting Co., 1981

Lagerlof, Selma

>   **Emperor of Portugallia**   [Kejsarn av Portugallien; en
>   Varmlandsherattelse]
>
>   >   The Tower of Lies (*)
>   >   Metro-Goldwyn-Mayer, Inc., 1925
>
>   **This Woman and This Man** (S)
>
>   >   Guilty of Love (*)
>   >   Paramount Pictures Corp., 1920

Lamb, Ginger and Dana Lamb

>   **Quest for a Lost City** (NF)
>
>   >   Quest for the Lost City
>   >   Sol Lesser Prod./RKO Radio Pictures, Inc., 1955

Lambert, Reita

>   **Clipped Wings** (S)
>
>   >   Hello Sister
>   >   James Cruze, Inc./Sono Art Prod.-World Wide, 1930
>
>   **Widow's Night** (S)
>
>   >   Careless Lady
>   >   Fox Film Corp., 1932

Lamplugh, Lois

>   **Rockets in the Dunes**
>
>   >   Rockets in the Dunes (G. B.)
>   >   Anvil/Children's Film Foundation, 1960

Landon, Margaret

>   **Anna and the King of Siam** (NF)
>
>   >   Anna and the King of Siam

Louis D. Lighton Prod./ Twentieth Century-Fox Film
Corp., 1946

The King and I (also based on the musical play The King
and I, by Richard Rogers)
Twentieth Century-Fox Film Corp., 1956

Landrau, Grace Hodgson

Being Respectable

Being Respectable (*)
Warner Brothers Pictures, Inc., 1924

Lane, Rose Wilder

Let the Hurricane Roar

Young Pioneers (TVM) (also based on the novel Young
Pioneers, by Lane)
American Broadcasting Co. Circle Films/American
Broadcasting Co., 1976

Young Pioneers

Young Pioneers (TVM) (also based on the novel Let the
Hurricane Roar, by Lane)
American Broadcasting Co. Circle Films/American
Broadcasting Co., 1976

Langley, Adria Locke

A Lion is in the Streets

A Lion is in the Streets
Warner Brothers Pictures, Inc., 1953

Laski, Marghanita

Little Boy Lost

Little Boy Lost
Paramount Pictures Corp., 1953

Lathan, Jean Lee

Jack and the Beanstalk (S) (fairy tale retold by Lathan)

Fun and Fancy Free (anim. and live) ("Jack and the
Beanstalk" segment of AF)

201

Walt Disney, Prod./RKO Radio Pictures, Inc., 1947

Lathrop, Harriet Mulford (see Margaret Sidney)

Laughlin, Clara E.

The Penny Philanthropist: A Story that Could be True

The Penny Philanthropist (*)
Wholesome Films Corp./State Rights, 1917

Laurence, Margaret

A Jest of God

Rachel, Rachel
Kayos Prod./Warner Brothers Pictures, Inc.-Seven Arts,
Inc., 1968

Laurey, Joy

Joy

Joy (Fra./Can.)
ATC 3000-RSL Films/Union Generale Cinematographique,
1983

Lauro, Shirley

Open Admissions (P)

Open Admissions (TVM)
Columbia Broadcasting System, 1988

Lavin, Nora and Molly Thorp

The Hop Dog

Adventure in the Hopfields (G. B.)
Vandyke/British Lion-Children's Film Foundation, 1954

Lawrence, Josephine

The Years are So Long

Make Way for Tomorrow (also based on the play The Years
are So Long, by Helen Leary and Nolan Leary, which was
derived from Lawrence's novel)

Paramount Pictures Corp., 1937

Lawrence, Margery

Interrupted Melody (NF)

Interrupted Melody
Metro-Goldwyn-Mayer, Inc., 1955

The Madonna of the Seven Moons

Madonna of the Seven Moons
Gainsborough Prod./Eagle Lion, 1944

The Woman Who Needed Killing

A Dangerous Woman
Paramount Pictures Corp., 1929

Lawson, Jonell

Roses are for the Rich

Roses are for the Rich (TVM)
Columbia Broadcasting System, 1987

Lea, F. H. (Fanny Heaslip)

Four Marys

Man-proof
Metro-Goldwyn-Mayer, Inc., 1937

The Peacock Screen (S)

Cheaters
Liberty Pictures Corp./Hollywood, 1934

With This Ring

With This Ring (*)
B. P. Schulberg Prod., 1925

Leake, Grace Sothcote

House of Refuge

Bondage
Fox Film Corp., 1933

Lear, Martha Weinman

    Heartsounds (NF)

        <u>Heartsounds</u> (TVM)
        Embassy Television/American Broadcasting Co., 1984

Leary, Helen and Nolan Leary

    The Years are So Long (P)

        <u>Make</u> <u>Way</u> <u>for</u> <u>Tomorrow</u> (also based on the novel <u>The</u>
        <u>Years</u> <u>are</u> <u>So</u> <u>Long</u>, by Josephine Lawrence, from which
        the play was derived)
        Paramount Pictures Corp., 1937

Leduc, Violette

    Therese et Isabelle

        <u>Therese</u> <u>and</u> <u>Isabelle</u> (U. S./Ger.)
        Amsterdam Film Corp.-Berolina Films/Audubon Films, 1968

Lee, Edna
    (pseud. of Edna H. Turpin)

    Queen Bee

        <u>Queen</u> <u>Bee</u>
        Columbia Pictures Corp., 1955

Lee, Gypsy Rose
    (pseud. of Rose Louise Hovick)
    (also see Louise Hovick)

    G—String Murders (ghost written by Craig Rice)

        <u>Lady</u> <u>of</u> <u>Burlesque</u>
        Hunt Stromberg Prod./United Artists Film Corp., 1943

    Gypsy, a Memoir (NF)

        <u>Gypsy</u> (also based on the musical play <u>Gypsy</u>, by Arthur
        Laurents, which was derived from Lee's book)
        Warner Brothers Pictures, Inc., 1962

Lee, Harper
    (pseud. of Nelle Harper Lee)

    To Kill a Mockingbird

<u>To</u> <u>Kill</u> <u>a</u> <u>Mockingbird</u>
Pakula-Mulligan Prod.--Brentwood Prod./Universal
International Motion Pictures, 1962

Lee, Jennette Barbour Perry

   Simeon Tetlow's Shadow

      <u>Ruler</u> <u>of</u> <u>the</u> <u>Road</u> (*)
      Pathe Exchange, Inc., 1918

Lee, Laurel

   Walking Through the Fire (NF)

      <u>Walking</u> <u>Through</u> <u>the</u> <u>Fire</u> (TVM)
      Time-Life Television Prod./Columbia Broadcasting
      System, 1979

Lee, Nelle Harper (see Harper Lee)

Lee, Reba and Mary Hastings Bradley
   (Reba Lee: unidentified pseud.)

   I Passed for White (NF)

      <u>I</u> <u>Passed</u> <u>for</u> <u>White</u>
      Allied Artists, 1960

Lees, Hanna and Laurence P. Bachmann
   (Hanna Lees: pseud. of Elizabeth Head Fetter)

   Death in the Doll House

      <u>Shadow</u> <u>on</u> <u>the</u> <u>Wall</u>
      Metro-Goldwyn-Mayer, Inc., 1950

LeGuin, Ursula K.

   The Lathe of Heaven

      <u>The</u> <u>Lathe</u> <u>of</u> <u>Heaven</u> (TVM)
      National Educational Television/WNET--Thirteen Non-
      Broadcast, 1980

Lehmann, Rosamond

The Weather in the Streets

> The Weather in the Streets (TVM) (G. B.)
> Rediffusion/British Broadcasting Corp. 2, 1983

Leighton, Florence
  (pseud. of Florence Leighton Pfalzgraf)

Heaven's Gate (S)

> Our Little Girl
> Twentieth Century-Fox Film Corp., 1935

Leitzbach, Adeline and Theodore A. Liebler, Jr.

Success (P)

> Success (*)
> Murray W. Garsson/Metro Pictures Corp., 1923

Lenihan, Winifred and Vera Caspary

Blind Mice (P)

> Working Girls
> Paramount Pictures Corp., 1931

Lennart, Isobel

Funny Girl (MP)

> Funny Girl
> Rastar Prod./Columbia Pictures Corp., 1968

Lerner, Mary

The Living Dead (S)

> The Breaking Point (*)
> J. L. Frothingham/Hodkinson, 1921

Leslie, Doris
  (pseud. of Lady Hannay Fergusson)

Polonaise (NF)

> A Song to Remember
> Columbia Pictures Corp., 1944

Leslie, Josephine (see R. A. Dick)

Leslie-Melville, Betty and Jock Leslie-Melville

    Raising Daisy Rothschild (NF)

        The Last Giraffe (TVM)
        Westfall Prod./Columbia Broadcasting System, 1979

Lessing, Doris

    The Grass is Singing

        The Grass is Singing (G. B./Swed.)
        Chibote-Swedish Film Institute/Mainline, 1982

    Memoirs of a Survivor

        Memoirs of a Survivor (G. B.)
        Memorial-Electrical and Musical Industries/Columbia
        Pictures Corp.-Electrical and Musical Industries-Warner
        Brothers Pictures, Inc. 1981

Lestrange, David (also see Constance Collier and Ivor Novello)
    (joint pseud. of Constance Collier and Ivor Novello)

    When Boys Leave Home (P)

        Downhill (*) (G. B.)
        Gainsborough Prod./World Wide Films, Ltd., 1927

Lette, Kathy and Gabrielle Cary

    Puberty Blues

        Puberty Blues (Austr.)
        Limelight/Universal Classics, 1983

Lever, (Lady) Arthur

    Brown Sugar (P)

        Brown Sugar (*) (G. B.)
        British Super/Jury Imperial Pictures, 1922

        Brown Sugar (G. B.)
        Twickenham/Warner Brothers Pictures, Inc., 1931

Levin, Edwina
     (pseud. of Edwina Le Vin Dickerson MacDonald)

   The Devil's Riddle

          The Devil's Riddle (*)
          Fox Film Corp., 1920

   False Gods (S)

          Reputation (*)
          Universal-Jewel Prod., Inc., 1921

   Happiness a La Mode (S)

          Happiness a La Mode (*)
          Select Pictures, Corp., 1919

   Leona Goes A-Hunting (S)

          Help Wanted -- Male! (*)
          Pathe Exchange, Inc., 1920

Levinson, Norma

   The Room Upstairs

          The Room Upstairs (TVM)
          Columbia Broadcasting System, 1987

Lewis, Ethelreda and Alfred Aloysius Horn

   Trader Horn

          Trader Horn
          Metro-Goldwyn-Mayer, Inc., 1931

Lewis, Helen Prothero

   As God Made Her

          As God Made Her (*) (G. B.)
          Anglo-Hollandia/National, 1920

   Love and the Whirlwind: a Novel

          Love and a Whirlwind (*) (G. B.)
          Alliance Prod./Cosmograph, 1922

   The Silver Bridge

          The Silver Bridge (*) (G. B.)

Cairns Torquay Films, 1920

Lewis, Hilda

The Day is Ours

Mandy (G. B.)
Ealing Studios/General Film Dist., Inc., 1952

Lewis, Mary Christianna Milne (see Christianna Brand)

Lewis, Mary E. and Samuel G. Lewis

The Making of Maddalena or The Compromise (P)

The Making of Maddalena (*)
The Oliver Morosco Photoplay, Co./Paramount Pictures
Corp., 1916

Leycester, Laura and Wyn Weaver

The Rising Generation (P)

The Rising Generation (*) (G. B.)
Westminster Pictures/Williams and Pritchard Films, 1928

Libby, Laura Jean

When Love Grows Cold (S)

When Love Grows Cold (*)
R-C Pictures, 1925

Lieferant, Sylva and Henry Lieferant

Doctor's Wives

Doctor's Wives
Twentieth Century-Fox Film Corp., 1931

Lightner, Frances

Puppets (P)

Puppets (*)
Al Rockett Prod./First National, 1926

Liljencrantz, Ottilia

The Thrall of Leif the Lucky; a Story of Viking Days

The Viking (*)
Metro-Goldwyn-Mayer, Inc., 1929

Lincoln, Natalie Sumner

The Man Inside

The Man Inside (*)
Universal Film Manufacturing Co./Universal Film
Manufacturing Co.-a Broadway Universal Feature , 1916

Lincoln, Victoria

February Hill

Primrose Path (also based on the play The Primrose
Path, by Robert L. Buckner)
RKO Radio Pictures, Inc., 1940

Linden, Margaret and John Colton

Under Capricorn (P)

Under Capricorn (G. B.) (also based on the novel Under
Capricorn, by Helen Simpson from which the play was
derived)
Sidney Bernstein-Alfred Hitchcock, 1949

Lindop, Audrey Erskine

I Start Counting

I Start Counting (G. B.)
Triumvirate/United Artists Film Corp., 1969

I Thank a Fool

I Thank a Fool (G. B.)
Metro-Goldwyn-Mayer British, 1962

The Singer Not the Song

The Singer Not the Song (G. B.)
J. Arthur Rank Film Prod./J. Arthur Rank Film Dist.,
1961

The Tall Headlines

Tall Headlines (G. B.)
Raymond Stross/Grand National Pictures, 1952

Lindsay, Joan

Picnic at Hanging Rock

Picnic at Hanging Rock (Austr.)
Atlantic Releasing Co., 1975

Linford, Dee

Man Without a Star

Man Without a Star
Universal International Motion Pictures, 1955

A Man Called Gannon
Universal Motion Pictures Co., 1969

Linington, Barbara Elizabeth (see Anne Blaisdell)

Lippmann, Julie M.

Burkeses Amy

The Hoodlum (*)
Mary Pickford/First National, 1919

List, Julie Autumn

**The Day the Loving Stopped: a Daughter's View of Her
Parent's Divorce (NF)**

The Day the Loving Stopped (TVM)
Monash-Zeitman Prod./American Broadcasting Co., 1981

Littlewood, Joan

Oh What a Lovely War (P)

Oh! What a Lovely War (G. B.) (also based upon the
play The Long Long Trail, by Charles Chilton)
Accord/Paramount Pictures Corp., 1969

Livingston, Florence Bingham

The Custard Cup

> The Custard Cup (*)
> Fox Film Corp., 1923

Livingston, Hazel

Rosemary

> The Secret Studio (*)
> Fox Film Corp., 1927

Stolen Love

> Stolen Love (*)
> FBO Prod., Inc., 1928

Livingston, Mae and Jane Allen

Thanks, God! I'll Take It From Here

> Without Reservations
> RKO Radio Pictures, Inc., 1946

Lockhart, Caroline

The Dude Wrangler

> The Dude Wrangler
> Independent/Sono Art-World Wide Pictures, 1930

The Fighting Shepherdess

> The Fighting Shepherdess (*)
> Louis B. Mayer Prod.- Anita Steward Prod., Inc./First
> National, 1920

The Man from the Bitter Roots

> The Man from Bitter Roots (*)
> Fox Film Corp., 1916

Loewengard, Heidi Huberta Freybe (see Martha Albrand)

Lofts, Nora (also see Peter Curtis)

Chinese Finale (S)

> Seven Women
> John Ford Prod.-Bernard Smith Prod./Metro-Goldwyn-

Mayer, Inc., 1966

Heartburn

Heartburn
Paramount Pictures Corp., 1986

Jassy

Jassy (G. B.)
Gainsborough Prod./General Film Dist., Inc., 1947

Logan, Gwendolen and Philip Hubbard

East is East (P)

East is East (*) (G. B.)
Turner Films/Butcher's Films Service, 1916

Lomax, Bliss

The Leather Burners

The Leather Burners
United Artists' Film Corp., 1943

London, Charmian

The Book of Jack London (NF)

Jack London
United Artists Film Corp., 1943

Long, Amelia Reynolds

The Thought Monster (S)

Fiend Without a Face (G. B.)
MLC Prod. Associates/Eros, 1958

Long, Gabrielle Margaret Vere Campbell (see George Preedy and Joseph Shearing)

Loos, Anita (also see the two entries below)

But Gentlemen Marry Brunettes

Gentlemen Marry Brunettes
United Artists' Film Corp., 1955

Gentleman Prefer Blondes: the Illuminating Diary of a Professional Lady

> Gentlemen Prefer Blondes (*) (also based on the same named musical play, by Loos and Joseph Fields, which was derived from the same named play, by Loos and Emerson)
> Paramount Pictures Corp./Famous Players Film Co., 1928

Gigi (P, based on the novel, Gigi, by Colette)

> Gigi
> Metro-Goldwyn-Mayer, Inc., 1958

Loos, Anita and John Emerson (also see the entry above and the entry below)

The Fall of Eve (P)

> The Fall of Eve
> Columbia Pictures Corp., 1929

Gentlemen Prefer Blondes (P, based on the novel "Gentlemen Prefer Blondes": the Illuminating Diary of a Professional Lady, by Anita Loos)

> Gentlemen Prefer Blondes (*) (also based on the musical play Gentlemen Prefer Blondes, by Loos and Joseph Fields, which was derived from the novel Gentlemen Prefer Blondes: the Illuminating Diary of a Professional Lady, by Loos, and the play Gentlemen Prefer Blondes, by Loos and Emerson)
> Paramount Pictures Corp./Famous Players Film Co., 1928

Social Register (P)

> Social Register
> Columbia Pictures Corp., 1934

The Whole Town's Talking, a Farce in Three Acts (P)

> The Whole Town's Talking (*)
> Universal Motion Pictures Co., 1926

> Ex-Bad Boy
> Universal Motion Pictures Co., 1931

Loos, Anita and Joseph Fields (also see the two entries above)

Gentlemen Prefer Blondes (MP)

Gentlemen <u>Prefer</u> <u>Blondes</u> (*) (also based on the novel
<u>Gentlemen</u> <u>Prefer</u> <u>Blondes;</u> <u>the</u> <u>Illuminating</u> <u>Diary</u> <u>of</u> <u>a</u>
<u>Professional</u> <u>Lady</u>, by Anita Loos, from which the
play <u>Gentlemen</u> <u>Prefer</u> <u>Blondes</u>, by Loos and Emerson,
and the musical play <u>Gentlemen</u> <u>Prefer</u> <u>Blondes</u>, was
derived)
Paramount Pictures Corp./Famous Players Film Co., 1928

Gentlemen <u>Prefer</u> <u>Blondes</u>
Twentieth Century-Fox Film Corp., 1953

Lord, Arline

The Majo (S)

<u>A</u> <u>Romance</u> <u>of</u> <u>Seville</u> (*) (G. B.)
British International Pictures/First National-Pathe
Exchange, 1929

Lord, Gabrielle

Fortress

<u>Fortress</u> (TVM)
Crawford Prod.-Home Box Office Premiere Films/Home Box
Office, 1985

Lorimer, Norma

On Desert Altars

<u>Woman,</u> <u>Woman!</u> (*)
Fox Film Corp./Fox Film Corp.-A Standard Picture, 1919

The Shadow of Egypt

<u>The</u> <u>Shadow</u> <u>of</u> <u>Egypt</u> (*) (G. B.)
Astra Films-National, 1924

There Was a King in Egypt

<u>The</u> <u>Lure</u> <u>of</u> <u>Egypt</u> (*)
Federal Photoplays of California/Pathe Exchange, Inc.,
1921

Lowell, Joan

Adventure Girl (NF)

<u>Adventure</u> <u>Girl</u>
RKO Radio Pictures, Inc., 1934

Lowndes, Mrs. Belloc

> ### The Chink in the Armour
>
> > The <u>House</u> <u>of</u> <u>Peril</u> (*) (G. B.) (also based on the same
> > named play, by Horace Annesley Vachell, which was
> > derived from Lowndes' novel)
> > Astra Films, 1922
>
> ### Letty Lynton
>
> > <u>Letty</u> <u>Lynton</u>
> > Metro-Goldwyn-Mayer, Inc., 1932
>
> ### The Lodger (S/N)
>
> > <u>The</u> <u>Lodger</u> (*) (G. B.)
> > Gainsborough Prod./Woolf and Freedman Film Service,
> > 1926
> >
> > <u>The</u> <u>Lodger</u> (G. B.)
> > Twickenham/Woolf and Freedman Film Service, 1932
> >
> > <u>The</u> <u>Lodger</u>
> > Twentieth Century-Fox Film Corp., 1944
> >
> > <u>The</u> <u>Man</u> <u>in</u> <u>the</u> <u>Attic</u>
> > Panoramic Prod./Twentieth Century-Fox Film Corp., 1953
>
> ### Shameful Behavior (S)
>
> > <u>Shameful</u> <u>Behavior</u> (*)
> > Preferred Pictures, 1926
>
> ### The Story of Ivy
>
> > <u>Ivy</u>
> > Inter-Wood Prod./Universal International Motion
> > Pictures, 1947

Lowenstein, Wendy

> ### Dead Men Don't Dig Coal
>
> > <u>Strikebound</u> (Austr.)
> > TRM/Mainline, 1984

Lucas, Cleo

> ### I, Jerry Take Thee Joan

<u>Merrily</u> <u>We</u> <u>Go</u> <u>to</u> <u>Hell</u>
Paramount Pictures Corp., 1932

Luce, Alethea

   Amos Judd, a Play in a Prologue and Four Acts (P)

      <u>The</u> <u>Young</u> <u>Rajah</u> (*) (also based on the novel <u>Amos</u> <u>Judd</u>,
      by John Ames Mitchell, from which the play was derived)
      Famous Players-Lasky Corp., 1922

Luce, Clare Boothe (married name of Clare Boothe) (also see Clare
   Boothe)

   Kiss the Boys Goodbye (P)

      <u>Kiss</u> <u>the</u> <u>Boys</u> <u>Goodbye</u>
      Paramount Pictures Corp., 1941

   The Women (P)

      <u>The</u> <u>Women</u>
      Metro-Goldwyn-Mayer, Inc., 1939

      <u>The</u> <u>Opposite</u> <u>Sex</u>
      Metro-Goldwyn-Mayer, Inc., 1956

Lund, Doris

   Eric (NF)

      <u>Eric</u> (TVM)
      Lorimar Prod./National Broadcasting Co., 1975

Lurie, Alison

   The War Between the Tates (N)

      <u>The</u> <u>War</u> <u>Between</u> <u>the</u> <u>Tates</u> (TVM)
      Talent Associates, Ltd./National Broadcasting Co., 1977

Luther, Barbara

   Moon Walk (S)

      <u>A</u> <u>Ticklish</u> <u>Affair</u>
      Euterpe, Inc./Metro-Goldwyn-Mayer Inc., 1963

Lutz, Grace Livingston Hill

The Best Man (S)

    The Best Man (*)
    Jesse D. Hampton Prod./W. W. Hodkinson Corp.-Pathe
    Exchange, Inc., 1919

The Enchanted Barn

    The Enchanted Barn (*)
    Vitagraph Co. of America-a Blue Ribbon Feature/
    Vitagraph Co. of America, 1919

Lynn, Loretta and George Vecsey

    Coal Miner's Daughter (NF)

        Coal Miner's Daughter
        Universal Motion Pictures Co., 1980

Lyon, Dana (also see Theo Durrant)
    (pseud. of Mabel Dana Lyon)

    The Frightened Child

        House on Telegraph Hill
        Twentieth Century-Fox Film Corp., 1951

Lyon, Mabel Dana (see Dana Lyon and Theo Durrant)

Lyon, Nan and Ivan Lyons

    Someone is Killing the Great Chefs of Europe

        Who is Killing the Great Chefs of Europe? (U. S./Ger.)
        Aldrich-Lorimar Prod.-Geria-Bavaria/Warner Brothers
        Pictures, Inc., 1978

Mabie, Louise Kennedy

Wings of Pride

> Wings of Pride (*)
> Jans Pictures, Inc./Jans Pictures, Inc.-State Rights,
> 1920

Macardle, Dorothy

Uneasy Freehold

> The Uninvited
> Paramount Pictures Corp., 1944

MacCraken, Mary

A Circle of Children (NF)

> A Circle of Children (TVM)
> Edgar J. Sherick Prod.-Twentieth Century-Fox
> Television/Columbia Broadcasting System, 1977

Lovey: a Very Special Child (NF)

> Lovey: a Circle of Children, Part II (TVM)
> Time-Life Television Prod./Columbia Broadcasting
> System, 1978

MacDonald, (Mrs.) Barry

What Should a Woman Do to Promote Youth and Happiness? (N, which may be unpublished)

> What Should a Woman Do to Promote Youth and Happiness?
> (*)
> Barry MacDonald Film Co., (1915?)

Mac Donald, Betty

The Egg and I (NF)

> The Egg and I
> Universal Motion Pictures Co., 1947

MacDonald, Edwina Le Vin Dickerson (see Edwina Levin)

MacDonell, Margaret and Gordon MacDonell

    To Catch a Thief (P)

        To Catch a Thief (G. B.)
        GS Enterprises/RKO Radio Pictures, Inc., 1936

Mac Gerr, Patricia

    Follow as the Night

        One Step to Eternity
        Ellis Films, Inc., 1955

MacGowan, Alice

    Judith of the Cumberlands

        Judith of the Cumberlands (*)
        Signal Film Corp./Mutual Film Corp.-a Mutual Star
        Prod., 1916

        The Moonshine Menace (*)
        American Film Co., 1921

MacGrath, Leueen and Abe Burrows and George S. Kaufaman

    Silk Stockings (MP)

        Silk Stockings
        Metro-Goldwyn-Mayer, Inc., 1957

MacInnes, Helen

    Above Suspicion

        Above Suspicion
        Metro-Goldwyn-Mayer, Inc./Loew's, Inc., 1943

    Assignment in Brittany

        Assignment in Brittany
        Metro-Goldwyn-Mayer, Inc., 1943

    The Salzburg Connection

The Salzburg Connection
Twentieth Century-Fox Film Corp., 1972

The Venetian Affair

The Venetian Affair
Jerry Thorpe Prod./Metro-Goldwyn-Mayer, Inc., 1967

Mackaye, Dorothy and Carlton Miles

Gangstress, or Women in Prison (P)

Ladies They Talk About
Warner Brothers Pictures Co., 1933

Lady Gangster
Warner Brothers Pictures Co., 1942

MacKintosh, Elizabeth (see Josephine Tey)

MacLaine, Shirley

Out on a Limb (NF)

Out on a Limb (TVM)
American Broadcasting Co., 1987

MacLane, Mary

I, Mary MacLane (NF)

Men Who Have Made Love to Me (*)
Essanay Film Manufacturing Co.-a George K. Spoor/Ultra
Picture Corp.-Perfection Pictures/George Kiline System,
1918

Macpherson, Jean du Rocher

Evidence (P)

Evidence (*)
F. Ray Comstock Film Corp., 1915

MacVean, Phyllis (see Phyllis Hambledon)

MacVeigh, Sue
(pseud. of Elizabeth Custer Nearing)

Grand Central Murder

<u>Grand</u> <u>Central</u> <u>Murder</u>
Metro-Goldwyn-Mayer, Inc., 1942

Macy, Dora (also see Grace Perkins)
     (pseud. of Grace Perkins)

   Ex-Mistress

          <u>My</u> <u>Past</u>
          Warner Brothers Pictures, Inc., 1931

   Night Nurse

          <u>Night</u> <u>Nurse</u>
          Warner Brothers Pictures, Inc., 1931

Maddux, Rachel

   The Orchard Children

          <u>Who'll</u> <u>Save</u> <u>Our</u> <u>Children?</u> (TVM)
          Time-Life Television Prod./Columbia Broadcasting
          System, 1978

   A Walk in the Spring Rain

          <u>A</u> <u>Walk</u> <u>in</u> <u>the</u> <u>Spring</u> <u>Rain</u>
          Pingree Prod./Columbia Pictures Corp., 1970

Madison, Martha and Eva Kay Flint
     (Martha Madison: pseud. of Martha O'Dwyer; Eva Kay Flint:
     pseud. of Eva Finklestein)

   Subway Express (P)

          <u>Subway</u> <u>Express</u>
          Columbia Pictures Corp., 1931

   The Up and Up (P)

          <u>Reckless</u> <u>Living</u> (Note: Nash and Ross claim the picture
          was also based on the story "Twenty Grand," which the
          authors derived from their play. We find no
          verification it is a short story and not just a story
          idea.)
          Universal Motion Pictures Co., 1931

Magruder, Mary

   Courage (S)

222

Satan and the Woman (*)
Excellent Pictures Corp., 1928

Mahan, Patte Wheat

Three for a Wedding

Doctor, You've Got to be Kidding
Trident Prod./Metro-Goldwyn-Mayer, Inc., 1967

Majerus, Janet

Grandpa and Frank

Home to Stay (TVM)
Time-Life Television Prod./Columbia Broadcasting
System, 1978

Malleson, Lucy B. (see Anthony Gilbert)

Malloy, Doris and Gertrude Orr

Women Like Men (S)

Mad Parade
Liberty Pictures Corp./Paramount Pictures Corp., 1931

Maniates, Belle K.

Amarilly of Clothes-Line Alley

Amarilly of Clothesline Alley (*)
Mary Pickford/Famous Players-Lasky Corp.--Artcraft
Pictures Corp., 1918

The Littlest Scrub Lady (S)

Mirandy Smiles (*)
Famous Players-Lasky Corp., 1918

Penny of Top Hill Trail

Penny of Top Hill Trail (*)
Andrew J. Callaghan/Federated Film Exchange, 1921

Mann, Peggy

There are Two Kinds of Terrible

Two Kinds of Love (TVM)
Orgolini-Nelson Prod.-CBS Entertainment/Columbia
Broadcasting System, 1983

Mannes, Margaret

   The Woman who was Scared (S)

      Forever Darling
      Metro-Goldwyn-Mayer, Inc., 1956

Mannin, Ethel

   Dancing Boy

      Beloved Imposter (G. B.)
      Stafford/RKO Radio Pictures, Inc., 1936

Manning, Mary

   **Finnegans Wake, A Dramatization in Six Scenes of the Book
   of James Joyce** (P)

      Finnegans Wake   (also based on the novel Finnegans
      Wake, by James Joyce, from which the play was derived)
      Expanding Cinema/Grove Press, 1965

Marcin, Natalie

   You Can't Fool a Marine (S)

      Anchors Aweigh
      Metro-Goldwyn-Mayer, Inc., 1945

Mardignian, Aurora

   **Ravished Armenia; the Story of Aurora Mardiganian, the
   Christian Girl, Who Lived Through the Great Massacres** (NF)

      Auction of Souls (*)
      Selig Studios/First National, 1919

Marion, Frances

   The Fisher-Girl (S)

      A Daughter of the Sea (*)
      World, 1915

Mollie, Bless Her

> Molly and Me
> Twentieth Century-Fox Film Corp., 1945

A Movie Romance (S)

> A Girl's Folly (*)
> Paragon/World, 1917

The Secret Six

> The Secret Six
> Metro-Goldwyn-Mayer, Inc., 1931

Marquette, Doris and Leon Gordon

The Garden of Weeds (P)

> The Garden of Weeds (*)
> Famous Players-Lasky Corp./Paramount Pictures Corp.,
> 1924

Marraden, Beatrice

Ships that Pass in the Night

> Ships that pass in the Night (*) (G. B.)
> Screen Plays/British Exhibitor's Films, 1921

Marshall, Armina and Lawrence Langner

The Pursuit of Happiness (P)

> The Pursuit of Happiness
> Paramount Pictures Corp., 1934

Marshall, Catherine

A Man Called Peter: The Story of Peter Marshall (NF)

> A Man Called Peter
> Twentieth Century-Fox Film Corp., 1954

Marshall, Rosamond

The Bixby Girls

> All the Fine Young Cannibals

Metro-Goldwyn-Mayer, Inc., 1960

Kitty

<u>Kitty</u>
Paramount Pictures Corp., 1946

Martin, Gillian

Living Arrows

<u>Between Two Women</u> (TVM)
Jon Avnet Co./American Broadcasting Co., 1986

Martin, Helen Reimensnyder

Barnabetta

<u>Erstwhile Susan</u> (*) (also based on the play <u>Erstwhile Susan</u>, by Marian De Forest, which was derived from Martin's novel)
Realart Pictures Corp., 1919

The Parasite

<u>The Parasite</u> (*)
B. P. Schulberg Prod., 1925

The Snob

<u>The Snob</u> (*)
Metro-Goldwyn-Mayer, Inc., 1924

Tillie, a Mennonite Maid

<u>Tillie</u> (*) (also based on the play <u>Tillie, a Mennonite Maid</u>, by Frank Howe, Jr., which was derived from Martin's novel)
Realart Pictures Corp./Paramount Pictures Corp., 1922

Martin, Nell

Lord Byron of Broadway

<u>Lord Byron of Broadway</u>
Metro-Goldwyn-Mayer, Inc., 1930

Martindale, May

Gamblers All

<u>Gamblers</u> <u>All</u> (*) (G. B.)
G. B. Samuelson/Granger, 1919

Marton, Sandra

Out of the Shadows

<u>Out</u> <u>of</u> <u>the</u> <u>Shadows</u> (TVM) (G. B.)
Independent Television Corp., 1988

Mason, Grace Sartwell

Clarissa and the Post Road (S)

<u>Man</u> <u>Crazy</u> (*)
Charles R. Rogers Prod./First National, 1927

The Shadow of Rosalie Byrnes

<u>The</u> <u>Shadow</u> <u>of</u> <u>Rosalie</u> <u>Byrnes</u> (*)
Selznick Pictures Corp., 1920

Speed (S)

<u>Speed</u> (*)
Banner Prod., 1925

Mason, Howard
(pseud. of Jennifer Ramage)

Photofinish

<u>Follow</u> <u>that</u> <u>Horse</u> (G. B.)
Cavalcade/Warner Brothers Pictures, Inc., 1959

Mather, Anne

Leopard in the Snow

<u>Leopard</u> <u>in</u> <u>the</u> <u>Snow</u> (G. B./Can.)
Harlequin-Seastone-Leopard in the Snow/Enterprise
Pictures, 1978

Mathers, Helen

Cherry Ripe

<u>Cherry</u> <u>Ripe</u> (*) (G. B.)
Astra Films, 1921

Comin' Thro' the Rye

> Comin' Thro' the Rye (*) (G. B.)
> Hepworth/Harma, 1916

> Comin' Thro' the Rye (*) (G. B.)
> Hepworth, 1923

Matthews, Adelaide and Anne Nichols (also see the entry below)

Just Married; a Comedy in Three Acts (P)

> Just Married (*)
> Paramount Famous Lasky Corp., 1928

Matthews, Adelaide and Martha M. Stanley (also see the entry above)

The First Mrs. Cheverick, a Play (P)

> Scrambled Wives (*)
> Marguerite Clark Prod./Associated First National, 1921

The Teaser (P)

> The Teaser (*)
> Universal Motion Pictures Co., 1925

Maxtone-Graham, Joyce (see Jan Struther)

May, Julian
(pseud. of Judy Dikty)

Dune Roller (S)

> The Cremators
> New World Cinema, 1972

May, Margery Land

The Bleeders (S)

> The Beauty Market (*)
> Katherine MacDonald Pictures Corp.-Attractions Dist.
> Corp./First National, 1919

Such as Sit in Judgement

> Those Who Judge (*)
> Banner Prod., 1924

Mayer, Jane Rothschild (see Clare Jaynes)

Maynard, Nan

This is my Street

This is my Street (G. B.)
Adder/Anglo-Amalgamated Film Dist., 1963

Mayo, Eleanor R.

Turn Home

Tarnished
Republic Pictures Corp., 1950

Mayo, Margaret (also see the two entries below)
(pseud. of Lillian Clatten)

Baby Mine (P)

Baby Mine (*)
Goldwyn Pictures Corp./Goldwyn Dist. Corp., 1917

Baby Mine (*)
Metro-Goldwyn-Mayer, Inc., 1928

Behind the Lines

Behind the Scenes (*)
Famous Players Film Co./Paramount Pictures Corp., 1914

Polly of the Circus (P)

Polly of the Circus (*)
Goldwyn Pictures Corp./Goldwyn Dist. Corp., 1917

Polly of the Circus
Metro-Goldwyn-Mayer, Inc., 1932

Poor Boob (P)

The Poor Boob (*)
Famous Players-Lasky Corp./Famous Players-Lasky Corp.-
Paramount Pictures Corp., 1919

Mayo, Margaret and Edward Salisbury Field (also see the entry
above and the entry below)
(Margaret Mayo: pseud. of Lillian Clatten)

Twin Beds (P)

>Twin Beds (*)
>Carter De Haven Prod./First National, 1920
>
>Twin Beds
>First National-Warner Brothers Pictures, Inc., 1929
>
>The Life of the Party (G. B.)
>Warner Brothers Pictures, Inc.-First National/First National, 1934
>
>Twins Beds
>Edward Small Prod./United Artists Film Corp., 1942

Mayo, Margaret and Mrs. Humphry (Mary Augusta) Ward (also see the two entries above)
(Margaret Mayo: pseud of Lillian Clatten)

The Marriage of William Ashe (P)

>The Marriage of William Ashe (*) (also based on the same named novel, by Mrs. Humphrey Ward, from which the play was derived)
>Metro Pictures Corp., 1921

McCall, Mary

Fraternity (S)

>On the Sunny Side
>Twentieth Century-Fox Film Corp., 1941

The Goldfish Bowl (S)

>It's Tough to be Famous
>First national/Warner Brothers Pictures, Inc., 1932

Revolt (S)

>Scarlet Dawn
>Warner Brothers Pictures, Inc., 1932

McCall, Sidney (also see Mary McNeil Fenollosa and the entry below)
(pseud. of Mary McNeil Fenollosa)

The Breath of God

>The Breath of the Gods (*)
>Universal Film Manufacturing Co./Universal Film

230

Manufacturing Co.--a Jewel Super-Prod., 1920

Red Horse Hill

The <u>Eternal</u> <u>Mother</u> (*)
Metro Pictures Corp./Metro Pictures Corp.-A Metro
Wonderplay, 1917

McCall, Sidney and William J. Hurlbut (also see Mary McNeil
    Fenollosa and the entry above)

The Strange Woman

The <u>Strange</u> <u>Woman</u> (*)   (also based on the same named
play, by Hurlbut)
Fox Film Corp., 1918

McCarthy, Mary

The Group

The <u>Group</u>
Famous Artists Prod.-Famartists Prod./United Artist's
Film Corp., 1966

McCauley, Sue

Other Halves

Other <u>Halves</u> (N. Z.)
Oringham, 1985

McCormick, Mona

Too Dangerous to Be at Large (NF)

<u>Dangerous</u> <u>Company</u> (TVM)
The Dangerous Co.-Finnegan Associates/Columbia
Broadcasting System, 1982

McCormick, Victoria (see Janet Green)

McCracken, Ester

No Medals (P)

The <u>Weaker</u> <u>Sex</u> (G. B.)
Two Cities Films, Ltd./General Film Dist., Inc., 1948

Quiet Wedding (P)

>   Quiet Wedding
>   Conqueror/Paramount Pictures Corp. British, 1941
>
>   Happy is the Bride (G. B.)
>   Panther/British Lion Film Corp., 1958

Quiet Weekend, A Comedy in Three Acts (P)

>   Quiet Weekend (G. B.)
>   Associated British Picture Corp./Pathe Exchange, Inc.,
>   1946

McCullers, Carson

The Heart is a Lonely Hunter

>   The Heart is a Lonely Hunter
>   Warner Brothers Pictures, Inc./Seven Arts, Inc., 1968

The Member of the Wedding (P, based on the novel The Member
of the Wedding, by Carson McCullers)

>   The Member of the Wedding
>   Columbia Pictures Corp., 1952

Reflections in a Golden Eye

>   Reflections in a Golden Eye
>   Warner Brothers Pictures, Inc., 1967

McCullough, Colleen

Tim

>   Tim (Austr.)
>   Pisces/Satori, 1979

McDonald, Anne and Rosemary Crossley

Annie's Coming Out (NF)

>   Annie's Coming Out (Austr.)
>   Film Australia/Universal Motion Pictures Co., 1985

McFadden, Cyra

Serial

>   Serial

Paramount Pictures Corp., 1980

McFadden, Elizabeth

   The Double Door (P)

        Double Door
        Paramount Pictures Corp., 1934

Mc Ilvaine, Jane

   It Happens Every Thursday (NF)

        It Happens Every Thursday
        Universal Motion Pictures Co., 1953

McIntyre, Heather

   Treble Trouble (P)

        Home and Away (G. B.)
        Conquest-Guest/Eros Films, 1956

McKenna, Marthe Cnockhaert

   I Was a Spy (NF)

        I Was a Spy (G. B.)
        Gaumont Co./Woolf and Freedman Film Service, 1934

   Lancer Spy

        Lancer Spy
        Twentieth Century-Fox Film Corp., 1937

Mc Laurin, Kate L.

   The Six-Fifty (P)

        The Six-Fifty (*)
        Universal Pictures, 1923

   Whispering Wires: a Play in Three Acts (P)

        Whispering Wires (*) (also based on the novel
        Whispering Wires, by Henry Leverage, from which the
        play was derived)
        Fox Film Corp., 1926

McLean, Kathryn Anderson (see Kathryn Forbes)

McNamara, Rachel

Lark's Gate

Tell Your Children (*) (G. B.)
International Artists, 1922

McNaughton, Sarah

The Fortune of Christina McNab

The Fortune of Christina McNab (*) (G. B.)
Gaumont-Westminister Pictures, 1921

McNeil, Elizabeth

9 1/2 Weeks

9 1/2 Weeks
Metro-Goldwyn-Mayer, Inc./United Artists Film Corp.,
1986

McNeill, Janet

Child in the House

Child in the House (G. B.)
Laureate/Eros Films, 1956

McNulty, Faith

The Burning Bed (NF)

The Burning Bed (TVM)
Tisch-Avnet Prod./National Broadcasting Co., 1984

McSwigan, Marie

All Aboard for Freedom

Snow Treasure
Sagittarius Prod./Allied Artists Pictures Corp.1968

Meaney, Lottie M. and Oliver D. Bailey

Pay-Day (P)

Pay Day (*)
Metro Pictures Corp./Metro Pictures Corp.-a Special
Prod. De Luxe-Screen Classics, Inc., 1918

A Stitch in Time (P)

A Stitch in Time (*)
Vitagraph Co. of America, 1919

Mears, Mary

The Forbidden Thing (S)

The Forbidden Thing (*)
Allan Dwan Prod./Associated Producers, Inc., 1920

Meherin, Elenore

**"Chickie"; a Hidden, Tragic Chapter From the Life of a Girl
of This Strange "Today"**

Chickie (*)
First National, 1925

Meiser, Edith (see "Xantippe")

Mercein, Eleanor (maiden name of Eleanor Mercein Kelly) (also see
Eleanor Mercein Kelly)

Basquerie

Their Mad Moment
Fox Film Corp., 1931

Meredyth, Bess and Wells Root

The Southerner (S)

The Prodigal
Metro-Goldwyn-Mayer, Inc., 1931

Merrick, Hope

Mary Girl (P)

Mary Girl (*) (G. B.)
Butcher's Film Service, 1917

Mertz, Barbara Louise Gross (see Barbara Michaels)

Messer, Mona (see Anne Hocking)

Metalious, Grace

Peyton Place

Peyton Place
Twentieth Century-Fox Film Corp., 1957

Return to Peyton Place

Return to Peyton Place
Jerry Wald Prod.-Associated Producers, Inc./Twentieth
Century-Fox Film Corp., 1961

Michael, Judith
(pseud. of Judith Bernard and Michael Fain)

Deceptions

Deceptions (TVM)
Louis Rudolph Prod.--Columbia Pictures Television/
National Broadcasting Co, 1985

Michaels, Barbara
(pseud. of Barbara Louise Gross Mertz)

Ammie, Come Home

The House That Would Not Die (TVM)
Aron Spelling Prod., 1970

Michelson, Miriam

In the Bishop's Carriage

In the Bishop's Carriage (*)
Famous Players Film Co./State Rights, 1913

She Couldn't Help It (*) (also based on the play In the
Bishop's Carriage, by Channing Pollock, which was
derived from Michelson's novel)
Realart Pictures Corp., 1920

Michael Thwaite's Wife

The Better Half (*)

Select Pictures Corp., 1918

Miller, Alice Duer (also see Clara Bartram and "Dorothy Fields
    and Otto Harbach" entry)

The Adventuress (S)

> The Keyhole
> Warner Brothers Pictures, Inc., 1933

And One was Beautiful

> And One was Beautiful
> Metro-Goldwyn-Mayer, Inc./Loew's, Inc., 1940

Are Parents People? (S)

> Are Parents People? (*)
> Famous Players-Lasky Corp./Paramount Pictures Corp.,
> 1925

Big Executive (S)

> Big Executive
> Paramount Pictures Corp., 1933

Calderon's Prisoner

> Something Different (*)
> Realart Pictures Corp., 1920

The Charm School (N and the play Charm School, by Miller and
Robert Milton, which was derived from Miller's novel) --
which served as the source for the following films is not
clear (the source we used for this section is The Paramount
Story by Eames)

> The Charm School (*)
> Paramount, 1921
>
> Someone to Love (*)
> Paramount Famous Lasky Corp., 1928
>
> Sweetie
> Paramount Pictures Corp., 1929
>
> Collegiate
> Paramount Pictures Corp., 1936
>
> College Swing
> Paramount Pictures Corp., 1938

Come Out of the Kitchen!   A Romance

Come Out of the Kitchen (*)
Famous Players-Lasky Corp./Famous Players-Lasky Corp.--
Paramount Pictures Corp., 1919

Honey (also based on the play Come Out of the Kitchen,
by A. E. Thomas, which was derived from Miller's
novel)
Paramount Famous Lasky Corp., 1930

Come Out of the Pantry (G. B.)
British and Dominions Film Corp./United Artists Film
Corp., 1935

Spring in Park Lane (G. B.) (this movie may be based on
the play only, but sources are not clear, so we have
listed   it)
Imperadio/British Lion, 1948

Gowns by Roberta

Roberta
RKO Radio Pictures, Inc., 1935

Ladies Must Live

Ladies Must Live (*)
Mayflower Photoplay Corp./Paramount Pictures Corp.,
1921

Less Than Kin

Less Than Kin (*)
Famous Players-Lasky Corp./Famous Players-Lasky Corp.--
Paramount Pictures Corp., 1918

Manslaughter

Manslaughter (*)
Cecil B. De Mille for Famous Players-Lasky
Corp./Paramount Pictures Corp., 1922

Manslaughter
Paramount Pictures Corp., 1930

And Sudden Death
Paramount Pictures Corp., 1936

The Princess and the Plumber (S)

The Princess and the Plumber
Twentieth Century-Fox Film Corp., 1930

The White Cliffs (Po)

The White Cliffs of Dover
Metro-Goldwyn-Mayer, Inc., 1944

Miller, Alice Duer and Robert Milton (see Charm School by Alice
    Duer Miller)

Miller, Helena and Anita Fairgrieve

    Purple and Fine Linen (P)

        Adventure in Manhattan (also based on the short story
        "Purple and Fine Linen," by May Edginton, from which
        the play was derived)
        Columbia Pictures Corp., 1936

Miller, Mary Ashe and John Fleming Wilson

    The Man Who Married His Own Wife (S)

        The Man Who Married His Own Wife (*)
        Universal Film Manufacturing Co., 1922

Miller, Sue

    The Good Mother

        The Good Mother
        Touchstone-Silver Screen Partners IV-Arnold
        Glimcher/Buena Vista Dist. Co., 1988

Millin, Sarah Gertrude

    Rhodes (NF)

        Rhodes of Africa (G. B.)
        Gaumont British, Ltd., 1936

Milne, Margery and Lorus J. Milne

    The Mating Instinct (NF)

        Love and the Animals
        Falcon International Corp./Dal-Art Films, 1969

Mitchell, Basil and Wallace Geoffrey
    (Basil Mitchell: pseud of Jeannie Francis Mitchell)

    The Perfect Woman (P)

The <u>Perfect</u> <u>Woman</u> (G. B.)
Two Cities Films, Ltd., 1950

Mitchell, Cathy and Dave Mitchell and Richard Ofshe

The Light on Synanon: How a Country Weekly Exposed a Corporate Cult -- and Won the Pulitzer Prize (NF)

<u>Attack</u> <u>on</u> <u>Fear</u> (TVM)
Tomorrow Entertainment, Inc./Columbia Broadcasting System, 1984

Mitchell, Frances Marion

Joan of Rainbow Springs

<u>Girl</u> <u>of</u> <u>My</u> <u>Heart</u> (*)
Fox Film Corp., 1920

Mitchell, Jeannie Francis (see "Basil Mitchell and Wallace Geoffrey" entry)

Mitchell, Margaret

Gone with the Wind

<u>Gone</u> <u>With</u> <u>the</u> <u>Wind</u>
Selznick International Pictures/Metro-Goldwyn-Mayer, Inc., 1939

Mitchell, Mary

A Warning to Wantons

<u>A</u> <u>Warning</u> <u>to</u> <u>Wantons</u> (G. B.)
Aquila/General Film Dist., Inc., 1949

Mitchell, Norma and Russell G. Medcraft

Cradle Snatchers, a Farce-Comedy in Three Acts (P) (also see <u>Let's</u> <u>Face</u> <u>It</u> by Dorothy Fields and Herbert Fields)

<u>The</u> <u>Cradle</u> <u>Snatchers</u> (*)
Fox Films Corp., 1927

<u>Why</u> <u>Leave</u> <u>Home</u>
Fox Films Corp., 1929

240

Mitchell, Ruth Comfort

Into Her Kingdom

Into Her Kingdom (*)
Corinne Griffith Prod./First National, 1926

Mitford, Nancy

The Blessing

Count Your Blessings
Metro-Goldwyn-Mayer, Inc., 1959

The Little Hut (P, based on the play Le Petit Hutte, by
Andre Roussin)

The Little Hut
Metro-Goldwyn-Mayer, Inc., 1957

Mithers, Carol Lynn

My Life as a Man (A)

Her Life as a Man (TVM)
LS Entertainment, Inc./National Broadcasting Co., 1984

Moggach, Deborah

To Have and to Hold

To Have and to Hold (TVM) (G. B.)
London Weekend Television, 1985

Montague, Margaret Prescott

Linda

Linda
Mrs. Wallace Reed Prod./Willis Kent Prod., 1929

In Calvert's Valley

Calvert's Valley (*)
Fox Film Corp., 1922

The Sowing of Alderson Cree

Seeds of Vengeance (*)
C. R. Macauley Photoplays, Inc./Select Pictures Corp.,

1920

Uncle Sam of Freedom Ridge (S)

Uncle Sam of Freedom Ridge (*)
Harvey Levey Prod./State Rights, 1920

Montgomery, Florence

Misunderstood

Misunderstood (also based on the Italian movie
Incompreso, 1967)
Metro-Goldwyn-Mayer, Inc.-United Artists Film Corp.,
1984

Montgomery, Lucy Maud

Anne of Avonlea

Anne of Green Gables (*) (also based on the novels Anne
of Green Gables, Anne of the Island, and the related
stories Chronicles of Avonlea, all by Montgomery)
Realart Pictures Corp., 1919

Anne of Avonlea (TVM) (Can.) (also based on the novels
Anne of the Island and Anne of Windy Poplars, both by
Montgomery)
Walt Disney Prod./Buena Vista Home Video, 1987

Anne of Green Gables

Anne of Green Gables (*) (also based on the novels Anne
of Avonlea, Anne of the Island, and the related stories
Chronicles of Avonlea, all by Montgomery)
Realart Pictures Corp., 1919

Anne of Green Gables
RKO Radio Pictures, Inc., 1934

Anne of Green Gables (TVM) (Can.)
Walt Disney Prod./Buena Vista Home Video, 1985

Anne of the Island

Anne of Green Gables (*) (also based on the novels Anne
of Green Gables, Anne of Avonlea, and the related
stories Chronicles of Avonlea, all by Montgomery)
Realart Pictures Corp., 1919

Anne of Avonlea (TVM) (Can.) (also based on the novels
Anne of Avonlea and Anne of Windy Poplars, both by
Montgomery)

242

Walt Disney Prod./Buena Vista Home Video, 1987

Anne of Windy Poplars

Anne of Windy Poplars
RKO Radio Pictures, Inc., 1940

Anne of Avonlea (TVM) (Can.) (also based on the novels
Anne of Avonlea and Anne of the Island, both by
Montgomery)
Walt Disney Prod./Buena Vista Home Video, 1987

Chronicles of Avonlea (RS)

Anne of Green Gables (*) (also based on the novels Anne
of Green Gables, Anne of Avonlea, and Anne of the
Island, both by Montgomery)
Realart Pictures Corp., 1919

Monti, Carlotta and Cy Rice

W. C. Fields and Me (NF)

W. C. Fields and Me
Universal Motion Pictures Co., 1976

Moody, (Mrs.) William Vaughn

The Faith Healer (P)

The Faith Healer (*)
Famous Players Film Co./Paramount, 1921

Moon, Lorna

Dark Star

Min and Bill
Metro-Goldwyn-Mayer, Inc., 1930

Moore, Grace

You're Only Human Once (NF)

So This is Love
Warner Brothers Pictures, Inc., 1953

Moore, Katherine Leslie

The Peacock Feather: a Romance

                Pennies from Heaven
                Columbia Pictures Corp., 1936

Moore, Olga

     Quintuplets to You (S)

                You Can't Beat Love
                RKO Radio Pictures, Inc., 1937

Moore, Ruth

     Spoonhandle

                Deep Waters
                Twentieth Century-Fox Film Corp., 1948

Moray, Helga

     Untamed

                Untamed
                Twentieth Century Fox Film Corp., 1955

Morgan, Beatrice Burton (married name of Beatrice Morgan) (also
     see Beatrice Burton)

     The Little Yellow House

                The Little Yellow House (*)
                Film Booking Office Prod., Inc., 1928

Morgan, Joan

     This was a Woman (P)

                This Was a Woman (G. B.)
                Excelsior Feature Film Prod., 1948

Morgan, Leota

     The Streets of New York (P)

                The Streets of New York (*)
                State/Arrow Pictures, 1922

Morris, Harriet

The Snowbird (S)

> The <u>Dancer's</u> <u>Peril</u> (*)
> World, 1917

Morris, Rebecca

The Good Humor Man (S)

> <u>One</u> <u>is</u> <u>a</u> <u>Lonely</u> <u>Number</u>
> Metro-Goldwyn-Mayer, Inc., 1972

Morrison, Anne [Anne Morrison Chapin] (also see entry below)

Love Flies in the Window (P)

> <u>This</u> <u>Man</u> <u>is</u> <u>Mine</u>
> RKO Radio Pictures, Inc., 1934

Morrison, Anne [Anne Morrison Chapin] and Patterson McNutt (also
    see entry above)

Pigs, Comedy in Three Acts (P)

> The <u>Midnight</u> <u>Kiss</u> (*)
> Fox Film Corp., 1926

Morrison, Emmeline

The Sins Ye Do

> The <u>Sins</u> <u>Ye</u> <u>Do</u> (*) (G. B.)
> Stoll, 1924

Morrison, Margaret

The Reverse be my Lot

> The <u>Reverse</u> <u>be</u> <u>my</u> <u>Lot</u> (G. B.)
> Rock Prod./Columbia Pictures Corp., 1938

Morrow, (Mrs.) Honore

On to Oregon

> <u>Seven</u> <u>Alone</u>
> Doty-Dayton, 1975

Morse, Anne Christensen (see Ann Head)

Mortimer, Lillian

No Mother to Guide Her (P)

No Mother to Guide Her (*)
Fox Film Corp., 1923

Mortimer, Penelope

A Bachelor's Romance (P)

The Bachelor's Romance (*)
Famous Players Film Co./Paramount Pictures Corp., 1915

The Pumpkin Eater

The Pumpkin Eater (G. B.)
Romulus Films/Columbia Pictures Corp., 1964

Morton, Martha

Her Lord and Master: a Comedy in Four Acts (P)

Her Lord and Master (*)
Vitagraph Co. of America, 1921

Morton, Victoria

The Whirlpool

The Whirlpool (*)
Select Pictures Corp., 1918

Mosco, Maisie

Happy Family (P)

Mumsy, Nanny, Sonny and Girly (G. B.)
Brigette-Fitzroy-Francis/CIRO, 1969

Mulholland, Clara

Kathleen Mavourneen

Kathleen Mavourneen
Argyle Enterprises-British/Wardour, 1937

246

Mumford, Ethel Watts

    Everything Money Can Buy (S)

        <u>After</u> <u>Business</u> <u>Hours</u> (*)
        Columbia Pictures Corp., 1925

    Sick Abed (P)

        <u>Sick</u> <u>Abed</u> (*)
        Famous Players-Lasky Corp./Famous Players-Lasky Corp.--
        Paramount Pictures Corp.--Artcraft Pictures Corp., 1920

    The Wedding Song

        <u>The</u> <u>Wedding</u> <u>Song</u> (*)
        Cinema Corp. of America/Producers Dist. Corp., 1925

Muni, Belle and Abem Finkel

    Unwanted (S)

        <u>The</u> <u>Deceiver</u>
        Columbia Pictures Corp., 1931

Munson, Audrey

    Life Story (A)

        <u>Heedless</u> <u>Moths</u> (*) (also based on the article "Studio
        Secrets," by Munson)
        Perry Plays/Equity Pictures, 1921

    Studio Secrets (A)

        <u>Heedless</u> <u>Moths</u> (*) (also based on the article "Life
        Story," by Munson)
        Perry Plays/Equity Pictures, 1921

Murdoch, Iris (also see the entry below)

    The Bell

        <u>The</u> <u>Bell</u> (TVM) (G. B.)
        British Broadcasting Corp. TV, 1982

    A Severed Head

        <u>A</u> <u>Severed</u> <u>Head</u> (G. B.) (also based on the same named
        play, by Murdoch and J. B. Priestly, which was derived

from Murdoch's novel)
Winkast/Columbia Pictures Corp., 1970

Murdoch, Iris and J. B. Priestly (also see the entry above)

A Severed Head (P)

A <u>Severed</u> <u>Head</u> (G. B.) (also based on the same named novel, by Murdoch, from which the play was derived)
Winkast/Columbia Pictures Corp., 1970

Murfin, Jane (also see the entry below)

Playthings of Destiny (P)

<u>Playthings</u> <u>of</u> <u>Destiny</u> (*)
Anita Stewart/Associated First National, 1921

The Right to Lie (P)

<u>The</u> <u>Right</u> <u>to</u> <u>Lie</u> (*)
Capellani/Pathe Exchange, Inc., 1919

Murfin, Jane and Jane Cowl (also see the entry above)

Daybreak (P)

<u>Daybreak</u> (*)
Metro Pictures Corp., 1918

Information Please (P)

A <u>Temperamental</u> <u>Wife</u> (*)
Constance Talmadge Film Co.-a John Emerson-Anita Loos Prod./First National, 1919

Lilac Time (P)

<u>Lilac</u> <u>Time</u> (*)
First National, 1928

Smilin' Through (P)

<u>Smilin'</u> <u>Through</u> (*)
Warner Brothers Pictures, Inc., 1922

<u>Smilin'</u> <u>Through</u>
Metro-Goldwyn-Mayer, Inc., 1932

<u>Smilin'</u> <u>Through</u>
Metro-Goldwyn-Mayer, Inc., 1941

Muzzy, Bertha Sinclair

    The Range Dwellers

        <u>The</u> <u>Taming</u> <u>of</u> <u>the</u> <u>West</u> (*)
        Universal Pictures, 1925

Myers, Elizabeth

    Mrs. Christopher

        <u>Blackmailed</u>
        HH Films/General Film Dist., Inc., 1951

Nearing, Elizabeth Custer (see Sue MacVeigh)

Nemirovsky, Irene

David Golder

<u>My</u> <u>Daughter</u> <u>Joy</u> (G. B.)
London Films-British Lion Prod. Assests/British Lion,
1950

Nepean, Edith

Gwyneth of the Welsh Hills

<u>Gwyneth</u> <u>of</u> <u>the</u> <u>Welsh</u> <u>Hills</u> (*) (G. B.)
Stoll, 1921

Nesbit, Edith (maiden name of Edith Nesbit Bland)

The Ballad of Splendid Silence (Po)

<u>A</u> <u>Ballad</u> <u>of</u> <u>Splendid</u> <u>Silence</u> (*)
Eric Williams Speaking Pictures-Barker, 1913

<u>The</u> <u>Ordeal</u> (*)
Life Photo, 1914

The Railway Children

<u>The</u> <u>Railway</u> <u>Children</u>
Electrical and Musical Industries-Associated
British/Metro-Goldwyn-Mayer British-Electrical and
Musical Industries, 1970

Nethersole, Olga

The Writing on the Wall (P)

<u>The</u> <u>Writing</u> <u>on</u> <u>the</u> <u>Wall</u> (*) (also based on the novel
<u>The</u> <u>Writing</u> <u>on</u> <u>the</u> <u>Wall:</u> <u>a</u> <u>Novel</u> <u>Founded</u> <u>on</u> <u>Olga</u>
<u>Nethersole's</u> <u>Play</u> <u>by</u> <u>William</u> <u>J.</u> <u>Hurlbut</u>, by Edward
Marshall and William J. Hurlbut)
Vitagraph Co. of America-A Blue Ribbon Feature/Greater
Vitagraph, 1916

250

Neumann, Beda and Ernest Neumann

    I Lost my Heart in Heidelburg (P)

        The <u>Student's</u> <u>Romance</u> (G. B.)
        British International Pictures/Wardour, 1935

Neville, Margot
    (joint pseud. of Margot Goyder and Anne Neville Goyder
    Joske)

    The Island of Despair

        The <u>Island</u> <u>of</u> <u>Despair</u> (*) (G. B.)
        Stoll, 1926

    Safety First

        <u>Safety</u> <u>First</u> (*) (G. B.)
        Stoll, 1926

        <u>Crazy</u> <u>People</u> (G. B.)
        British Lion Film Corp./Metro-Goldwyn-Mayer British,
        1934

Newell, Maude Woodruff

    Her Unknown Knight (S)

        <u>Impulse</u> (*)
        Berwilla Film Corp./Arrow Film Corp., 1922

Newman, Andrea

    Three into Two Won't Go

        <u>Three</u> <u>into</u> <u>Two</u> <u>Won't</u> <u>Go</u> (G. B.)
        Universal International Motion Pictures/J. Arthur Rank
        Film Dist., Ltd., 1969

Nichols, Anne (also see the entry below)

    Abie's Irish Rose (P)

        <u>Abie's</u> <u>Irish</u> <u>Rose</u>
        Paramount Famous Lasky Corp., 1929

        <u>Abie's</u> <u>Irish</u> <u>Rose</u>
        Bing Crosby Prod., Inc./United Artists Film Corp., 1946

Her Gilded Cage (P)

> Her Gilded Cage (*)
> Famous Players-Lasky Corp./Paramount Pictures Corp.,
> 1922

Linger Longer Lefty (P)

> Give Me a Sailor
> Paramount Pictures Corp., 1938

Nichols, Anne and Adelaide Matthews (also see the entry above)

Just Married; a Comedy in Three Acts (P)

> Just Married (*)
> Paramount Famous Lasky Corp., 1928

Nichols, Beverley (also see the entry below)

Evensong: a Novel

> Evensong (G. B.) (also based on the play Evensong, by
> Nichols and Edward Knoblock, which was derived from
> Nichols' novel)
> Gaumont British, Ltd., 1934

Nichols, Beverley and Edward Knoblock (also see the entry above)

Evensong (P)

> Evensong (G.B.) (also based on the novel Evensong: A
> Novel, by Nichols, from which the play was derived)
> Gaumont British, Ltd., 1934

Nicholson, Meredith

Broken Barriers

> Broken Barriers (*)
> Metro-Goldwyn Pictures, 1924

The Hopper (S)

> The Hopper (*)
> Triangle Film Corp., 1918

The House of a Thousand Candles

> The House of a Thousand Candles (*)

Selig Polyscope Co., 1915

Haunting Shadows (*)
Jesse D. Hampton Prod., 1920

The House of a Thousand Candles
Republic Pictures Corp., 1936

Lords of High Decision

Lords of High Decision (*)
Universal Film Manufacturing Co., 1916

The Port of Missing Men

The Port of Missing Men (*)
Famous Players Film Co., 1914

Nicklaus, Thelma

Tamahine

Tamahine (G. B.)
Associated British Picture Corp./WPD, 1963

Nielson, Helen

Gold Coast Nocturne

Murder by Proxy (G. B.)
Hammer Films/Exclusive Films, 1955

Niggli, Josefina

A Mexican Village (RS)

Sombrero
Metro-Goldwyn-Mayer, Inc., 1953

Niland, Darcy

The Shiralee

The Shiralee (G. B.)
Ealing Studios/Metro-Goldwyn-Mayer British, 1957

Nolan, Jeanette

Gather Ye Rosebuds

Isn't it Romantic
Paramount Pictures Corp., 1948

Nordstrom, Frances

   The Ruined Lady (P)

        One Woman to Another (*)
        Famous Players/Paramount Pictures Corp., 1927

Norman, Marsha

   The Laundromat (P)

        The Laundromat (TVM)
        Sandcastle 5 Film/Home Box Office, 1985

   'Night, Mother (P)

        'Night, Mother
        Universal Motion Pictures, 1986

Norris, Helen

   The Christmas Wife (S)

        The Christmas Wife (TVM)
        Home Box Office, 1988

Norris, Kathleen

   Beauty's Daughter

        Navy Wife
        Twentieth Century-Fox Corp., 1935

   Butterfly

        Butterfly (*)
        Universal Motion Pictures Co., 1924

   The Callahans and the Murphys

        The Callahans and the Murphys (*)
        Metro-Goldwyn-Mayer, Inc., 1927

   Christine of the Hungry Heart

        Christine of the Hungry Heart (*)
        First National, 1924

Flaming Passion

> Lucretia Lombard (*)
> Warner Brothers Pictures, Inc., 1923

Harriet and the Piper

> Harriet and the Piper (*)
> Louis B. Mayer Prod.-Anita Steward Prod.,
> Inc./Associated First National, 1920

The Heart of Rachael

> The Heart of Rachael (*)
> Bessie Barriscale Prod.-Paralta Plays, Inc./W. W.
> Hodkinson Corp.-General Film, 1918

Josselyn's Wife

> Josselyn's Wife (*)
> B. B. Features, Inc./Robertson-Cole--Exhibitor's Mutual
> Dist. Corp., 1919

> Josselyn's Wife (*)
> Tiffany Prod., 1926

The Luck of Geraldine Laird

> The Luck of Geraldine Laird (*)
> B. B. Features, Inc./Robert-Cole, 1920

Lucretia Lombard

> Lucretia Lombard (*)
> Warner Brothers Pictures, Inc., 1923

Manhattan Love (S)

> Change of Heart
> Fox Film Corp., 1934

Mother

> Mother (*)
> Film Booking Office Prod., Inc., 1927

My Best Girl

> My Best Girl (*)
> Mary Pickford/United Artists Film Corp., 1927

Passion Flower

> Passion Flower
> Metro-Goldwyn-Mayer, Inc., 1930

Poor Dear Margaret Kirby (S)

> Poor Dear Margaret Kirby (*)
> Selznick Pictures Corp., 1921

Rose of the World

> Rose of the World (*)
> Warner Brothers Pictures, Inc.,, 1925

Second Hand Wife

> Second Hand Wife
> Fox Film Corp., 1933

Sisters

> Sisters (*)
> International Film Service/American Releasing, 1922

Walls of Gold

> Walls of Gold
> Fox Film Corp., 1933

Norton, Mary

Bednob and Broomstick

> Bednobs and Broomsticks
> Walt Disney Prod./Buena Vista Dist. Co., 1971

The Borrowers

> The Borrowers (TVM)
> Charles M. Schulz Creative Associates--Walt DeFaria
> Prod.--Twentieth Century-Fox Television/National
> Broadcasting Co., 1973

- O -

Oates, Joyce Carol

Where are You Going, Where have You Been? (S)

Smooth Talk
Napenthe-American Playhouse/Spectrafilm, 1985

O'Brien, Edna

The Country Girls

The Country Girls (TVM) (G. B.)
London Films International-Channel 4 TV/Enterprise
Pictures, 1984

The Lonely Girl

Girl with Green Eyes (G. B.)
Woodfall Film Prod./United Artists Film Corp., 1964

A Woman by the Seaside (S)

Passage of Love (G. B.)
Partisan/J. Arthur Rank Film Dist., Ltd., 1965

O'Brien, Kate

That Lady

That Lady (G. B.)
Atalanta, 1955

O'Connor, Elizabeth

The Irishman

The Irishman (Austr.)
Forest Home/Greater Union, 1978

O'Connor, Flannery

Wise Blood

Wise Blood (U. S./Ger.)

Ithaca-Amthea/New Line, 1979

O'Connor, Mary H.

    The Little Savior (S)

        Souls Triumphant (*)
        Fine Arts Film Co./Triangle Dist. Corp., 1917

O'Dwyer, Martha (see "Martha Madison and Eva Kay Flint" entry)

Oemler, Marie Conway

    Slippy Mc Gee; Sometimes Known as the Butterfly Man

        Slippy McGee
        Republic Pictures Corp., 1947

Offord, Lenore Glen (see Theo Durrant)

Ogilive, Elizabeth

    High Tide at Noon

        High Tide at Noon (G. B.)
        J. Arthur Rank Film Prod./J. Arthur Rank Film Dist.,
        1957

O'Hara, Mary
    (pseud. of Mary O'Hara Alsop Sture-Vasa)

    Green Grass of Wyoming

        Green Grass of Wyoming
        Twentieth Century Fox Film Corp., 1948

    My Friend Flicka (S/N)

        My Friend Flicka
        Twentieth Century-Fox Film Corp., 1943

    Thunderhead, Son of Flicka

        Thunderhead, Son of Flicka
        Twentieth Century-Fox Film Corp., 1945

Olcott, Rita

Song in His Heart (NF)

> <u>My</u> <u>Wild</u> <u>Irish</u> <u>Rose</u>
> Warner Brothers Pictures Corp., 1947

Olsen, Tillie

Tell Me a Riddle

> <u>Tell</u> <u>Me</u> <u>a</u> <u>Riddle</u>
> Godmother/Filmways, 1980

Orczy, Baroness Emmuska (Emma Magdalena Rosalia Maria Josifa Barbara, Baroness Orczy)(also see the entry below)

Beau Brocade

> <u>Beau</u> <u>Brocade</u> (*) (G. B.)
> Lucoque Films/Artistic, 1916

The Celestial City

> <u>The</u> <u>Celestial</u> <u>City</u> (*) (G. B.)
> British Instructional Films/Jury-Metro-Goldwyn, 1929

Eldorado

> <u>The</u> <u>Scarlet</u> <u>Pimpernel</u> (TVM) (G. B.) (also based on the novel <u>The</u> <u>Scarlet</u> <u>Pimpernel</u>, by Orczy)
> London Films-Edgar J. Scherick, 1982

The Emperor's Candlesticks

> <u>The</u> <u>Emperor's</u> <u>Candlesticks</u>
> Metro-Goldwyn-Mayer, Inc., 1937

I Will Repay

> <u>I</u> <u>Will</u> <u>Repay</u> (*) (G. B.)
> Ideal, 1923

The Laughing Cavalier

> <u>The</u> <u>Laughing</u> <u>Cavalier</u> (*) (G. B.)
> Dreadnought/Jury's Imperial Pictures, 1917

Leatherface: a Tale of Old Flanders

> <u>Two</u> <u>Lovers</u> (*)
> Samuel Goldwyn Prod./United Artists Film Corp., 1928

The Old Man in the Corner (RS)

The Old Man in the Corner (*)
Stoll, 1924

The Scarlet Pimpernel

The Scarlet Pimpernel (*) (also based on the same named
play, by Orczy and Montagu Barstow, which was derived
from Orczy's novel)
Fox Film Corp./Fox Film Corp.-a Fox Special Feature,
1917

The Elusive Pimpernel (*) (G. B.)
Stoll, 1919

The Triumph of the Scarlet Pimpernel (*) (G. B.)
British and Dominion Films Corp./Woolf and Freedman
Film Service, 1928

The Scarlet Pimpernel (G. B.)
London Films/United Artists' Film Corp., 1935

The Return of the Scarlet Pimpernel (G. B.)
London Films/United Artists' Film Corp., 1937

Pimpernel Smith (G. B.)
British National/Anglo, 1942

The Elusive Pimpernel (G. B.)
London Films-British Lion Prod. Assets-Archers/British,
1950

The Scarlet Pimpernel (TVM) (G. B.) (also based on the
novel Eldorado, by Baroness Emmuska Orczy)
London Films-Edgar J. Schrick/Columbia Broadcasting
System, 1982

Spy of Napoleon

Spy of Napoleon (G. B.)
Joe Hamilton Prod./Wardour, 1936

Orczy, Baroness Emmuska (Emma Magdalena Rosalia Maria Josifa
Barbara, Baroness Orczy) and Montagu Barstow (also see the
entry above)

The Scarlet Pimpernel (P)

The Scarlet Pimpernel (*) (also based on the same named
novel, Orczy, from which the play was derived)
Fox Film Corp., 1917

Orgel, Doris

Devil in Vienna (NF)

>   A <u>Friendship</u> in <u>Vienna</u> (TVM)
>   Walt Disney Prod., 1988

Orr, Gertrude and Doris Malloy

Women Like Men (S)

>   <u>Mad</u> <u>Parade</u>
>   Liberty Pictures Corp./Paramount Pictures Corp., 1931

Orr, Mary [Mary Orr Denham] (also see the entry below)

The Wisdom of Eve (S)

>   <u>All</u> <u>about</u> <u>Eve</u> (also based on a radio play, by Orr,
>   which was derived from her short story)
>   Twentieth Century-Fox Film Corp., 1950

Orr, Mary [Mary Orr Denham] and Reginald Denham (also see the
entry above)

Wallflower (P)

>   <u>Wallflower</u>
>   Warner Brothers Pictures, Inc., 1948

O'Shaughnessy, Edith Louise

The Viennese Medley

>   <u>The</u> <u>Greater</u> <u>Glory</u> (*)
>   First National, 1926

Ostenso, Martha (also see the entry below)

Wild Geese

>   <u>Wild</u> <u>Geese</u> (*)
>   Riffany-Stahl Prod., 1927
>
>   <u>Wild</u> <u>Geese</u>
>   Majestic Pictures Corp., 1933

Ostenso, Martha and Elizabeth Kenny (also see the entry above)

And They Shall Walk (NF)

> Sister Kenny
> RKO Radio Pictures, Inc., 1946

Ostrander, Isabel

The Island of Intrigue

> The Island of Intrigue (*)
> Metro Pictures Corp., 1919

Suspense

> Suspense (*)
> Screencraft Pictures, Inc.-a Frank Reicher
> Prod./Independent Sales Corp.--Film Clearing House,
> Inc.--Ten-Twenty-Thirty Series, 1919

"Ouida"
    (pseud. of Marie Louise de la Ramee)

Bebee: or, Two Little Wooden Shoes

> The Little Dutch Girl (*)
> Shubert Film Co./World Film Corp., 1915

> Two Little Wooden Shoes (*) (G. B.)
> Progress/Butcher's Film Service, 1920

A Dog of Flanders

> A Dog of Flanders (*)
> Metro Pictures Corp., 1924

> A Dog of Flanders
> RKO Radio Pictures Corp., 1935

> A Dog of Flanders
> Twentieth Century-Fox Film Corp., 1959

Moths (P)

> Moths (*)
> Thanhouser Film Corp./Mutual Film Corp.-a Mutual
> Special, 1913

> Her Greatest Love (*)
> Fox Film Corp., 1917

Strathmore: Or, Wrought by His Own Hand

> Strathmore (*)
> Reliance Motion Picture Corp./Mutual Film Corp.-a
> Mutual Masterpiece, 1915

<u>Flames</u> <u>of</u> <u>Desire</u> (*)
Fox Film Corp., 1924

Under Two Flags

<u>Under</u> <u>Two</u> <u>Flags</u> (*)
Fox Film Corp., 1916

<u>Under</u> <u>Two</u> <u>Flags</u> (*)
Universal Film Manufacturing Co., 1922

<u>Under</u> <u>Two</u> <u>Flags</u>
Twentieth Century-Fox Film Corp., 1936

Owen, Jean Z.

Mrs. Hoyle of the Hotel Royalston (S)

<u>According</u> <u>to</u> <u>Mrs.</u> <u>Hoyle</u>
Monogram Pictures Corp., 1951

Owens, Rochelle

Futz and What Came After (P)

<u>Futz</u>
Guvnor Prod./Commonwealth United Entertainment, 1969

Packer, Joy

Nor the Moon by Night

> <u>Nor</u> <u>the</u> <u>Moon</u> <u>by</u> <u>Night</u> (G. B.)
> Independent Film Prod./J. Arthur Rank Film Dist., Ltd.,
> 1958

Page, Elizabeth

Tree of Liberty

> <u>The</u> <u>Howards</u> <u>of</u> <u>Virginia</u>
> Columbia Pictures Corp., 1940

Page, Gertrude

Edge o' Beyond

> <u>Edge</u> <u>o'</u> <u>Beyond</u> (*) (G. B.)
> G. B. Samuelson/General Film Dist., 1919

Love in the Wilderness

> <u>Love</u> <u>in</u> <u>the</u> <u>Wilderness</u> (*) (G. B.)
> G. B. Samuelson/General Film Dist., 1920

Paddy-the-Next-Best-Thing

> <u>Paddy</u> <u>the</u> <u>Next</u> <u>Best</u> <u>Thing</u> (*) (G. B.)
> Graham-Wilcox, 1923

> <u>Paddy</u> <u>the</u> <u>Next</u> <u>Best</u> <u>Thing</u>
> Fox Film Corp., 1933

Tree of Liberty

> <u>The</u> <u>Howards</u> <u>of</u> <u>Virginia</u>
> Columbia Pictures Corp., 1940

Paley, Grace

Enormous Changes at the Last Minute (S)

> <u>Enormous</u> <u>Changes</u> <u>at</u> <u>the</u> <u>Last</u> <u>Minute</u> ("Alxandra's

264

Story" segment of AF)
Ordinary Lives/Film Forum, 1985

Distance (S)

Enormous Changes at the Last Minute ("Virginia's
Story" segment of AF)
Ordinary Lives/Film Forum, 1985

Faith in the Afternoon (S)

Enormous Changes at the Last Minute ("Faith's Story"
segment of AF)
Ordinary Lives/Film Forum, 1985

Palmer, Minnie

My Sweetheart (P)

My Sweetheart (*) (G. B.)
Ideal, 1918

Papashvily, Helen and George Papashvily

Anything Can Happen (NF)

Anything Can Happen
Paramount Pictures Corp., 1952

Paradis, Marjorie Bartholomew

It Happened One Day

This Side of Heaven
Metro-Goldwyn-Mayer, Inc., 1934

Parent, Gail

Sheila Levine is Dead and Living in New York

Sheila Levine is Dead and Living in New York
Paramount Pictures Corp., 1975

Pargiter, Edith

The Assize of the Dying

The Spaniard's Curse (G. B.)
Wentworth/Independent Film Dist., 1958

265

Park, Ruth

Playing Beatie Bow

Playing Beatie Bow (Austr.)
South Australia Films, 1986

Parker, Dorothy (also see the entry below)

Horsie (S)

Queen for a Day (also based on the stories "The
Gossamer World," by Faith Baldwin, and "High Diver," by
John Ashworth)
United Artists' Film Corp., 1951

Parker, Dorothy and Bernice Brown, Elsie Janis, Sophie Kerr, and
Carolyn Wells and Robert Gordon Anderson, Louis Bromfield,
George Agnew Chamberlain, Frank Craven, Rube Goldberg,
Wallace Irwin, George Barr McCutcheon, Meade Minnigerode,
Gerald Mygatt, George Palmer Putnam, Kermit Roosevelt,
Edward Streeter, John V. A. Weaver, H. C. Witwer, and
Alexander Woollcott (also see the entry above)

Bobbed Hair

Bobbed Hair (*)
Warner Brothers Pictures, Inc., 1925

Parker, Lottie Blair (Lathrop)

Under Southern Skies (P)

Under Southern Skies (*)
Universal Film Manufacturing Co./Universal Film
Manufacturing Co.-a Broadway Universal Feature, 1915

Way Down East (P)

Way Down East (*)
D. W. Griffith/Road Show-United Artists Film Corp.,
1920

Way Down East
Twentieth Century-Fox Film Corp., 1935

Parker, Phyllis

Flight into Freedom (S)

Steel Fist
Monogram Pictures Corp., 1952

Parr, Louisa and C. E. Munro

Adam and Eve (P)

Queen's Evidence (*) (G. B.)
British and Colonial Kinematograph Co./Moss, 1919

Parrish, Ann

All Kneeling

Born to be Bad
RKO Radio Pictures, Inc., 1950

Parrott, (Katharine) Ursula (also see entry below)

Brilliant Marriage

Brilliant Marriage
Invincible Pictures Corp., 1936

Ex-Wife

The Divorcee
Metro-Goldwyn-Mayer, Inc., 1930

Love Affair (S)

Love Affair
Columbia Pictures Corp., 1932

Next Time we Live (RS)

Next Time we Love
Universal Motion Pictures Co., 1936

Strangers May Kiss

Strangers May Kiss
Metro-Goldwyn-Mayer, Inc., 1931

There's Always Tomorrow (P)

There's Always Tomorrow
Universal Motion Pictures Co., 1934

There's Always Tomorrow
Universal Motion Pictures Co., 1956

Parrott, Ursula and Gertrude Atherton, Vicki Baum, Vina Delmar, and Sophie Kerr and Polan Banks, Irvin S. Cobb, Zane Grey, Rupert Hughes, and J. P. Mc Evoy (also see entry above)

Woman Accused

> Woman Accused
> Paramount Pictures Corp., 1933

Patterson, Norma

Have You Come for Me?

> You Live and Learn (G. B.)
> Warner Brothers Pictures, Inc.-First National/Warner Brothers Pictures, Inc., 1937

Patton, Frances Gray

Good Morning, Miss Dove

> Good Morning, Miss Dove
> Twentieth Century-Fox Film Corp., 1955

Pedlar, Margaret

House of Dreams Come True

> House of Dreams (G. B.)
> Danubia, 1933

The Splendid Folly

> Splendid Folly (*) (G. B.)
> Windsor Pictures Corp./Walturdaw, 1919

Perdue, Virginia

He Fell Down Dead

> Shadow of a Woman
> Warner Brothers Pictures, Inc., 1946

Perelman, Laura and S. J. Perelman

All Good Americans (P)

> Paris Interlude

Metro-Goldwyn-Mayer, Inc., 1934

The Night Before Christmas (P)

Larceny Inc.
Warner Brothers Pictures, Inc., 1942

Perkins, Grace (maiden name of Grace Perkins Oursler) (also see
Dora Macy)

Mike (P)

Torch Singer
Paramount Pictures Corp., 1933

No More Orchids

No More Orchids
Columbia Pictures Corp., 1932

Personal Maid

Personal Maid
Paramount Pictures Corp., 1931

Peterson, Margaret

Dust of Desire

The Song of Love (*)
Norma Talmadge/Associated First National, 1923

Petit, E.
(pseud. of Mrs. Arthur Somers Roche)

The Rich are Always With Us

The Rich are Always With Us
First National-Warner Brothers Pictures, Inc., 1932

Pettus, Maude

A Gentle Ill Wind (S)

The Edge of the Law (*)
Universal Film Manufacturing Co.-a Butterfly
Picture/Universal Film Manufacturing Co., 1917

Peyton, Kathleen

The Right Hand Man

>The Right Hand Man (Austr.)
>Yarraman/New World Cinema, 1987

Pfalzgraf, Florence Leighton (see Florence Leighton)

Phelps, Pauline and Marion Short

The Girl from Out Yonder (P)

>Out Yonder (*)
>Selznick Pictures Corp./Select Pictures Corp., 1919

Phillips, Claire and Myron B. Goldsmith

Manila Expionage (NF)

>I Was an American Spy
>Monogram Pictures Corp.-Allied Artists, 1951

Philpotts, Adelaide and Eden Philpotts

Yellow Sands (P)

>Yellow Sands (G. B.)
>Associated British Picture, Corp., 1938

Pierson, Louise

Roughly Speaking (NF)

>Roughly Speaking
>Warner Brothers Pictures, Inc., 1945

Pinkerton, Katherine and Grace Drew Brown

Spring Fever (S)

>Nancy From Nowhere (*)
>Realart Pictures Corp./Paramount Pictures Corp., 1922

Piper, Anne

Marry at Leisure (S)

>A Nice Girl Like Me (G. B.)
>Partisan-Anglo-Embassy Pictures Corp./Avco Embassy,

1969

Yes, Giorgio

> Yes, Giorgio
> Metro-Goldwyn-Mayer, Inc.--United Artists Film Corp.,
> 1982

Piper, Evelyn
     (pseud. of Merriam Modell)

Bunny Lake is Missing

> Bunny Lake is Missing
> Wheel/Columbia Pictures Corp., 1965

The Nanny

> The Nanny (G. B.)
> Hammer Films-Seven Arts, Inc./WPD, 1965

Plath, Sylvia

The Bell Jar

> The Bell Jar
> Peerce-Goldston/Avco Embassy, 1978

Pollock, Alice Leal and Rita Weiman

The Co-Respondent (P)

> The Co-Respondent (*)
> Advanced Motion Pictures/Jewel Prod., Inc., 1917

> The Whispered Name (*)
> Universal Motion Pictures Co., 1924

Polson, Beth and Dr. Miller Newton

Not My Kid (NF)

> Not My Kid (TVM)
> Beth Polson-Finnegan Associates/Columbia Broadcasting
> System, 1985

Poole, Victoria

Thursday's Child (NF)

Thursday's Child (TVM)
Catalina Prod. Group-Viacom/Columbia Broadcasting
System, 1983

Popkin, Zelda

A Death of Innocence

A Death of Innocence (TVM)
Mark Carliner Prod./Columbia Broadcasting System, 1971

Porter, Eleanor H.

Dawn

Dawn (*)
J. Stuart Blackton/Pathe Exchange, Inc., 1919

Pollyanna

Pollyanna (*) (also based on the play Pollyanna, by
Catherine Chisholm Cushing, which was derived from
Porter's novel)
Mary Pickford/United Artists Film Corp., 1920

Pollyanna
Walt Disney Prod./Buena Vista Dist. Co., 1960

Porter, (Mrs.) Gene Stratton

Freckles

Freckles (*)
Jesse L. Laskey Feature Play Co./Paramount Pictures
Corp., 1917

Freckles (*)
Film Booking Office Prod., Inc., 1928

Freckles
RKO Radio Pictures, Inc., 1935

Freckles Comes Home
Monogram Pictures Corp., 1942

Freckles
Twentieth Century-Fox Film Corp., 1960

A Girl of the Limberlost

A Girl of the Limberlost (*)
Gene Stratton Porter Prod./Film Booking Office of

America, 1924

A <u>Girl</u> <u>of</u> <u>the</u> <u>Limberlost</u>
Monogram Pictures Corp., 1934

<u>Romance</u> <u>of</u> <u>the</u> <u>Limberlost</u>
Monogram Pictures Corp., 1938

A <u>Girl</u> <u>of</u> <u>the</u> <u>Limberlost</u>
Columbia Pictures Corp., 1945

The Harvester

<u>The</u> <u>Harvester</u> (*)
R-C Pictures/Film Booking Office, 1927

<u>The</u> <u>Harvester</u>
Republic Pictures Corp., 1936

Her Father's Daughter

<u>Her</u> <u>First</u> <u>Romance</u>
Monogram Picture Corp., 1940

The Keeper of the Bees

<u>The</u> <u>Keeper</u> <u>of</u> <u>the</u> <u>Bees</u> (*)
Film Booking Office, 1925

<u>The</u> <u>Keeper</u> <u>of</u> <u>the</u> <u>Bees</u>
Monogram Picture Corp., 1935

<u>The</u> <u>Keeper</u> <u>of</u> <u>the</u> <u>Bees</u>
Columbia Pictures Corp., 1947

Laddie

<u>Laddie</u> (*)
Film Booking Office, 1926

<u>Laddie</u>
RKO Radio Pictures, Inc., 1935

<u>Laddie</u>
RKO Radio Pictures, Inc., 1940

The Magic Garden

<u>The</u> <u>Magic</u> <u>Garden</u> (*)
Gene Stratton Porter Prod./Film Booking Office of
America, 1927

Michael O'Halloran

<u>Any</u> <u>Man's</u> <u>Wife</u>

273

Republic Pictures Corp., 1936

Michael O'Halloran
Republic Pictures Corp., 1937

Michael O' Halloran
Windsor Pictures Corp./Monogram Pictures Corp., 1948

Porter, Katherine Anne

Noon Wine (S)

Noon Wine (TVM)
Doro Bachrach-Merchant-Ivory Prod./WNET, 1985

Ship of Fools

Ship of Fools
Columbia Pictures Corp., 1965

Porter, Rose

Chrysalis (P)

All of Me
Paramount Pictures Corp., 1934

Potter, Jennifer

Strange Days

Flight to Berlin (G. B.)
Road Movies-British Film Institute Prod. Board-Channel
4 TV/British Film Institute, 1984

Powell, Dawn

Story of a Country Boy

Man of Iron
First National-Warner Brothers Pictures, Inc., 1935

Walking Down Broadway (P)

Hello Sister
Fox Film Corp., 1933

Poynter, Beulah

Dancing Man

<u>Dancing</u> <u>Man</u>
Pyramid, 1934

Lena Rivers (P, based on the same named novel, by Mary Jane
Holmes) (also see Mary Jane Holmes)

> <u>Lena</u> <u>Rivers</u> (*) (also based on the same named novel, by
> Mary Jane Holmes, from which the play was derived)
> Cosmos Feature Film Corp./Cosmos Feature Film Corp.-
> State Rights, 1914

The Little Girl That He Forgot (P)

> <u>The</u> <u>Little</u> <u>Girl</u> <u>That</u> <u>He</u> <u>Forgot</u> (*)
> Cosmos Feature Film Corp./State Rights, 1915

The Marrying of Emmy (S)

> <u>The</u> <u>Miracle</u> <u>of</u> <u>Money</u> (*)
> Hobart Henley Prod./Pathe Exchange, Inc., 1920

unidentified novel (Note: though some sources suggest <u>Her</u>
<u>Splendid</u> <u>Folly</u> may be the title, we found no record of such
a book: it may be unpublished, an unreprinted magazine
serial, a magazine serial published in book form with a
different title, or an original novel of a different title.)

> <u>Her</u> <u>Splendid</u> <u>Folly</u>
> Progressive Prod., 1933

Preedy, George (also see Marjorie Bowen and Joseph Shearing)
    (pseud. of Gabrielle Margaret Vere Campbell Long)

General Crack

> <u>General</u> <u>Crack</u>
> Warner Brothers Pictures, Inc., 1929

Price, Evadne (also see the two entries below)
    (pseud. of Helen Zenna Smith)

Red for Danger

> <u>Blondes</u> <u>for</u> <u>Danger</u> (G. B.)
> Wilcox/British Lion Film Corp., 1938

Price, Evadne and Joan Roy Byford (also see entry above and the
    entry below)
    (Evadne Price: pseud. of Helen Zenna Smith)

The Haunted Light (P, based on the novel <u>The</u> <u>Haunted</u> <u>Light</u>

275

by Price)

>The Phantom Light (G. B.)
>Gainsborough Prod./Gaumont British, Ltd., 1935

Price, Evadne and Ken Attiwill (also see the two entries above)
   (Evadne Price: pseud. of Helen Zenna Smith)

Once a Crook (P)

>Once a Crook (G. B.)
>Twentieth Century-Fox Film Corp., 1941

Wanted on Voyage (P)

>Not Wanted on Voyage (G. B.)
>Byron-Ronald Shiner/Renown Pictures Corp., 1957

Prichard, Hesketh and Prichard, Kate

Don Q's Love Story (S)

>Don Q, Son of Zorro (*)
>Elton Corp./United Artists Film Corp., 1925

Prichard, Kate and Hesketh Prichard

Don Q's Love Story (S)

>Don Q, Son of Zorro (*)
>Elton Corp./United Artists Film Corp., 1925

Prichard, Katherine Susannah

The Pioneers

>The Pioneers (*) (Austr.)
>Fraser Films, 1916

>The Pioneers (*) (Austr.)
>Australasian Films, 1926

Proctor, Adelaide Anne

Legend of Provence (Po)

>The Legend of Provence (*)
>Thanhouser Film Corp.-Thanhouser "Big" Prod./Mutual
>Film Corp., 1913

The <u>Broken</u> <u>Rosary</u> (G. B.)
Butcher Film Service, 1934

Prouty, Olive Higgins

Now, Voyager

<u>Now, Voyager</u>
Warner Brothers Pictures, Inc., 1942

Stella Dallas

<u>Stella</u> <u>Dallas</u> (*)
Samuel Goldwyn Prod./United Artists Film Corp., 1925

<u>Stella</u> <u>Dallas</u> (also based on the play of the same name,
by Gertrude Purcell and Harry Wagstaff Gribble, which
was derived from Prouty's novel)
United Artists Film Corp., 1937

Provost, Agnes Louise

Her Kingdom of Dreams (S)

<u>Her</u> <u>Kingdom</u> <u>of</u> <u>Dreams</u> (*)
Anita Stewart Prod., Inc./First National, 1919

Prumbs, Lucille S. and Sarah B. Smith

Ever the Beginning (P)

<u>My</u> <u>Girl</u> <u>Tisa</u>
United States Pictures, Inc./Warner Brothers Pictures,
Inc., 1948

Pulver, Mary Brecht

The Man Hater (S)

<u>The</u> <u>Man</u> <u>Hater</u> (*)
Triangle Film Corp./Triangle Dist. Corp., 1917

Purcell, Gertrude and Harry Wagstaff Gribble

Stella Dallas (P, based on the same named novel, by Olive
Higgins Prouty)

<u>Stella</u> <u>Dallas</u> (also based on the same named novel, by
Olive Higgins Prouty, from which it was derived)
United Artists Film Corp., 1937

277

Putnam, Nina Wilcox (also see the entry below)

Doubling for Cupid (S)

The Beautiful Cheat (*)
Universal Motion Pictures Co., 1926

The Grandflapper (S)

Slaves of Beauty (*)
Fox Film Corp., 1927

In Search of Arcady

In Search of Arcady (*)
National Film Corp. of America/Robertson-Cole--
Exhibitors Mutual Dist. Corp., 1919

Two Weeks with Pay (S)

Two Weeks with Pay (*)
Realart Pictures Corp., 1921

Putnam, Nina Wilcox and Norman Jacobsen (also see the entry above)

The Price of Applause (S)

The Price of Applause (*)
Triangle Film Corp./Triangle Dist. Corp., 1918

Quinn, Theodora

    Ishi in Two Worlds

        <u>Ishi:</u> <u>the</u> <u>Last</u> <u>of</u> <u>His</u> <u>Tribe</u> (TVM)
        Edward and Mildred Lewis Prod./National Broadcasting
        Co., 1978

Quoirez, Francoise (see Francoise Sagan)

Ragsdale, Lulah

Miss Dulcie from Dixie

> Miss Dulcie from Dixie (*)
> Vitagraph Co. of America, 1919

Ramage, Jennifer (see Howard Mason)

Ramsay, Rina

Barnaby. A Novel.

> Barnaby (*) (G. B.)
> Reginald Barker Prod., 1919

Ramsey, Alicia

Bridge (P, which may not have been produced)

> Social Hypocrites (*)
> Metro Pictures Corp./Metro Pictures Corp.--Metro All-
> Star Series, 1918

Eve's Daughter (P)

> Eve's Daughter (*)
> Famous Players-Lasky Corp./Famous Players-Lasky Corp.--
> Paramount Pictures Corp., 1918

A Prince of Lovers (P)

> A Prince of Lovers (*) (G. B.)
> Gaumont British, Ltd.-British Screencraft, 1922

Rand, Ayn

The Fountainhead

> The Fountainhead
> Warner Brothers Pictures, Inc., 1949

The Night of January 16th (P)

The <u>Night</u> <u>of</u> <u>January</u> <u>16th</u>
Paramount Pictures Corp., 1941

Rand, Judy

   He's Fired, She's Hired (unpublished novel)

      <u>He's</u> <u>Fired,</u> <u>She's</u> <u>Hired</u> (TVM)
      Columbia Broadcasting System Entertainment/Columbia
      Broadcasting System, 1984

Randall, Florence Engel

   The Watcher in the Woods

      <u>The</u> <u>Watcher</u> <u>in</u> <u>the</u> <u>Woods</u> (G. B.)
      Walt Disney Prod., 1982

Rath, E. J.
   (joint pseud. of Mrs. Edith Rathbone Jacobs Brainerd and
   Chauncey Corey Brainerd)

   The Dark Chapter, a Comedy of Class Distinctions

      <u>Asi</u> <u>Es</u> <u>La</u> <u>Vida</u> (also based on the play <u>They</u> <u>All</u> <u>Want</u>
      <u>Something;</u> <u>a</u> <u>Comedy</u> <u>in</u> <u>a</u> <u>Prologue</u> <u>and</u> <u>Three</u> <u>Acts</u>, by
      Courtenay Savage, which was derived from the Raths'
      novel) (Note: this is the Spanish language version --
      with a different cast -- of <u>What</u> <u>a</u> <u>Man</u>.)
      Sono-Art Prod., 1930

      <u>What</u> <u>a</u> <u>Man</u> (also based on the play <u>They</u> <u>All</u> <u>Want</u>
      <u>Something;</u> <u>a</u> <u>Comedy</u> <u>in</u> <u>a</u> <u>Prologue</u> <u>and</u> <u>Three</u> <u>Acts</u>, by
      Courtenay Savage, which was derived from the Raths'
      novel)
      Sono-Art Prod., 1930

   Elope If You Must

      <u>Elope</u> <u>If</u> <u>You</u> <u>Must</u> (*)
      Fox Film Corp., 1922

   Good References

      <u>Good</u> <u>References</u> (*)
      First National, 1920

   Let's Go

      <u>Fast</u> <u>Life</u>
      Metro-Goldwyn-Mayer, Inc., 1932

Mister 44

> Mister 44 (*)
> Yorke Film Corp./Metro Pictures Corp.-a Metro
> Wonderplay, 1916

The Nervous Wreck

> The Nervous Wreck (*) (also based on the play The
> Nervous Wreck, a Comedy in Three Acts, by Owen Davis,
> which was derived from Rath's novel)
> Christie Film Co./Producers Dist. Corp., 1926

Sam

> The River of Romance (*)
> Yorke Film Corp./Metro Pictures Corp., 1916

Too Many Crooks

> Too Many Crooks (*)
> Vitagraph Co. of America, 1919

> Too Many Crooks (*)
> Famous Players-Lasky Corp./Paramount Pictures Corp.,
> 1927

When the Devil was Sick

> Clear the Decks (*)
> Universal Motion Pictures Co., 1929

Rath, Virginia (see Theo Durrant)

Ratzka-Wendler, Clara

Das Benkenntnis

> Whirl of Youth
> World Wide Pictures, 1929

Rau, Margaret and Neil Rau

I'm Giving Them Up for Good (unpublished novel)

> Cold Turkey
> United Artists Film Corp., 1971

Rawlings, Marjorie Kinnan

Cross Creek (NF)

<u>Cross Creek</u>
Universal Motion Pictures Co., 1983

Gal Young Un (S)

<u>Gal Young Un</u>
Nunez Films, 1979

A Mother in Mannville (S) (Note: the movie maybe also based on parts of other stories in Rawlings' collection <u>When the Whippoorwill</u>.)

<u>The Sun Comes Up</u>
Metro-Goldwyn-Mayer, Inc., 1949

The Yearling

<u>The Yearling</u>
Metro-Goldwyn-Mayer, Inc., 1946

Ray, Rene
    (Pseud. of Irene Creese)

The Strange World of Planet X

<u>The Strange World of Planet X</u> (G. B.) (also based on the television serial of the same name, which was derived from Ray's novel)
Eros Films, 1958

Rayman, Sylvia

Women of Twilight (P)

<u>Women of Twilight</u> (G. B.)
Daniel Angel-Romulus Films/Independent Film Dist., 1952

Rebeta-Burditt, Joyce

The Cracker Factory

<u>The Cracker Factory</u> (TVM)
Roger Gimbel Prod.-Electrical and Musical Industries Television/American Broadcasting Co., 1979

Reed, Myrtle

At the Sign of the Jack O'Lantern

<u>At the Sign of the Jack O'Lantern</u> (*)
Renco Film Co., 1922

Flower of the Dusk

> Flower of the Dusk (*)
> Metro Pictures Corp., 1918

Lavender and Old Lace

> Lavender and Old Lace (*)
> Renco Film Co./W. W. Hodkinson Corp., 1921

Spinner in the Sun

> Veiled Woman (*)
> Renco Film Co./W. W. Hodkinson Corp., 1922

A Weaver of Dreams

> A Weaver of Dreams (*)
> Metro Pictures Corp./Metro Pictures Corp.--All-Star
> Series, 1918

Reid, Virginia

Black Market Babies (A)

> Black Market Babies
> Monogram Pictures Corp., 1945

Reiling, Netty (see Anna Seghers)

Reilly, Patricia and H. N. Swanson

Big Business Girl (S)

> Big Business Girl
> Warner Brothers Pictures, Inc./First National, 1931

Rendell, Ruth

Ginger and the Kingsmarkham Chalk Circle (S)

> No Crying He Makes (TVM) (G. B.)
> Graham Benson-Television South Picture/Arts and
> Entertainment Network, 1988

The Housekeeper

> The Housekeeper (Can.)
> Rawifilm-Schultz/Castlehill-Kodiak, 1987

Resnik, Muriel

Any Wednesday, a Comedy (P)

> Any Wednesday
> Warner Brothers Pictures, Inc., 1966

The Girl in the Turquoise Bikini

> How Sweet it Is
> Cherokee-National General Pictures/National General
> Pictures, 1968

Reynolds, Mrs. Baille
    (pseud. of Gertrude M. Robins Reynolds)

Confession Corner

> Confessions (*) (G. B.)
> Stoll, 1925

The Daughter Pays

> The Daughter Pays (*)
> Selznick Pictures Corp./Select Pictures Corp., 1920

The Man Who Won

> The Man Who Won (*) (G. B.)
> G. B. Samuelson/Granger, 1918

The Notorious Miss Lisle

> The Notorious Miss Lisle (*)
> Katherine MacDonald Pictures Corp./First National, 1920

Reynolds, Gertrude M. Robins (see Mrs. Baille Reynolds)

Rhodes, Kathlyn

Afterwards

> Afterwards (*) (G. B.)
> Bushey Studios/Associated Producers and Dist., 1928

Rhys, Jean
    (pseud. of Ella Gwendolen Rees Williams)

Quartet

Quartet (G. B./Fra.)
Merchant Ivory-Lyric International/Gem-Toby
Organisation, 1981

Ricardel, Molly and William Du Bois

I Loved You Wednesday

I Loved You Wednesday
Twentieth Century-Fox Film Corp., 1933

Rice, Alice Hegan (also see Anne Crawford Flexner)

Calvary Alley

Sunshine Nan (*)
Famous Players-Lasky Corp./Famous Players-Lasky Corp.--
Paramount Pictures Corp., 1918

Lovey Mary

Mrs. Wiggs of the Cabbage Patch (*) (also based on the
novel Mrs. Wiggs of the Cabbage Patch, by Rice, and the
play Mrs. Wiggs of the Cabbage Patch, by Anne Crawford
Flexner, which was derived from Rice's novel)
California Motion Picture Corp., 1914

Lovey Mary (*)
Metro-Goldwyn-Mayer, Inc., 1926

Mr. Opp.

Mr. Opp. (*)
Bluebird Photoplays, Inc., 1917

Mrs. Wiggs of the Cabbage Patch

Mrs. Wiggs of the Cabbage Patch (*) (also based on the
novel Lovey Mary, by Rice, and the play Mrs. Wiggs of
the Cabbage patch, by Anne Crawford Flexner)
California Motion Picture Corp./World Film, 1914

Mrs. Wiggs of the Cabbage Patch (*) (also based on the
same named play, by Anne Crawford Flexner, which was
derived from Rice's novel)
Famous Players-Lasky Corp./Famous Players-Lasky Corp.--
Paramount Pictures Corp., 1919

Mrs. Wiggs of the Cabbage Patch (also based on the same
named play, by Anne Crawford Flexner, which was derived
from Rice's novel)
Paramount Pictures Corp., 1934

> > *Mrs. Wiggs of the Cabbage Patch* (also based on the same
> > named play, by Anne Crawford Flexner, which was derived
> > from Rice's novel)
> > Paramount Pictures Corp., 1942

> ## Romance of Billy Goat Hill

> > *Romance of Billy Goat Hill* (*)
> > Universal Film Manufacturing Co./Universal Film
> > Manufacturing Co.-Red Feather Photoplays, 1916

> ## Sandy

> > *Sandy* (*)
> > Famous Players-Lasky Corp./Famous Players-Lasky Corp.--
> > Paramount Pictures Corp., 1918

Rice, Craig
> (pseud. of Georgiana Ann Randolph Craig)
> (also see Gypsy Rose Lee)

> ## Big Story

> > *The Underworld Story*
> > United Artists Film Corp., 1950

> ## Having a Wonderful Crime

> > *Having a Wonderful Crime*
> > RKO Radio Pictures, Inc., 1945

> ## Home Sweet Homicide

> > *Home, Sweet Homicide*
> > Twentieth Century-Fox Film Corp., 1946

> ## The Lucky Stiff

> > *The Lucky Stiff*
> > Amusement Enterprises/United Artists Film Corp., 1949

Rice, Louise

> ## The Alien Blood (S)

> > *The Alien Blood* (*)
> > Balboa Amusement Prod. Co.-a Fortune Photoplay/General
> > Film, 1917

Rice, Suzanne (see Kathleen Shepard)

Richards, Caroline

Sweet Country

Sweet Country
Playmovie/Cinema Group C., 1987

Richards, Laura Elizabeth

Captain January

Captain January (*)
Sol Lesser Prod./Principal Pictures, 1924

Captain January
Twentieth Century-Fox Film Corp., 1936

Richards, Rene and John Ames

The Renee Richards Story: Second Serve (NF)

Second Serve (TVM)
Linda Yellin Prod.-Lorimar Telepictures Prod./Columbia
Broadcasting System, 1986

Richards, Sylvia

Gunsight Whitman (S)

Rancho Notorious
Fidelity Pictures, Inc./RKO Radio Pictures, Inc., 1952

Richardson, Abby Sage and Grace Livingston Furniss

The Pride of Jennico (P)

The Pride of Jennico (*)
Famous Players Film Co., 1914

Richardson, Anna S. and Edmund Breese (also see the entry below)

A Man's Home (P)

A Man's Home (*)
Selznick Pictures Corp./Select Pictures Corp., 1921

Richardson, Anna S. and Sophie Kerr (also see the entry above)

Big Hearted Herbert (P)

Big-Hearted Herbert
Warner Brothers Pictures, Inc., 1934

Father is a Prince
First National/Warner Brothers Pictures, Inc., 1940

Rigdon, Gertrude

The Department Store (S)

Hold Me Tight
Twentieth Century-Fox Film Corp., 1933

Rinehart, Mary Roberts (also see the entry below)

Acquitted (S)

Acquitted (*)
Fine Arts Film Co./Triangle Film Corp., 1916

Affinities (S)

Affinities (*)
Ward Lascell Prod., 1922

Bab's Burglar (S)

Bab's Burglar (*)
Famous Players Film Co./Paramount Pictures Corp., 1917

The Breaking Point

The Breaking Point (*)
Famous Players/Paramount, 1924

The Circular Staircase

The Circular Staircase (*)
Selig Polyscope Co.-Selig Red Seal Plays/Greater
Vitagraph, 1915

The Bat Whispers (also based on the play The Bat, by
Rinehart and Avery Hopwood, which was derived from
Rinehart's novel)
Art Cinema Corp./United Artists Film Corp., 1931

The Bat (also based on the play The Bat, by Rinehart
and Avery Hopwood, which was derived from Rinehart's
novel)
Liberty Pictures Corp./Allied Artists Film Corp., 1957

Dangerous Days

<u>Dangerous</u> <u>Days</u> (*)
Eminent Authors Pictures, Inc.-a Reginald Barker
Prod./Goldwyn Dist. Corp., 1920

Empire Builders (S)

<u>It's</u> <u>a</u> <u>Great</u> <u>Life</u> (*)
Eminent Authors Pictures, Inc./Goldwyn Dist. Corp.,
1920

The G. A. C. (S)

<u>Her</u> <u>Country</u> <u>First</u> (*)
Famous Players-Lasky Corp./Famous Players-Lasky Corp.--
Paramount Pictures Corp., 1918

Her Diary (S)

<u>Bab's</u> <u>Diary</u> (*)
Famous Players Film Co./Paramount Pictures Corp., 1917

Her Majesty, the Queen (S)

<u>Her</u> <u>Love</u> <u>Story</u> (*)
Famous Players-Lasky Corp./Paramount Pictures Corp.,
1924

In the Pavilion (S)

<u>The</u> <u>Glorious</u> <u>Fool</u> (*) (also based on the short story
"Twenty-Two," by Rinehart)
Goldwyn Pictures Corp., 1922

K -- the Unknown

<u>The</u> <u>Doctor</u> <u>and</u> <u>the</u> <u>Woman</u> (*)
Lois Weber Prod./Jewel Prod., Inc., 1918

<u>K</u> <u>--</u> <u>the</u> <u>Unknown</u> (*)
Universal Motion Pictures, 1924

Long Live the King

<u>Long</u> <u>Live</u> <u>the</u> <u>King</u> (*)
Metro Pictures Corp., 1923

Lost Ecstasy

<u>I</u> <u>Take</u> <u>This</u> <u>Woman</u>
Paramount Pictures Corp., 1931

Make Them Happy (S)

<u>Finders</u> <u>Keepers</u> (*)

290

Universal Motion Pictures Co., 1928

Mind Over Motor (S)

Mind over Motor (*)
Ward Lascelle Prod./Principal Pictures, 1923

Miss Pinkerton (RS)

Miss Pinkerton
First National-Warner Brothers Pictures, Inc./ Warner
Brothers Pictures, Inc., 1932

The Nurse's Secret
Warner Brothers Pictures Ltd., 1941

Mr. Cohen Takes a Walk (S)

Mr. Cohen Takes a Walk (G. B.)
Warner Brothers Pictures, Inc.-First National, 1935

The State versus Elinor Norton

Elinor Norton
Twentieth Century-Fox Film Corp., 1935

The Street of Seven Stars

The Street of Seven Stars (*)
De Luxe Pictures, Inc., 1918

Theme: the Celebrity (S)

Bab's Matinee Idol (*)
Famous Players Film Co./Paramount Pictures Corp., 1917

Tish (RS)

Tish
Metro-Goldwyn-Mayer, Inc., 1942

Twenty-Three and a Half Hours' Leave (S)

23 1/2 Hours' Leave (*)
Thomas H. Ince Prod./Famous Players-Lasky Corp.--
Paramount Pictures Corp.-Artcraft Pictures Corp., 1919

23 1/2 Hours' Leave
Grand National Pictures, 1937

What Happened to Father (S)

What Happened to Father (*)
Vitagraph Co. of America-a Blue Ribbon Feature/Greater
Vitagraph, 1915

What Happened to Father (*)
Warner Brothers Pictures, Inc., 1927

Rinehart, Mary Roberts and Avery Hopwood (also see the entry
    above)

   The Bat (P, based on the novel The Circular Staircase, by
   Rinehart)

      The Bat (*)
      United Artists Film Corp., 1926

      The Bat Whispers (also based on the novel The Circular
      Staircase, by Roberts, from which the play was derived)
      Art Cinema Corp./United Artists Film Corp., 1931

      The Bat (also based on the novel The Circular
      Staircase, by Roberts, from which the play was derived)
      Liberty Pictures Corp./Allied Artists Film Corp., 1957

   Tumble In (P)

      Seven Days (*)
      Union Film Dist., 1925

Rita
      (Pseud. of Eliza Margaret J. Gollan Humphreys)

   Calvary

      Calvary (*) (G. B.)
      Master Films/British Exhibitors' Films, 1920

   Darby and Joan

      Darby and Joan (G. B.)
      Rock Studios/Metro-Goldwyn-Mayer British), 1937

   Grim Justice

      Grim Justice (*) (G. B.)
      Turner Films/Butcher's Film Service, 1916

   Half a Truth

      Half a Truth (*) (G. B.)
      Stoll, 1922

   The Iron Stair

      The Iron Stair (*) (G. B.)
      Stoll, 1920

The Iron Stair (G. B.)
Realart Pictures Corp./RKO Radio Pictures, Inc., 1933

My Lord Conceit

My Lord Conceit (*) (G. B.)
Stoll, 1921

Petticoat Loose

Petticoat Loose (*) (G. B.)
Stoll, 1922

The Pointing Finger

The Pointing Finger (G. B.)
Realart Pictures Corp./RKO Radio Pictures, Inc., 1933

Sheba

Sheba (*) (G. B.)
Hepworth/Butcher's Film Service, 1919

Rives, Amelie
(pseud. of Princess Troubetzkoy)

The Fear Market (P)

The Fear Market (*)
Realart Pictures Corp., 1920

Rives, Hallie Erminie

The Long Lane's Turning

The Long Lane's Turning (*)
National Film Corp. of America/Robertson-Cole-
Exhibitors Mutual Dist. Corp., 1919

Satan Sanderson

Satan Sanderson (*)
Rolfe Photoplays, Inc./Metro Pictures Corp., 1915

The Valiants of Virginia

The Valiants of Virginia (*)
Selig Polyscope Co.-a Red Seal Play/Greater Vitagraph,
1916

Robbins, Katherine Leiser (also see the entry below)

The Gilded Dream (S)

> The Gilded Dream (*)
> Universal Film Manufacturing Co./Universal Film
> Manufacturing Co.-New Star Series, 1920

Her Fling (S)

> The Risky Road (*)
> A Dorothy Phillips Prod.-Universal Film Manufacturing
> Co./Universal Film Manufacturing Co., 1918

In Folly's Trail (S)

> In Folly's Trail (*)
> Universal Film Manufacturing Co./Universal Film
> Manufacturing Co.-New Star Series, 1920

Robbins, Katherine Leiser and Lorne H. Fontaine (also see the
entry above)

The Scarlet Stain (S)

> The Scarlet Shadow (*)
> Universal Film Manufacturing Co., 1919

Roberts, Alice M.

When Fate Leads Trump (N, which may be unpublished)

> When Fate Leads Trump (*)
> Excelsior Feature Film Co./Alliance Films Corp., 1914

Roberts, Edith Kneipple

That Hagen Girl

> That Hagen Girl
> Warner Brothers Pictures, Inc., 1947

Roberts, Elizabeth Maddox

The Great Meadow

> The Great Meadow
> Metro-Goldwyn-Mayer, Inc., 1931

Robertson, Eileen Arnot

Four Frightened People

>Four Frightened People
>DeMille Prod./Paramount Pictures Corp., 1934

Robins, Elizabeth

A Dark Lantern

>A Dark Lantern (*)
>Realart Pictures Corp., 1920

My Little Sister

>My Little Sister (*)
>Fox Film Corp., 1919

Robinson, Jill Schary

Bedtime Story

>A Cry for Love (TVM)
>Charles Fries Prod.-Alan Sacks Prod./National
>Broadcasting Co., 1980

Robinson, Marilynne

Housekeeping

>Housekeeping
>Columbia Pictures Corp., 1987

Robinson, Martha and Cecil Maiden

Show Flat (P)

>Show Flat
>British and Dominions Film Corp.-Paramount Pictures
>Corp. British, 1936

Robson, May and Charles T. Dazey

The Three Lights (P)

>A Night Out (*)
>Vitagraph Co. of America-a Blue Ribbon Feature/Greater
>Vitagraph, 1916

Roche, Mrs. Arthur Sommers (see E. Petit)

Rodger, Sarah Elizabeth

    Person-To-Person Call (S)

        Girl Overboard
        Universal Motion Pictures Co., 1937

Rodgers, Mary

    Freaky Friday

        Freaky Friday
        Walt Disney Prod./Buena Vista Dist. Co., 1976

Roe, Vingie Eve

    The Alchemy of Love (S)

        Twilight (*)
        De Luxe Pictures, Inc./William L. Sherry Service-Film
        Clearing House, Inc., 1919

    The Golden Tide

        A Perilous Journey
        Republic Pictures Corp., 1953

    The Heart of the Night Wind

        Big Timber (*)
        Universal Motion Pictures Corp., 1924

    The Primal Lure: a Romance of Fort Lu Cerne

        The Primal Lure (*)
        New York Motion Picture Corp.--Kay-Bee/Triangle Film
        Corp., 1916

    The Splendid Road

        The Splendid Road (*)
        Frank Lloyd Prod./First National, 1925

    Tharon of Lost Valley

        The Crimson Challenge (*)
        Famous Players-Lasky Corp./Paramount Pictures Corp.,
        1922

    Val of Paradise

        North of the Rio Grande (*)
        Famous Players-Lasky Corp./Paramount Pictures Corp.,
        1922

    Wild Honey (S)

        Wild Honey (*)
        De Luxe Pictures, Inc./William L. Sherry Service, 1918

Rogers, Betty

    Will Rogers; his Wife's Story (NF)

        The Story of Will Rogers
        Warner Brothers Pictures, Inc., 1952

Roiphe, Anne Richardson

    Up the Sandbox!

        Up the Sandbox
        First Artists/National General Pictures, 1972

Rollin, Betty

    First You Cry (NF)

        First You Cry (TVM)
        MTM Enterprises-Company Four/Columbia Broadcasting
        System, 1978

Roos, Kelley
        (joint pseud. of Audrey Kelley and William Roos)

    The Frightened Stiff

        A Night to Remember
        Columbia Pictures Corp., 1942

    If the Shroud Fits

        Dangerous Blondes
        Columbia Pictures Corp., 1943

    To Save His Life

        Dead Men Tell No Tales (TVM)
        Twentieth Century-Fox Television/Columbia Broadcasting
        System, 1971

Rorick, Isabel Scott

    Mr. and Mrs. Cugat

        <u>Are</u> <u>Husbands</u> <u>Necessary?</u>
        Paramount Pictures Corp., 1942

Rose, Anna Perrott
    (pseud. of Anna Maria Rose Wright)

    Room for One More (NF)

        <u>Room</u> <u>for</u> <u>One</u> <u>More</u>
        Warner Brothers Pictures. Inc., 1952

Ross, Ishbel

    Promenade Deck

        <u>Three</u> <u>on</u> <u>a</u> <u>Honeymoon</u>
        Fox Film Corp., 1934

Ross, Lillian Bos

    The Stranger

        <u>Zandy's</u> <u>Bride</u>
        Warner Brothers Pictures, Inc., 1974

Rossner, Judith

    Looking for Mr. Goodbar

        <u>Looking</u> <u>for</u> <u>Mr.</u> <u>Goodbar</u>
        Paramount Pictures Corp., 1977

Roth, Lillian and Mike Connolly and Gerald Frank

    I'll Cry Tomorrow (NF)

        <u>I'll</u> <u>Cry</u> <u>Tomorrow</u>
        Metro-Goldwyn-Mayer, Inc., 1955

Roth, Lois and Jalal Din

    The Wild Elephant (S)

        <u>Maya</u>
        Metro-Goldwyn-Mayer, Inc., 1966

Roth, Virginia (see Theo Durrant)

Rothberg, Marie and Mel White

    David (NF)

        <u>David</u> (TVM)
        Donald March Prod.-American Broadcasting Co., 1988

Rothstein, (Mrs.) Arnold

    Now I'll Tell (NF)

        <u>Now</u> <u>I'll</u> <u>Tell</u>
        Fox Film Corp., 1934

Rouverol, Aurania

    Skidding (P)

        <u>A</u> <u>Family</u> <u>Affair</u>
        Metro-Goldwyn-Mayer, Inc., 1937

Roy, Julie and Lucy Freeman

    Betrayal: the True Story of the First Woman to Successfully Sue her Psychiatrist for Using Sex in the Guise of Therapy (NF)

        <u>Betrayal</u> (TVM)
        Roger Gimbel Prod./Electrical and Musical Industries
        Television/National Broadcasting Co., 1978

Roy, Olivia

    The Husband Hunter

        <u>The</u> <u>Husband</u> <u>Hunter</u> (*) (G. B.)
        G. B. Samuelson/Granger, 1920

Rubens, Bernice

    Madame Sousatzka

        <u>Madame</u> <u>Sousatzka</u> (G. B.)
        Sousatzka-Cineplex Odeon/Universal International Motion
        Pictures, 1988

Ruck, Berta [Amy Roberta Ruck Oliver]

His Official Fiancee

His <u>Official</u> <u>Fiancee</u> (*)
Famous Players-Lasky Corp./Famous Players-Laskey
Corp.--Paramount Pictures Corp.-Artcraft Pictures
Corp., 1919

In Another Girl's Shoes

In <u>Another</u> <u>Girl's</u> <u>Shoes</u> (*) (G. B.)
G. B. Samuelson--Alexander Butler, 1917

Sir or Madam

<u>Sir</u> <u>or</u> <u>Madam</u> (*) (G. B.)
Foremost Prod./Warner Brothers Pictures, Inc., 1928

Ruggles, Eleanor

Prince of Players (NF)

<u>Prince</u> <u>of</u> <u>Players</u>
Twentieth Century-Fox Film Corp., 1954

Rule, Jane

Desert of the Heart

<u>Desert</u> <u>Hearts</u>
Desert Hearts/Goldwyn Dist. Corp., 1985

Russell, Elizabeth

Princess Priscilla's Fortnight

The <u>Runaway</u> <u>Princess</u> (*) (G. B.)
British Instructional Films-Laender Film/Jury-Metro-
Goldwyn, 1929

Russell, Gloria

The Night Life of a Virile Potato (P)

<u>Stork</u> <u>Talk</u> (G. B.)
Unifilms, 1962

Russell, Mary Annette Beauchamp (see "Elizabeth")

Russell, Rosalind and Larry Marcus

    The Gentle Web (S)

        The <u>Unguarded</u> <u>Moment</u>
        Universal Motion Pictures Co., 1956

Russell, Sheila MacKay

    A Lamp is Heavy

        The <u>Feminine</u> <u>Touch</u> (G. B.)
        Ealing Studios/J. Arthur Rank Film Dist., Ltd., 1956

Ryan, Kathryn Morgan and Cornelius Ryan

    A Private Battle (NF)

        A <u>Private</u> <u>Battle</u> (TVM)
        Procter and Gamble Prod.-Robert Halmi Prod./Columbia
        Broadcasting System, 1980

Ryan, Marah Ellis

    For the Soul of Rafael

        <u>For</u> <u>the</u> <u>Soul</u> <u>of</u> <u>Rafael</u> (*)
        Garson Studios, Inc./Equity Pictures Corp., 1920

    That Girl Montana

        <u>That</u> <u>Girl</u> <u>Montana</u> (*)
        Jesse D. Hampton Prod./Pathe Exchange, Inc., 1921

    Told in the Hills

        <u>Told</u> <u>in</u> <u>the</u> <u>Hills</u> (*)
        Famous Players-Lasky Corp./Famous Players-Lasky Corp.--
        Paramount Pictures Corp.-Artcraft Pictures Corp., 1919

Ryerson, Florence [Florence Ryerson Clements] (also see the entry
    below)

    Willie the Worm (S)

        <u>Love</u> <u>Makes</u> <u>'em</u> <u>Wild</u> (*)
        Twentieth Century-Fox Film Corp., 1927

Ryerson, Florence [Florence Ryerson Clements] and Colin Clements
(also see the entry above)

Borrowed Love (S)

Call of the West
Columbia Pictures Corp., 1930

June Mad (P)

Her First Beau
Columbia Pictures Corp., 1941

Ryley, Madeline Lucette

An American Citizen (P)

An American Citizen (*)
Famous Players Film Co./State Rights, 1914

Mice and Men (P)

Mice and Men (*)
Famous Players Film Co./Paramount Pictures Corp., 1916

Sagan, Francoise
  (pseud. of Francoise Quoirez)

  Aimez-Vous Brahms?[Do you Love Brahms?]

      <u>Goodbye</u> <u>Again</u>
      Argus Films/United Artists Film Corp., 1961

  Bonjour Tristesse

      <u>Bonjour</u> <u>Tristesse</u> (G. B.)
      Wheel Prod., Ltd./Columbia British 1958

  A Certain Smile

      <u>A</u> <u>Certain</u> <u>Smile</u>
      Twentieth Century-Fox Film Corp., 1958

Sand, George
  (pseud. of Mme. Dudevant: Amandine-Aurore Lucille Dupin)

  La Petite Fadette

      <u>Fanchon</u> <u>the</u> <u>Cricket</u> (*)
      Famous Players Film Co./Paramount Pictures Corp., 1915

Sanders, George (Note: Sanders is a man, but "his" novel was
  ghosted by a woman.)

  Stranger at Home (ghost written by Leigh Brackett) (also see
  Leigh Brackett)

      <u>The</u> <u>Stranger</u> <u>Came</u> <u>Home</u> (G. B.)
      Hammer Films/Exclusive Films, 1954

Sandler, Susan

  Crossing Delancy (P)

      <u>Crossing</u> <u>Delancy</u>
      Warner Brothers Pictures, Inc., 1988

Sandoz, Mari

303

Cheyenne Autumn

> Cheyenne Autumn
> Warner Brothers Pictures, Inc., 1964

Sandstrom, Flora

Madness of the Heart

> Madness of the Heart (G. B.)
> Two Cities Films, Ltd./General Film Dist., Inc., 1949

The Midwife of Pont Clery

> Jessica (U. S./Ita./Fra.)
> Arts and Artists/United Artist's Film Corp., 1962

The Milk White Unicorn

> The White Unicorn (G. B.)
> John Corfield Prod./General Film Dist., Inc., 1947

Sangster, Margaret Elizabeth

The Island of Faith

> The New Teacher (*)
> Fox Film Corp., 1922

Sarlabous, Marie Antoinette (see Jean Bart)

Savage, Georgia

Slate and Wyn and Blanche McBride

> Slate, Wyn & Me (Austr.)
> Hemdale-International Film Management-Ukiyo/Hemdale,
> 1987

Savage, Juanita

The Spaniard

> The Spaniard (*)
> Famous Players-Lasky/Paramount Pictures, 1925

Savage, Mildred (see Jane Barrie)

Saxton, Martha

    Jayne Mansfield and the American Fifties (NF)

        The <u>Jayne</u> <u>Mansfield</u> <u>Story</u> (TVM)
        Alan Landsburg Prod./Columbia Broadcasting System, 1980

Sawyer, Ruth

    The Primrose Ring

        The <u>Primrose</u> <u>Ring</u> (*)
        Jesse L. Lasky Feature Play Co./Paramount Pictures
        Corp., 1917

Sayers, Dorothy L. (also see entry below)

    Busman's Honeymoon

        <u>Busman's</u> <u>Holiday</u> (G. B.) (also based on the samed named
        play, by Dorothy Sayers and Muriel St. Clare Byrne,
        which was derived from Sayer's novel)
        Metro-Goldwyn-Mayer British, 1940

    The Silent Passenger

        The <u>Silent</u> <u>Passenger</u> (G. B.)
        Phoenix Films/Associated British Film Dist., 1935

Sayers, Dorothy L. and Muriel St. Clare Byrne (also see entry
    above)

    Busman's Honeymoon (P)

        <u>Busman's</u> <u>Holiday</u> (G. B.) (also based on the same named
        novel, by Sayers, from which the play was derived)
        Metro-Goldwyn-Mayer British, 1940

Scarberry, Alma Sioux

    The Flat Tire

        <u>Hired</u> <u>Wife</u>
        Pinnacle, 1934

Scarborough, Dorothy

    The Wind

        The <u>Wind</u>

Metro-Goldwyn-Mayer, Inc., 1928

Schauffler, Elsie T.

Parnell (P)

> Parnell
> Metro-Goldwyn-Mayer, Inc., 1937

Schwartz, Sheila

Like Mother, Like Me

> Like Mom, Like Me (TVM)
> CBS Entertainment/Columbia Broadcasting System, 1978

Scott, Winfred Mary (see Pamela Wynne)

Screiber, Flora R.

Sybil (NF)

> Sybil (TVM)
> Lorimar Prod./National Broadcasting System, 1976

Sears, Zelda (also see the entry below)

The Clinging Vine (P)

> The Clinging Vine (*)
> DeMille Prod./Producers Dist. Corp., 1926

Sears, Zelda and Dodson Mitchell (also see the entry above)

Cornered (P)

> Cornered (*)
> Warner Brothers Pictures, Inc., 1924
>
> Road to Paradise
> First National, 1930

Seawell, Molly Elliot

The Fortunes of Fifi (P)

> The Fortunes of Fifi (*)
> Famous Players Film Co./Paramount Pictures Corp., 1917

Sedgwick, (Mrs.) Alfred

The Kinsman

> The Kinsman (*) (G. B.)
> Hepworth/Butcher's Film Service, 1919

Sedgwick, Anne Douglas

The Little French Girl

> The Little French Girl (*)
> Famous Players-Lasky Corp./Paramount Pictures Corp.,
> 1925

Tante

> The Impossible Woman (*) (G. B.) (also based on the
> play The Impossible Woman, by Haddon Chambers, which
> was derived from Sedgwick's novel)
> Ideal, 1919

Segall, Dorothy and Harry Segall

Windy (S)

> For Heaven's Sake (also based on the play May We Come
> In?, by Harry Segall)
> Twentieth Century-Fox Film Corp., 1950

Seghers, Anna
   (pseud. of Netty Reiling)

The Seventh Cross

> The Seventh Cross
> Metro-Goldwyn-Mayer, Inc., 1944

Selinko, Annemarie

Desiree

> Desiree
> Twentieth Century-Fox Film Corp., 1954

Senesh, Hanna

The Diaries of Hanna Senesh (D)

Hanna's War (also based on the nonfiction book A Great
Wind Cometh, by Yoel Palgi)
Golan-Globus Film Corp./Cannon Screen Entertainment,
1988

Seton, Anya

   Dragonwyck

      Dragonwyck
      Twentieth Century-Fox Film Corp., 1946

   Foxfire

      Foxfire
      Universal Motion Pictures Co., 1955

Seward, Florence A.

   Gold for the Caesars

      Gold for the Caesars
      Adelphia Campagnia/Metro-Goldwyn-Mayer, Inc., 1964

Sewell, Anna

   Black Beauty

      Black Beauty (*)
      Vitagraph Co. of America, 1921

      Black Beauty
      Chadwick/Monogram Pictures Corp., 1933

      Black Beauty
      Twentieth Century-Fox Film Corp., 1946

      Courage of Black Beauty
      Twentieth Century-Fox Film Corp., 1957

      Black Beauty (G. B.)
      Tigon British-Chilton/Tigon, 1971

      Black Beauty (TVM)
      Universal Television/National Broadcasting Co., 1978

Shaffer, Rosalind Keating

   The Finger Man (S)

Lady Killer
Warner Brothers Pictures, Inc., 1933

Sharman (Bolton), Maisie

Death Goes to School

Death Goes to School (G. B.)
Independent Artists/Eros Films, 1953

Sharp, Hilda Mary

The Stars in Their Courses

A Mother's Sin (*)
Vitagraph Co. of America-a Blue Ribbon Feature/Greater
Vitagraph, 1918

Sharp, Margery

Britannia Mews

Britannia Mews (G. B.)
Twentieth Century Prod., 1949

Cluny Brown

Cluny Brown
Twentieth Century-Fox Film Corp., 1946

Miss Bianca

The Rescuers (also based on the novel The Rescuers, by
Sharp)
Walt Disney Prod., 1977

Notorious Tenant (S)

The Notorious Landlady
Columbia Pictures Corp., 1962

The Nutmeg Tree

Julia Misbehaves
Metro-Goldwyn-Mayer, Inc., 1948

The Rescuers

The Rescuers (also based on the novel Miss Bianca, by
Sharp)
Walt Disney Prod., 1977

Sharpe, Madeleine

    The Chessboard (S)

        <u>Dangerous</u> <u>Business</u> (*)
        Norma Talmadge Film Corp., 1920

Shearing, Joseph (also see Marjorie Bowen and George Preedy)
    (pseud. of Gabrielle Margaret Vere Campbell Long)

    Airing in a Closed Carriage

        <u>Mark</u> <u>of</u> <u>Cain</u> (G. B.)
        Two Cities Films, Ltd./General Film Dist., Inc., 1948

    Blanche Fury

        <u>Blanche</u> <u>Fury</u> (G. B.)
        Independent Film Producers-Cineguild, Ltd.,
        Prod./General Film Dist., Inc., 1948

    For Her to See

        <u>So</u> <u>Evil</u> <u>my</u> <u>Love</u> (G. B.)
        Paramount Pictures Corp., 1948

    Moss Rose

        <u>Moss</u> <u>Rose</u>
        Twentieth Century-Fox Film Corp., 1947

Sheklow, Edna

    The Plant (P)

        <u>Promises,</u> <u>Promises</u>
        NTD, Inc., 1963

Shelley, Elsa

    Pick Up Girl; a Play in Three Acts (P)

        <u>Too</u> <u>Young</u> <u>to</u> <u>Love</u> (G. B.)
        Beaconsfield/J. Arthur Rank Film Dist., Ltd., 1960

Shelley, Mary

    Frankenstein: Or, the Modern Prometheus (we include those
    films which are claimed to be based on the novel or ideas in
    the novel and exclude those based on the characters only)

Life Without Soul (*)
Ocean Film Corp./State Rights, 1915

Frankenstein (also based on the play Frankenstein, by
Peggy Webling, which was derived from Shelley's novel)
Universal Motion Pictures Co., 1931

Bride of Frankenstein
Universal Motion Pictures Co., 1935

The Curse of Frankenstein (G. B.)
Hammer Films-Clarion/Warner Brothers Pictures, Inc., 1957

I Was a Teenage Frankenstein
American International Pictures, 1957

Frankenstein 1970
Allied Artists Pictures Corp., 1958

Frankenstein (TVM)
Dan Curtis Prod./American Broadcasting Co., 1973

Frankenstein: The True Story (TVM) (G. B.)
Universal International Motion Pictures-Cinema
International Corp./National Broadcasting Co., 1973

Victor Frankenstein (Swed./Ire.)
Aspect/Films Around the World, 1975

Doctor Franken (TVM)
Titus Prod.-Janus Prod.-National Broadcasting Co.
Entertainment/National Broadcasting Co., 1980

The Bride (G. B.)
Colgems-Delphi III/Columbia British, 1985

Frankenstein General Hospital
New Star, 1988

Shepard, Kathleen
     (pseud. of Suzanne Rice)

   I Will be Faithful

          Human Cargo
          Twentieth Century-Fox Film Corp., 1936

Sherbourne, Zoa

     Stranger in the House

          Memories Never Die (TVM)

311

Groverton Prod.-Scholastic Prod.-Universal Television/
Columbia Broadcasting System, 1982

Sherrill, Elizabeth and Corrie ten Boom and John Sherill (also
   see the entry below)

   The Hiding Place (NF)

         The Hiding Place
         World Wide, 1975

Sherrill, Elizabeth and John Sherrill and David Wilkerson (also
   see the entry above)

   The Cross and the Switchblade (NF)

         The Cross and the Switchblade
         Dick Ross Associates, 1970

Sherry, Edna

   Sudden Fear

         Sudden Fear
         RKO Radio Pictures, Inc., 1952

Shiber, Etta and Anne Dupre and Paul Dupre and Oscar Ray

   Paris-Underground (NF)

         Paris-Underground
         United Artists Film Corp., 1945

Shivers, Louise

   Here to Get My Baby Out of Jail

         Summer Heat
         Atlantic, 1987

Shore, Viola Brothers (also see the entry below)

   Notices (S)

         Hit of the Show (*)
         Film Booking Office Prod., Inc., 1928

   On the Shelf (S)

Let Women Alone (*)
Peninsula Studios/Producers Dist. Corp., 1925

Shore, Viola Brothers and Garrett Fort (also see the entry above)

The Prince of Headwaiters (S)

The Prince of Headwaiters (*)
Sam E. Rork Prod./First National, 1927

Sidney, Margaret
(pseud. of Harriet Mulford Lathrop)

Five Little Peppers and How they Grew

Five Little Peppers and How They Grew
Columbia Pictures Corp., 1939

Five Little Peppers at Home
Columbia Pictures Corp., 1940

Five Little Peppers in Trouble
Columbia Pictures Corp., 1940

Out West with the Peppers
Columbia Pictures Corp., 1940

Sifton, Claire and Paul Sifton

Midnight (P)

Midnight
All-Star/Universal Motion Pictures Co., 1934

Silver, Christine

Doorsteps (P)

Chicken Casey (*)
Triangle Film Corp., 1917

Silver, Joan and Linda Gottlieb

Limbo

Limbo
Universal Motion Pictures Co., 1972

Simmonds, Posy

The Frog Prince (S)

> <u>French</u> <u>Lesson</u>
> Enigma-Goldcrest Films and Television, Ltd./Warner
> Brothers Pictures, Inc., 1986

Simonton, Ida Vera

Hell's Playground

> <u>White</u> <u>Cargo</u> (*) (G. B.) (also based on the play <u>White</u>
> <u>Cargo</u>, by Leon Gordon, which was derived from
> Simonton's novel)
> Neo-Art Prod./Williams and Pritchard Films, 1929

> <u>White</u> <u>Cargo</u> (also based on the play <u>White</u> <u>Cargo</u>, by
> Leon Gordon, which was derived from Simonton's novel)
> Metro-Goldwyn-Mayer, Inc., 1942

Simpson, (Mrs.) C. Fraser

Footsteps in the Night

> <u>Footsteps</u> <u>in</u> <u>the</u> <u>Night</u> (G. B.)
> Associated Talking Pictures/RKO Radio Pictures, Inc.,
> 1932

Simpson, Helen (also see the entry below)

Saraband for Dead Lovers

> <u>Saraband</u> <u>for</u> <u>Dead</u> <u>Lovers</u> (G. B.)
> Ealing Studios/General Film Dist., Inc., 1949

Under Capricorn

> <u>Under</u> <u>Capricorn</u> (G. B.) (also based upon the same named
> play, by Margaret Linden and John Linden, which was
> derived from Simpson's novel)
> Capricorn-Transatlantic/Warner Brothers Pictures, Inc.,
> 1949

Simpson, Helen and Clemence Dane (also see the entry above)
  (Clemence Dane: pseud. of Winifred Ashton)

Enter Sir John (N/P)

> <u>Murder</u> (G. B.)
> British International Pictures/Wardour, 1930

Sims, Dorothy Rice and Valentine Williams

    Fog

        <u>Fog</u>
        Columbia Pictures Corp., 1934

Sinclair, Bertha Muzzy (see B. M. Bower)

Sinclair, Mary

    Kitty Tailleur

        <u>Kitty</u> <u>Tailleur</u> (*) (G. B.)
        Granger-Binger, 1921

Sjowall, Maj and Per Wahloo

    The Laughing Policeman

        <u>The</u> <u>Laughing</u> <u>Policeman</u>
        Twentieth Century-Fox Film Corp., 1973

Skinner, Constance Lindsay

    The Noose (S)

        <u>The</u> <u>Green</u> <u>Temptation</u> (*)
        Famous Players-Lasky Corp./Paramount Pictures Corp.,
        1922

Skinner, Cornelia Otis and Emily Kimbrough (also see the entry
    below)

    Our Hearts Were Young and Gay (NF)

        <u>Our</u> <u>Hearts</u> <u>Were</u> <u>Young</u> <u>and</u> <u>Gay</u>
        Paramount Pictures Corp., 1944

Skinner, Cornelia Otis and Samuel Taylor (also see the entry
    above)

    The Pleasure of His Company (P)

        <u>The</u> <u>Pleasure</u> <u>of</u> <u>His</u> <u>Company</u>
        Perlsea-Paramount Pictures Corp./Paramount Pictures
        Corp., 1961

Slade, Christine Jope

Caretakers Within (S)

Life's Darn Funny (*)
Metro Pictures Corp., 1921

Slater, Beverly

Stranger in My Bed (NF)

Stranger in My Bed (TVM)
National Broadcasting Co., 1986

Slesinger, Tess

The Answer on the Magnolia Tree (S)

Girl's School
Columbia Pictures Corp., 1938

Smith, Alice M. and Charlotte Thompson

The Strength of the Weak (P)

The Strength of the Weak (*)
Bluebird Photoplays, Inc., 1916

Smith, Betty

Joy in the Morning

Joy in the Morning
Metro-Goldwyn-Mayer, Inc., 1965

A Tree Grows in Brooklyn

A Tree Grows in Brooklyn
Twentieth Century-Fox Film Corp., 1945

A Tree Grows in Brooklyn (TVM)
Norman Rosemont Prod.--Twentieth Century-Fox
Television/National Broadcasting Co., 1974

Smith, Dodie (Dorothy Gladys) (also see C. L. Anthony)

Call It a Day (P)

Call It a Day
Warner Brothers Pictures, Inc., 1937

Dear Octopus (P)

Dear Octopus (G. B.)
Gainsborough Prod./General Film Dist., Inc., 1943

The One Hundred and One Dalmations

One Hundred and One Dalmations
Walt Disney Prod./Buena Vista Dist. Co., 1960

Smith, (Lady) Eleanor

Ballerina

Men in her Life
Columbia Pictures Corp., 1941

Caravan

Caravan
Fox Film Corp., 1934

Caravan (G. B.)
Gainsborough Prod./General Film Dist., Inc., 1946

The Man in Grey, a Regency Romance

The Man in Grey (G. B.)
Gainsborough Prod./General Film Dist., Inc., 1943

Red Wagon

Red Wagon (G. B.)
British International Pictures/Wardour, 1934

Red Wagon
Alliance Prod., 1938

Tzigane

Gypsy (G. B.)
Warner Brothers Pictures, Inc.-First National/Warner
Brothers Pictures, Inc., 1937

Smith, Mrs. G. Castle (see "Brenda")

Smith, Harriet Lummis

Agatha's Aunt

A Heart to Let (*) (also based on the play Agatha's

Aunt, a Comedy in Three Acts, by Sidney Toler, which
was derived from Smith's novel)
Realart Pictures Corp., 1921

Smith, Helen Zenna (see Evadne Price)

Smith, Sara (see Hesba Stretton)

Smith, Sarah B. and Lucille S. Prumbs

Ever the Beginning (P)

My Girl Tisa
United States Pictures, Inc./Warner Brothers Pictures,
Inc., 1948

Smith, Sheila Kaye
(pseud. of Sheila Kaye-Smith)

Joanna Godden

Loves of Joanna Godden (G. B.)
Ealing Studios/General Film Dist., Inc., 1947

Smith, Shelley
(pseud. of Nancy H. Bodington)

Ballad of the Running Man

The Running Man (G. B.)
Peet Prod./Columbia British, 1963

Somerville, Edith and Martin Ross

Experiences of an Irish RM

Experiences of an Irish RM (TVM)
Channel 4 TV, 1982

Sommer, Edith

A Roomful of Roses (P)

Teenage Rebel
Twentieth Century-Fox Film Corp., 1956

Southard, Ruth

No Sad Songs for Me

> No Sad Songs for Me
> Columbia Pictures Corp., 1950

Spark, Muriel

The Abbess of Crewe

> Nasty Habits (G. B.)
> Bowden-Brut/Scotia-Barber, 1977

The Prime of Miss Jean Brodie

> The Prime of Miss Jean Brodie (G. B.) (also based on
> the same named play, by Jay Presson Allen, which was
> derived from Spark's novel)
> Twentieth Century-Fox Film Corp., 1969

Spaulding, Susan Marr

Two Shall be Born (S)

> Two Shall be Born (*)
> Twin Pictures/Vitagraph Co. of America, 1924

Speare, Dorothy and Charles Beahan

Don't Fall in Love (P)

> One Night of Love
> Columbia Pictures Corp., 1934

Spencer, Elizabeth

I, Maureen (S)

> I, Maureen (Can.)
> Jandu-P. W. S./New World Cinema, 1978

Light in the Piazza

> Light in the Piazza (G. B.)
> Metro-Goldwyn-Mayer British, 1961

Spewack, Bella and Samuel Spewack

Boy Meets Girl (P)

> Boy Meets Girl
> Warner Brothers Pictures, Inc., 1938

Clear All Wires (P)

> Clear All Wires
> Metro-Goldwyn-Mayer, Inc., 1933

Kiss Me Kate (MP, music and lyrics by Cole Porter)

> Kiss Me Kate
> Metro-Goldwyn-Mayer, Inc., 1953

My Three Angels (P, based on a foreign language play, by Albert Husson)

> We're No Angels
> Paramount Pictures Corp., 1955

Solitaire Man; a Melodrama in Three Acts (P)

> The Solitaire Man
> Metro-Goldwyn-Mayer, Inc., 1933

Sprague, Bessie Toulouse (see Priscilla Wayne)

Spyri, Johanna

Heidi

> Heidi
> Darryl F. Zanuck Prod./Twentieth Century-Fox Film Corp., 1937

> Heidi's Song
> Hanna-Barbera/Paramount Pictures Corp., 1982

Squier, Emma Lindsay

The Angry God and the People of Corn (S)

> The Angry God
> Arlisle Prod./United Artists Film Corp., 1948

Glorious Buccaneer (S)

> Dancing Pirate
> RKO Radio Pictures, Inc., 1936

Stabel, Thelma

You Were There (Note: Nash and Ross and Silver and Ward claim this is a novel, other sources disagree.)

        <u>Undercurrent</u>
        Metro-Goldwyn-Mayer, Inc./Loew's, Inc., 1946

Stanford, Sally

    Lady of the House (NF)

        <u>Lady of the House</u> (TVM)
        William Kayden Prod.-Metromedia Prod. Corp./National
        Broadcasting Co., 1978

Stanley, Caroline Abbot

    A Modern Madonna

        <u>The Forgotten Law</u> (*)
        Graf Prod./Metro Pictures Corp., 1922

Stanley, Martha M. (also see the entry below)

    My Son, a Play in Three Acts (P)

        <u>My Son</u> (*)
        First National, 1925

        <u>Tarnished Youth</u>
        World Wide, 1932

Stanley, Martha M. and Adelaide Matthews (also see the entry above)

    Scrambled Wives (P)

        <u>Scrambled Wives</u> (*)
        Marguerite Clark Prod./Associated First National, 1921

    The Teaser (P)

        <u>The Teaser</u> (*)
        Universal Motion Pictures Co., 1925

Stanton, Doralie and E. Hoskin

    The World's Best Girl

        <u>The Romance of a Movie Star</u> (*) (G. B.)
        Broadwest/Walturdaw, 1920

Starr, Catherine

Paperhouse

> Paperhouse (G. B.)
> Working Title/Vestron, 1988

St. Dennis, Madelon

The Death Kiss

> The Death Kiss
> KBS/World Wide, 1930

Stead, Christina

For Love Alone

> For Love Alone (Austr.)
> Waranta-UAA/UAA, 1986

Steel, Danielle

Now and Forever

> Now and Forever (Aust.)
> Inter Planetary, 1983

Stein, Gertrude

Q. E. D.

> Quest for Love (S. Afr.)
> Elegant/Filmstrust, 1988

Steinem, Gloria

I was a Playboy Bunny (A)

> A Bunny's Tale (TVM)
> Stan Margulies Co.-American Broadcasting Co. Circle
> Films/American Broadcasting Co., 1985

Stern, Gladys Bronwyn

Long Lost Father (P)

Long Lost Father
RKO Radio Pictures, Inc., 1934

The Ugly Dachshund

The Ugly Dachshund
Walt Disney Prod./Buena Vista Dist. Co., 1966

The Woman in the Hall

The Woman in the Hall (G. B.)
Independent Producers-Wessex/General Film Dist., Inc.,
1947

Sterrett, Frances Roberta

Up the Road with Sallie

Up the Road with Sallie (*)
Select Pictures Corp., 1918

Stevenson, Janet and Philip Stevenson

Counter Attack (P, based on a foreign language play, by Ilya
Vershinin and Mickhail Ruderman)

Counter-Attack
Columbia Pictures Corp., 1945

Stewart, Mary

The Moon-Spinners

The Moon-Spinners (G. B.)
Walt Disney Prod., 1964

Stewart, Ramona

Desert Fury

Desert Fury
Paramount Pictures Corp., 1947

The Possession of Joel Delaney

The Possession of Joel Delaney
Haworth/Paramount Pictures Corp., 1972

Stinetorf, Louise A.

White Witch Doctor

> White Witch Doctor
> Twentieth Century-Fox Film Corp., 1953

St. John, Adela Rogers

A Free Soul

> A Free Soul (also based on the play A Free Soul, by
> Willard Mack, which was derived from St. John's novel)
> Metro-Goldwyn-Mayer, Inc., 1931

> The Girl Who Had Everything
> Metro-Goldwyn-Mayer, Inc., 1953

Government Girl

> Government Girl
> RKO Radio Pictures, Inc., 1943

Great God Fourflush (S)

> Woman's Man
> Monogram Pictures Corp., 1934

The Haunted Lady (S)

> Scandal
> Universal Motion Pictures Co., 1929

Love O' Women (S)

> Singed (*)
> Fox Film Corp., 1927

Pretty Ladies (S)

> Pretty Ladies (*)
> Metro-Goldwyn-Mayer, Inc., 1925

The Single Standard

> The Single Standard (*) (Note: sound effects and
> musical score added.)
> Metro-Goldwyn-Mayer, Inc., 1929

The Skyrocket

> Skyrocket (*)
> Celebrity/Associated Exhibitors, 1926

The Worst Woman in Hollywood (S)

Inez from Hollywood (*)
Sam E. Rork Prod./First National, 1924

Stockdale, Sybil and James B. Stockdale

In Love and War (NF)

In Love and War (TVM)
Tisch-Avnet Prod./National Broadcasting Co., 1987

Stockley, Cynthia

April Folly

April Folly (*)
Marion Davies Film Corp.--Cosmopolitan Prod.--
International Film Service Co./Famous Players-Lasky
Corp.--Paramount Pictures Corp.-Artcraft Pictures
Corp., 1920

The Claw

The Claw (*)
C. K. Y. Film Corp./Select Pictures Corp., 1918

The Claw (*)
Universal Motion Pictures Co., 1927

Dalla, the Lion Cub

The Female (*)
Famous Players-Lasky Corp./Paramount Pictures Corp.,
1924

Ponjola

Ponjola (*)
Sam E. Rork Prod./Associated First National, 1923

Poppy

Poppy (*) (also based on the same named play, by Ben
Teal and John P. Ritter, which was derived from
Stockley's novel)
Norma Talmadge Film Corp./Lewis J. Selznick
Enterprises, Inc.-Selznick Pictures Corp., 1917

Rozanne Ozanne (S)

Sins of Rozanne (*)
Famous Players-Lasky Corp./Famous Players-Lasky Corp.--
Paramount Pictures Corp., 1920

Stone, Grace Zaring
     (also see Ethel Vance)

     The Bitter Tea of General Yen

          The Bitter Tea of General Yen
          Columbia Pictures Corp., 1933

Stone, Mary

     A Social Highwayman (P)

          The Social Highwayman (*)
          Shubert Film Corp./World Film, 1916

Storm, Lesley
     (pseud. of Mabel Margaret Clark)

     The Day's Mischief (P)

          Personal Affair (G. B.)
          Two Cities Film, Ltd./General Film Dist., Inc., 1953

     Great Day (P)

          Great Day (G. B.)
          RKO Radio Pictures, Inc., 1945

     Heart of the City (P)

          Tonight and Every Night
          Columbia Pictures Corp., 1945

     Tony Draws a Horse (P)

          Tony Draws a Horse (G. B.)
          Pinnacle/General Film Dist., Inc., 1951

Stout, (Mrs.) E. Almaz

     Women who Win

          Women who Win (*) (G. B.)
          T. H. Davison, 1919

Stowe, Harriet Beecher

     My Wife and I

          My Wife and I (*)

Warner Brothers Pictures, Inc., 1925

The Pearl of Orr's Island, a Story of the Coast of Maine

> The Pearl of Love (*)
> Paul W. Whitcomb Prod./Lee-Bradford Corp., 1925

Uncle Tom's Cabin

> Uncle Tom's Cabin (*)
> Imp, 1913
>
> Uncle Tom's Cabin (*) (also based on the same named
> play, by George L. Aiken, which was derived from
> Stowe's novel)
> World Prod. Corp./World Film, 1914
>
> Uncle Tom's Cabin (*)
> Famous Players-Lasky Corp./Famous Players-Lasky Corp.--
> Paramount Pictures Corp., 1918
>
> Uncle Tom's Cabin (*) (Note: musical score added on
> some prints.)
> Universal Motion Pictures Co., 1927
>
> Uncle Tom's Cabin (TVM)
> Edgar J. Scherick/Showtime, 1987

Strabel, Thelma

Reap the Wild Wind

> Reap the Wild Wind
> Paramount Pictures Corp., 1942

Streshinsky, Shirley and Lauren Elder

And I Alone Survived (NF)

> And I Alone Survived (TVM)
> Jerry Leider-OJL Prod./National Broadcasting Co., 1978

Stretton, Hesba
(pseud. of Sara Smith)

Little Meg's Children

> Little Meg's Children (*) (G. B.)
> Seal/Lester, 1921

Struther, Jan

(pseud. of Joyce Maxtone-Graham)

Mrs. Miniver

> <u>Mrs.</u> <u>Miniver</u>
> Metro-Goldwyn-Mayer, Inc., 1942

Stuart, Aimee (also see the entry below)

Jeannie (P)

> <u>Jeannie</u> (G. B.)
> Tansa Films/General Film Dist., Inc., 1941

> <u>Let's</u> <u>be</u> <u>Happy</u> (G. B.)
> Marcel Hellman/Associated British and Pathe Film Dist.,
> 1957

Stuart, Aimee and Philip Stuart (also see the entry above)

Her Shop (P)

> <u>Borrowed</u> <u>Clothes</u> (G. B.)
> Maude Prod./Columbia Pictures Corp. 1934

Nine Till Six (P)

> <u>Nine</u> <u>Till</u> <u>Six</u> (G. B.)
> Associated Talking Pictures/RKO Radio Pictures, Inc.,
> 1932

Sture-Vasa, Mary O'Hara Alsop (see Mary O'Hara)

Sullivan, Kate

The Reluctant Grandmother (P)

> <u>She</u> <u>Knows</u> <u>Y'Know</u> (G. B.)
> Eternal/Grand National Pictures, 1962

Sumner, (Mrs.) Cid Ricketts

Quality

> <u>Pinky</u>
> Twentieth Century-Fox Film Corp., 1949

Tammy Out of Time

> <u>Tammy</u> <u>and</u> <u>the</u> <u>Millionaire</u> (also based on the novel

Tammy, Tell Me True, by Sumner)
Uni-Bet Prod./Universal Motion Pictures Co., 1963

Tammy, Tell Me True

Tammy Tell Me True
Ross Hunter Prod./Universal International Motion
Pictures, 1961

Tammy and the Millionaire (also based on the novel
Tammy Out of Time, by Sumner)
Uni-Bet Prod./Universal Motion Picture Co., 1963

Susann, Jacqueline

The Love Machine

The Love Machine
Columbia Pictures Corp., 1971

Once is not Enough

Once is not Enough
Paramount Pictures Corp., 1975

Valley of the Dolls

Valley of the Dolls
Red Lion/Twentieth Century-Fox Film Corp., 1967

Jacqueline Susann's "Valley of the Dolls 1981" (TVM)
Twentieth Century-Fox Television/Columbia Broadcasting
System, 1981

Sutherland, Evelyn Greenleaf and Beulah Marie Dix   (also see the
    entry below)

The Breed of the Treshams (P)

The Breed of the Treshams (*) (G. B.)
Astra Films, 1920

The Road to Yesterday (P)

The Road to Yesterday (*)
DeMille Prod./Producers Dist. Corp., 1925

Sutherland, Evelyn Greenleaf and Booth Tarkington (also see the
    entry above)

Monsieur Beaucaire (S/P/N)

Monsieur Beaucaire (*)
Famous Players Film Co./Paramount Pictures Corp., 1924

Sutherland, Joan

Fettered

Fettered (*) (G. B.)
Windsor Pictures Corp./Walturdaw, 1919

Wyngate Sattib

Fantee (*) (G. B.)
Anglo-Indian Films, 1920

Suyin, Han
(pseud. of Elizabeth Chou)

A Many Splendoured Thing

Love is a Many Splendoured Thing
Twentieth Century-Fox Film Corp., 1955

Swarthout, Gladys

Bless the Beasts and Children

Bless the Beasts and Children
Columbia Pictures Corp., 1971

Swatridge, Irene Maude Mossop (see Theresa Charles)

Swift, Kay

Who Could Ask for Anything More

Never a Dull Moment
RKO Radio Pictures, Inc., 1950

Syrett, Netta

Portrait of a Rebel

A Woman Rebels
RKO Radio Pictures, Inc., 1936

Tate, Sylvia

The Fuzzy Pink Nightgown

The Fuzzy Pink Nightgown
United Artists Film Corp., 1957

Man on the Run (S)

Woman on the Run
Fidelity Pictures, Inc./Universal Motion Pictures Co.,
1950

Taylor, Joan

Asking for It

An Invasion of Privacy (TVM)
Dick Berg-Stonehenge Prod.--Embassy Television/Columbia
Broadcasting System, 1983

Taylor, Katherine Haviland

Cecilia of the Pink Roses

Cecilia of the Pink Roses (*)
Marion Davies Film Co./Select Pictures Corp., 1918

The Failure (S)

One Man's Journey
RKO Radio Pictures, Inc., 1933

A Man to Remember
RKO Radio Pictures, Inc., 1938

Taylor, Mary Imlay

Candle in the Wind (S)

Conquest
Warner Brothers Pictures, Inc., 1929

The Wild Fawn

The Good-Bad Wife (*)
Vera McCord Prod. Inc./State Rights, 1920

Taylor, Renee and Joseph Bologna

Lovers and Other Strangers (P)

Lovers and Other Strangers
American Broadcasting Co./Cinerama, 1970

Taylor, Rosemary

Chicken Every Sunday

Chicken Every Sunday (also based on the same named
play, by Julius J. Epstein and Philip J. Epstein, which
was derived from Taylor's novel)
Twentieth Century-Fox Film Corp., 1948

The Hefferan Family
Twentieth Century-Fox Film Corp., 1956

Telfer, Dariel

The Caretakers

The Caretakers
United Artists Film Corp., 1963

Tell, Alma and Harriet Ford

Main Street (P)

Main Street (*) (also based on the same named novel, by
Sinclair Lewis, from which play was derived)
Warner Brothers Pictures, Inc., 1923

Temple, Irene (see Temple Bailey)

Temple, Joan

No Room at the Inn (P)

No Room at the Inn (G. B.)
British National Films, Ltd./Pathe Exchange, Inc., 1948

The Primrose Path (S)

The Primrose Path (G. B.)

British and Dominion Films Corp./Paramount Pictures
Corp. British, 1934

ten Boom, Corrie and Elizabeth Sherrill and John Sherill

The Hiding Place (NF)

The Hiding Place
World Wide, 1975

Terasaki, Gwen

Bridge to the Sun (NF)

Bridge to the Sun
Metro-Goldwyn-Mayer, Inc., 1961

Terrett, Courtenay

Public Relations (S)

Made on Broadway
Metro-Goldwyn-Mayer, Inc., 1933

Terrill, Lucy Stone

Clothes (S)

Clothes
Pathe Exchange, Inc., 1929

Face (S)

Unguarded Women (*)
Famous Players-Lasky Corp./Paramount Pictures Corp.,
1924

Tervapaa, Juhani
(pseud. of Hella Helsinki Wuolijoki)

Juurakon Hulda (P)

The Farmer's Daughter
RKO Radio Pictures, Inc., 1947

Tey, Josephine
(pseud. of Elizabeth MacKintosh)

Brat Farrar

Brat Farrar (TVM) (G. B.)
Terrance Dicks/British Broadcasting Corp., 1985

The Franchise Affair

The Franchise Affair (G. B.)
Associated British Picture Corp./Associated British and
Pathe Film Dist., 1951

A Shilling for Candles

Young and Innocent (G. B.)
Gaumont British, Ltd./General Film Dist., Inc., 1937

Thompkins, Juliet Wilbur

Fanny Foley Herself (S)

Fanny Foley Herself
RKO Radio Pictures, Inc., 1931

Thompson, "Boxcar" Bertha and Dr. Ben L. Reitman

Sisters of the Road (NF)

Boxcar Bertha
American International Pictures, 1972

Thompson, Charlotte (also see the two entries below)

In Search of a Sinner (P)

In Search of a Sinner (*)
Constance Talmadge Film Co./First National, 1920

Thompson, Charlotte and Alice M. Smith (also see the entry above
and the entry below)

The Strength of the Weak (P)

The Strength of the Weak (*)
Bluebird Photoplays, Inc., 1916

Thompson, Charlotte and Kate Douglas Wiggin (also see the two
entries above)

Rebecca of Sunnybrook Farm (P)

Rebecca of Sunnybrook Farm (*) (also based on the same

334

named novel, by Wiggin, from which the play was derived)
Mary Pickford/Artcraft Pictures Corp., 1917

Thompson, Maravene

Persuasive Peggy

Persuasive Peggy (*)
Mayfair Film Corp., 1917

The Woman's Law

The Woman's Law (*)
Arrow Film Corp., 1916

The Net (*)
Fox Film Corp., 1923

Thompson, Mary Agnes

A Call from Mitch Miller (S)

Loving You
Paramount Pictures Corp., 1957

Thorp, Molly and Nora Lavin

The Hop Dog

Adventure in the Hopfields (G. B.)
Vandyke/British Lion Film Corp.-Children's Film
Foundation, 1954

Thurman, Judith

Isak Dinesen: The Life of a Storyteller (NF)

Out of Africa (also based on the nonfiction books Out of Africa, by Isak Dinesen, and Silence Will Speak, by Errol Trzebinski)
Universal Motion Pictures Co., 1985

Thurston, Katherine Cecil

The Masquerader

The Masquerader (also based on the same named play, by John Hunter Booth, which was derived from Thurston's novel)

Samuel Goldwyn Prod./United Artists Film Corp., 1933

Tighe, Eileen and Graeme Lorimer

    Feature for June (P)

        June <u>Bride</u>
        Warner Brothers Pictures, Inc., 1948

Tildesley, Alice L.

    What Can you Expect? (S)

        <u>Short</u> <u>Skirts</u> (*)
        Universal Motion Pictures Co., 1921

Titus, Eve

    Basil of Baker Street

        <u>The</u> <u>Great</u> <u>Mouse</u> <u>Detective</u>
        Walt Disney, Prod.-Silver Screen Partners, 1986

Toll, Judy and Wendy Goldman

    Casual Sex? (P)

        <u>Casual</u> <u>Sex?</u>
        Jascat/Universal Motion Pictures Co., 1988

Tompkins, Juliet Wilbur

    A Girl Named Mary

        A <u>Girl</u> <u>Named</u> <u>Mary</u> (*)
        Famous Players-Lasky Corp./Famous Players-Lasky Corp.--
        Paramount Pictures Corp.-Artcraft Pictures Corp., 1919

    Once There Was a Princess (S)

        <u>Misbehaving</u> <u>Ladies</u>
        Warner Brothers Pictures, Inc./First National, 1931

    The Two Benjamins

        <u>Little</u> <u>Comrade</u> (*)
        Famous Players-Lasky Corp./Famous Players-Lasky Corp.--
        Paramount Pictures Corp., 1919

Tonkonogy, Gertrude

Three Cornered Moon; a Comedy in Three Acts (P)

>Three Cornered Moon
>Paramount Pictures Corp., 1933

Topkins, Katherine

Kotch

>Kotch
>Kotch-American Broadcasting Co./Cinerama, 1972

Townsend, Sue

Secret Diary of Adrian Mole, Aged 13 3/4

>Secret Diary of Adrian Mole, Aged 13 3/4 (TVM) (G. B.)
>Peter Sasdy/Thames TV, 1985

Tracy, Margaret

Mrs. White

>White of the Eye (G. B./U. S.)
>Cinema Group-Cannon Screen Entertainment, 1987

Trahey, Jane

Life with Mother Superior

>The Trouble with Angels
>Columbia Pictures Corp., 1965

Travers, Pamela L.

Mary Poppins; from A to Z

>Mary Poppins
>Walt Disney Prod./Buena Vista Dist. Co., 1964

Tree, Viola and Gerald Du Maurier

The Dancers (P)

>The Dancers
>Fox Film Corp., 1930

Trenker, Lois

    The Doomed Batallion (S)

        The Doomed Batallion
        Universal Motion Pictures Co., 1932

Troubetzkoy, Princess (see Amelie Rives)

Trowbridge, (Lady)

    The Golden Cage (P)

        The Golden Cage (G. B.)
        Sound City Films/Metro-Goldwyn-Mayer British, 1933

    His Grace Gives Notice

        His Grace Gives Notice (*) (G. B.)
        Stoll, 1924

        His Grace Gives Notice (G. B.)
        Realart Pictures Corp./RKO Radio Pictures, Inc., 1933

Troy, Una

    We are Seven

        She Didn't Say No! (G. B.)
        GW Films/Associated British and Pathe Film Dist., 1958

Truesdell, June

    Be Still my Love

        The Accused
        Paramount Pictures Corp., 1949

Tuchman, Barbara W.

    August 1914 (NF)

        The Guns of August
        Universal Motion Pictures Co., 1964

Tucker, Augusta

    Miss Susie Slagle's

Miss <u>Susie</u> <u>Slagle's</u>
Paramount Pictures Corp., 1945

Tully, May

Mary's Ankle (P)

<u>Mary's</u> <u>Ankle</u> (*)
Thomas H. Ince/Famous Players-Lasky Corp.--Paramount
Pictures Corp.-Artcraft Pictures Corp., 1920

Tupper, Edith S. (Sessions)

The House of the Tolling Bell (N, which may be unpublished)

<u>The</u> <u>House</u> <u>of</u> <u>the</u> <u>Tolling</u> <u>Bell</u> (*)
J. Stuart Blackton Features Pictures, Inc./Pathe
Exchange, Inc., 1920

Whispering Pines

<u>Wilful</u> <u>Youth</u> (*)
Capitol Film Exchange, 1927

Turnbull, Margaret (also see the entry below)

Looking After Sandy

<u>Bad</u> <u>Little</u> <u>Angel</u>
Metro-Goldwyn-Mayer, Inc./Loew's, Inc., 1939

Turnbull, Margaret and William C. DeMille (also see the entry
above)

Classmates; a Play in Four Acts (P)

<u>Classmates</u> (*)
Klaw and Erlanger-Biograph Co./General Film, 1914

<u>Classmates</u> (*)
Inspirational Pictures/First National, 1924

Turner, Ethel

One Way Ticket

<u>One</u> <u>Way</u> <u>Ticket</u>
Columbia Pictures Corp., 1935

Turney, Catherine

The Other One

> Back from the Dead
> Regal Films International/Twentieth Century-Fox Film
> Corp., 1957

Turpin, Edna H. (see Edna Lee)

Tuttiett, Mary Gleed (see Maxwell Gray)

Tuttle, Margaretta

Feet of Clay

> Feet of Clay (*)
> Famous Players-Lasky Corp./Paramount Pictures Corp.,
> 1924

Tyler, Anne

The Accidental Tourist

> The Accidental Tourist
> Warner Brothers Pictures, Inc., 1988

Tynan, Kathleen

Agatha

> Agatha (G. B.)
> Sweetwal/Warner Brothers Pictures, Inc. and First
> Artists, 1979

- U -

Uhnak, Dorothy

    The Bait

        The <u>Bait</u> (TVM)
        Spelling-Goldberg Prod.--American Broadcasting Co.
        Circle Films/American Broadcasting Co., 1973

    The Investigation

        <u>Kojak: The Price of Justice</u> (TVM)
        Universal Televsion/Columbia Broadcasting System, 1987

    Law and Order

        <u>Law and Order</u> (TVM)
        P. A. Prod.-Paramount Television/National Broadcasting
        Co., 1976

    The Ledger

        <u>Get Christie Love!</u> (TVM)
        David L. Wolper Prod./American Broadcasting Co., 1974

Unger, Gladys (also see the two entries below)

    The Goldfish; a Comedy of Many Manners in Three Acts (P,
    based on the foreign language play, by Armont and Gerbiden)

        The <u>Goldfish</u> (*)
        Constance Talmadge Prod./Associated First National,
        1924

    Starlight (P)

        The <u>Divine Woman</u> (*)
        Metro-Goldwyn-Mayer, Inc., 1927

Unger, Gladys and Arthur Lyons (also see the entry above and the
    entry above)

    London Pride (P)

        <u>London Pride</u> (*) (G. B.)
        London Films/Jury's Imperial Pictures, 1920

Unger, Gladys and Jesse Lasky (also see the two entries above)

    Private Beach (P)

        <u>Music</u> <u>is</u> <u>Magic</u>
        Twentieth Century-Fox Film Corp., 1935

Upright, Blanche

    The Valley of Content

        <u>Pleasure</u> <u>Mad</u> (*)
        Louis B. Mayer Prod./Metro Pictures Corp., 1923

Vale, Martin
    (pseud. of Marguerite Veiller)

  The Two Mrs. Carrolls (P)

        The Two Mrs. Carrolls
        Warner Brothers Pictures, Inc., 1947

Valland, Rose

  Le Front de l'Art

        The Train (Fra./Ita./U. S.)
        Les Prod. Artistes-Ariane-Dear Film/United Artists Film
        Corp., 1965

Van Atta, Winfred

  Shock Treatment

        Shock Treatment
        Arcola Pictures/Twentieth Century-Fox Film Corp., 1964

Van Campen, Helen

  The Man Who Beat Dan Dolan (S)

        The Man Who Beat Dan Dolan (*)
        Gotham Film Co./State Rights-Gotham Film Co., 1915

Vance, Ethel (also see Grace Zaring Stone)
    (pseud. of Grace Zaring Stone)

  Escape

        Escape
        Metro-Goldwyn-Mayer, Inc., 1940

  Winter Meeting

        Winter Meeting
        Warner Brothers Pictures, Inc.-First National, 1948

Van de Water, Virginia Terhune

The Two Sisters

> The Two Sisters (*)
> Trem Carr Prod./Rayart Pictures, 1929

Van Nuys, Laura Bower

Nebraska 1888 (NF)

> The One and Only, Genuine, Original Family Band
> Walt Disney Prod./Buena Vista Dist. Co., 1968

Van Slyke, Helen

The Best Place to Be

> The Best Place to Be (TVM)
> Ross Hunter Prod./National Broadcasting Co., 1979

Van Slyke, Lucille

Little Miss By-the-Day

> The Stolen Kiss (*)
> Realart Pictures Corp., 1920

Van Vorst, Marie

David Tremaine

> Big Tremaine (*)
> Yorke Film Corp./Metro Pictures Corp., 1916

The Girl from His Town

> The Girl from His Town (*)
> American Film Manufacturing Co./Mutual Film Corp.-a
> Mutual Star Prod., 1915

Mary Moreland

> Mary Moreland (*)
> Frank Powell Prod. Corp./Mutual Film Corp.-A Mutual
> Star Prod., 1917

Varley, Isabella (see Mrs. Linnaeus Banks)

Veiller, Marguerite (see Martin Vale)

Vermilye, Mrs. F. M (see Kate Jordan)

Victoire, Amere (see Rene Hardy)

Vinton, Iris

    Flying Ebony

        The Mooncussers (TVM)
        Walt Disney Prod./National Broadcasting Co., 1962

Vollmer, Lula

    Sun-Up (P)

        Sun-Up (*)
        Metro-Goldwyn-Mayer Inc., 1925

    Trigger (P)

        Spitfire
        RKO Radio Pictures, Inc., 1934

von Meck, Barbara and Catherine Drinker Bowen

    The Music Lovers (NF)

        The Music Lovers
        Russfilms/United Artist's Film Corp., 1970

Vroman, Mary Elizabeth

    See How They Run (S)

        Bright Road
        Metro-Goldwyn-Mayer, Inc., 1953

- W -

Wadsley, Olive

Belonging

> Belonging (*) (G. B.)
> Stoll, 1922

> In Every Woman's Life (*)
> Associated First National, 1924

The Flame

> The Flame (*) (G. B.)
> Stoll, 1920

Frailty

> Frailty (*) (G. B.)
> Stoll, 1921

Possession

> Possession (*) (G. B.)
> Hepworth/Butcher's Film Service, 1919

Wagnalls, Mabel

The Rosebush of a Thousand Years (S)

> Revelation (*)
> Metro Pictures Corp.-Special Prod. De Luxe/Metro
> Pictures Corp.-Screen Classics, Inc., 1918

> Revelation (*)
> Metro-Goldwyn Pictures, 1924

Walker, Alice

The Color Purple

> The Color Purple
> Peter Gruber Prod.-Jon Peters Prod./Warner Brothers
> Pictures, Inc., 1985

Walker, Dolores and Andrew Piotrowski

Recess (P)

Recess
Edwin, 1967

Walker, Laura

Dr. Monica (P, based on a foreign language play, by Marja Morozowicz Szczepkowska)

Dr. Monica
Warner Brothers Pictures, Inc., 1934

Wallace, Pamela

Dreams Lost, Dreams Found

Dreams Lost, Dreams Found (TVM) (U. S./G. B.)
Atlantic Videoventures Prod.-Yorkshire Television, Ltd./Paramount Pictures Corp., 1987

Love With a Perfect Stranger

Love with a Perfect Stranger (TVM)
Yorkshire Television, Ltd.-Atlantic Videoventures Prod./Showtime, 1986

Tears in the Rain

Tears in the Rain (TVM) (G. B.)
Independent Television Corp., 1988

Walsh, Sheila

Only a Mill Girl (P) (Note: Gifford lists this picture twice; we use the earlier date.)

Only a Mill Girl (*) (G. B.)
Foxwell/Ideal, 1919

Walton, (Mrs.) O. F.

The Old Arm Chair

The Old Arm Chair (*) (G. B.)
Screen Plays/British Exhibitors' Films, 1920

A Peep Behind the Scenes

A Peep Behind the Scenes (*) (G. B.)

Master Films/New Bio, 1918

A <u>Peep</u> <u>Behind</u> <u>the</u> <u>Scenes</u> (*) (G. B.)
British and Dominion Films Corp./Woolf and Freedman
Film Service, 1929

Ward, (Mrs.) Humphrey (Mary Augusta) (also see the entry below)

Lady Rose's Daughter

<u>Lady</u> <u>Rose's</u> <u>Daughter</u> (*)
Famous Players-Lasky Corp./Famous Players-Lasky Corp.--
Paramount Pictures Corp.--Artcraft Pictures Corp., 1920

The Marriage of William Ashe

<u>The</u> <u>Marriage</u> <u>of</u> <u>William</u> <u>Ashe</u> (*) (G. B.)
Hepworth/Harma, 1916

<u>The</u> <u>Marriage</u> <u>of</u> <u>William</u> <u>Ashe</u> (*) (also based on the
same named play, by Ward and Margaret Mayo, which was
derived from Ward's novel)
Metro Pictures Corp., 1921

Missing

<u>Missing</u> (*)
J. Stuart Blackton/Famous Players-Lasky Corp.--Parmount
Pictures Corp., 1918

Ward, (Mrs.) Humphrey (Mary Augusta) and Margaret Mayo (also see
the entry above)

The Marriage of William Ashe (P)

<u>The</u> <u>Marriage</u> <u>of</u> <u>William</u> <u>Ashe</u> (*) (also based on the
novel <u>The</u> <u>Marriage</u> <u>of</u> <u>William</u> <u>Ashe</u>, by Mrs. Humphrey
Ward, from which the play was derived)
Metro Pictures Corp., 1921

Ward, Mary Jane

The Snake Pit

<u>The</u> <u>Snake</u> <u>Pit</u>
Twentieth Century-Fox Film Corp., 1948

Ward-Thomas, Evelyn Bridget Patricia Stephens (see Evelyn Anthony)

Warde, Estrella

Cherokee Rose (S)

> The Fighting Hombre (*)
> Bob Custer Prod./Film Booking Office of America, 1927

Warde, Shirley and Vivian Cosby and Harry Wagstaff

Trick for Trick (P)

> Trick for Trick
> Fox Film Corp., 1933

Warden, Florence
(pseud. of Florence Alice Price James)

The Dazzling Miss Davison

> The Dazzling Miss Davison (*)
> Frank Powell Prod. Corp./Mutual Film Corp.-a Mutual
> Star Prod., 1917

The House on the Marsh

> The House on the Marsh (*) (G. B.)
> London Films/Jury's Imperial Pictures, 1920

Warner, Anne [Anne Warner French]

The Rejuvenation of Aunt Mary (P)

> The Rejuvenation of Aunt Mary (*)
> Klaw and Erlanger-Biograph Co./General Film Co., 1914

> The Rejuvenation of Aunt Mary (*)
> Metro Picture Corp./Producers Dist. Corp., 1927

Warren, Maude Radford

The House of Youth

> The House of Youth (*)
> Regal Films International/Producers Dist. Corp., 1924

The Road Through the Dark (S)

> The Road Through the Dark (*)
> Clara Kimball Young Film Corp./Select Pictures Corp.,
> 1918

Watkins, Mary T.

>	**Stolen Thunder** (S)

>>	<u>Oh, for a Man!</u>
>>	Fox Film Corp., 1930

Watkins, Maurine

>	**Chicago** (P)

>>	<u>Chicago</u> (*)
>>	De Mille/Pathe Exchange, Inc., 1928

>>	<u>Roxie Hart</u>
>>	Twentieth Century-Fox Film Corp., 1942

>	**The Tinsel Girl** (P)

>>	<u>The Strange Love of Molly Louvain</u>
>>	First National-Warner Brothers Pictures, Inc., 1932

Watts, Mary S.

>	**The Rise of Jennie Cushing**

>>	<u>The Rise of Jennie Cushing</u> (*)
>>	Artcraft Pictures Corp., 1917

Wayne, Priscilla
	(pseud. of Bessie Toulouse Sprague)

>	**Love Past Thirty**

>>	<u>Love Past Thirty</u>
>>	Monarch Film Corp., 1934

>	**Marriage on Approval**

>>	<u>Marriage on Approval</u>
>>	Freuler Film Associates/Monarch Film Corp., 1934

Webb, Mary

>	**Gone to Earth**

>>	<u>Gone to Earth</u> (G. B.)
>>	London Films-British Lion-Vanguard/British Lion, 1950

Webling, Peggy

Boundary House

> Boundary House (*) (G. B.)
> Hepworth/Moss, 1918

Frankenstein (P)

> Frankenstein (also based on the novel Frankenstein:
> Or, the Modern Prometheus, by Mary Shelley, from which
> the play was derived)
> Universal Motion Pictures Co., 1931

Webster, Alice Jane Chandler (see Jean Webster)

Webster, Jean
     (pseud. of Alice Jane Chandler Webster)

Daddy Long Legs (N/P)

> Daddy-Long-Legs (*)
> Mary Pickford/First National, 1919

> Daddy Long Legs
> Fox Pictures Corp., 1931

> Curly Top
> Twentieth Century-Fox Film Corp., 1935

> Daddy Long Legs
> Twentieth Century-Fox Film Corp., 1955

Weiman, Rita (also see the two entries below)

The Acquittal (P)

> The Acquittal (*)
> Universal Motion Pictures Co., 1923

Curtain (S)

> Curtain (*)
> Katharine MacDonald Pictures Corp./First National, 1920

Footlights (S)

> Footlights (*)
> Famous Players-Lasky Corp./Paramount Pictures Corp.,
> 1921

> The Spotlight (*)
> Paramount Famous Lasky Corp., 1927

Madame Peacock (S)

> Madame Peacock (*)
> The Nazimova Prod./Metro Pictures Corp., 1920

On Your Back (S)

> On Your Back
> Fox Film Corp., 1930

One Man's Secret (S)

> Possessed
> Warner Brothers Pictures, Inc., 1947

The Stage Door (S)

> After the Show (*)
> Famous Players-Lasky Corp./Paramount Pictures Corp.,
> 1921

To Whom it May Concern (S)

> The Social Code (*)
> Metro Pictures Corp., 1923

Upstage (S)

> Rouged Lips (*)
> Metro Pictures Corp., 1923

The Witness Chair (S)

> The Witness Chair
> RKO Radio Pictures, Inc., 1936

Weiman, Rita and Alice Leal Pollock (also see the entry above and
the entry below)

The Co-Respondent (P)

> The Co-Respondent (*)
> Advanced Motion Pictures/Jewel Prod., Inc., 1917
>
> The Whispered Name (*)
> Universal Motion Pictures Co., 1924

Weiman, Rita and Anthony Abbot, Samuel Hopkins Adams, John
Erskine, Rupert Hughes, and S. S. Van Dine (also see the two
entries above)

The President's Mystery

> The President's Mystery
> Republic Pictures Corp., 1936

Weisman, Mary-Lou

Intensive Care (NF)

> Intensive Care (TVM)
> Inc. Television Co. Prod.-Blue Andre Prod./National
> Broadcasting Co., 1985

Welles, Jennifer

The Memoirs of Jennifer Welles (NF)

> Inside Jennifer Welles
> Evart Releasing, 1977

Wells, Carolyn (also see the entry below)

Vicky Van

> The Woman Next Door (*)
> Famous Players-Lasky Corp./Famous Players-Lasky Corp.--
> Paramount Pictures Corp., 1919

Wells, Carolyn and Bernice Brown, Elsie Janis, Sophie Kerr, and
Dorothy Parker and Robert Gordon Anderson, Louis Bromfield,
George Agnew Chamberlain, Frank Craven, Rube Goldberg,
Wallace Irwin, George Barr McCutcheon, Meade Minnigerode,
Gerald Mygatt, George Palmer Putnam, Kermit Roosevelt,
Edward Streeter, John V. A. Weaver, H. C. Witwer, and
Alexander Woollcott (also see the entry above)

Bobbed Hair

> Bobbed Hair (*)
> Warner Brothers Pictures, Inc., 1925

Wells, Charlotte E. and Dorothy Donnelly

The Riddle: Woman (P, based on a foreign language play, by
Carl Jacobi)

> The Riddle: Woman (*)
> Associated Exhibitors, Inc./Pathe Exchange, Inc., 1920

353

Wells, Emma B. C. Wells and Gladys Hurlbut

    By Your Leave (P)

        By Your Leave
        RKO Radio Pictures, Inc., 1934

Wells, Leila Burton

    The Naked Truth (S)

        The Perfect Lover (*)
        Selznick Pictures Corp./Select Pictures Corp., 1919

West, Jessamyn

    Except for Me and Thee

        Friendly Persuasion (TVM) (also based on the novel
        Friendly Persuasion, by West)
        International Television Prod.-Allied Artists Film
        Corp./American Broadcasting Co., 1975

    Friendly Persuasion

        Friendly Persuasion
        William Wilder Prod./United Artists Film Corp., 1956

        Friendly Persuasion (TVM) (also based on the novel
        Except for Me and Thee, by West)
        International Television Prod./Allied Artists Film
        Corp./American Broadcasting Co., 1975

West, Mae

    Diamond Lil (P)

        She Done Him Wrong
        Paramount Pictures Corp., 1933

    Frisco Kate (P)

        Klondike Annie (also based on the unpublished story
        "Halleluyah I'm a Saint," by Marion Morgan, and the
        short story "Lulu was a Lady," by Frank Mitchell Dazey)
        Paramount Pictures Corp., 1936

    Sextette (P)

        Sextette
        Briggs and Sullivan/Crown International, 1978

West, Rebecca
    (pseud. of Cecily Isabel Fairfield)

    Abiding Vision (S)

        <u>A</u> <u>Life</u> <u>of</u> <u>Her</u> <u>Own</u>
        Metro-Goldwyn-Mayer, Inc., 1950

    Return of the Soldier

        <u>Return</u> <u>of</u> <u>the</u> <u>Soldier</u> (G. B.)
        Skreba Films-Cooper/United Kingdom Photoplays, 1983

Westman, Lolita Ann (also see the entry below)

    Lawless Honeymoon (S)

        <u>The</u> <u>Perfect</u> <u>Clue</u>
        Majestic Pictures Corp., 1935

Westman, Lolita Ann and H. H. Van Loan (also see the entry above)

    Cooking Her Goose (P)

        <u>The</u> <u>Runaway</u> <u>Bride</u>
        RKO Radio Pictures, Inc., 1930

Weston, Carolyn

    Poor, Poor Ophelia

        <u>The</u> <u>Streets</u> <u>of</u> <u>San</u> <u>Francisco</u> (TVM)
        Quinn Martin Prod.-Warner Brothers Television/American
        Broadcasting Co., 1972

Wharton, Edith (also see the entry below)

    The Age of Innocence

        <u>The</u> <u>Age</u> <u>of</u> <u>Innocence</u> (*)
        Warner Brothers Pictures, Inc., 1924

        <u>Age</u> <u>of</u> <u>Innocence</u> (also based on the same named play, by
        Margaret Ayer Barnes, which was derived from Wharton's
        novel)
        RKO Radio Pictures, Inc., 1934

    Bread Upon the Waters

        <u>Strange</u> <u>Wives</u>

Universal Motion Pictures Co., 1934

The Children

> Marriage <u>Playground</u>
> Paramount Famous Lasky Corp., 1929

The Glimpses of the Moon

> <u>The</u> <u>Glimpses</u> <u>of</u> <u>the</u> <u>Moon</u> (*)
> Famous Players-Lasky Corp./Paramount Pictures Corp.,
> 1923

The House of Mirth

> <u>The</u> <u>House</u> <u>of</u> <u>Mirth</u> (*) (also based on the same named
> play, by Wharton and Clyde Fitch, which was derived
> from the novel)
> Metro Pictures Corp., 1918

The Old Maid (S)

> <u>The</u> <u>Old</u> <u>Maid</u> (also based on the same named play, by Zoe
> Adkins, which was derived from Wharton's novelette)
> First National-Warner Brothers Pictures, Inc., 1939

Wharton, Edith and Clyde Fitch (also see the entry above)

The House of Mirth (P)

> <u>The</u> <u>House</u> <u>of</u> <u>Mirth</u> (*) (also based on the same named
> novel, by Wharton, from which the play was derived)
> Metro Pictures Corp., Inc./Metro Pictures Corp.--All-
> Star Series, 1918

Wherry, Edith

**The Red Lantern: Being the Story of the Goddess of the Red
Lantern Light**

> <u>The</u> <u>Red</u> <u>Lantern</u> (*)
> The Nazimova Prod.-Metro Pictures Corp./Metro Pictures
> Corp., 1919

Whipple, Dorothy

The Great Mr. Knight

> <u>They</u> <u>Knew</u> <u>Mr.</u> <u>Knight</u> (G. B.)
> Independent Producers-Gregory Hake and Walker
> Prod./General Film Dist., Inc., 1945

They were Sisters

>They were Sisters (G. B.)
>Gainsborough Prod./General Film Dist., Inc., 1945

White, Ethel Lina

Her Heart in Her Throat

>The Unseen
>Paramount Pictures Corp., 1945

Some Must Watch

>The Spiral Staircase
>RKO Radio Pictures, Inc.-Vanguard/RKO Radio Pictures,
>Inc., 1945

>The Spiral Staircase (G. B.)
>Raven/Columbia Pictures Corp.-Warner Brothers Pictures,
>Inc., 1975

The Wheel Spins

>The Lady Vanishes (G. B.)
>Gainsborough Prod./Metro-Goldwyn-Mayer, Inc., 1938

>The Lady Vanishes (G. B.)
>Hammer Films/J. Arthur Rank Film Dist., 1979

White, Grace Miller

From the Valley of the Missing

>From the Valley of the Missing (*)
>Fox Film Corp., 1915

Judy of Rogue's Harbour

>Judy of Rogue's Harbour (*)
>Realart Pictures Corp., 1920

Rose O' Paradise

>Rose O' Paradise (*)
>Paralta Plays, Inc./W. W. Hodkinson Corp.-General Film
>Co., 1918

The Secret of the Storm Country

>The Secret of the Storm Country (*)
>Norma Talmadge Film Corp./Select Pictures Corp., 1917

Tess of the Storm Country

> Tess of the Storm Country (*)
> Famous Players Film Co./State Rights, 1914

> Tess of the Storm Country (*)
> Mary Pickford/United Artists Film Corp., 1922

> Tess of the Storm Country
> Fox Film Corp., 1932

> Tess of the Storm Country
> Twentieth Century-Fox Film Corp., 1960

White, Maud Reeves

Sue of the South

> Sue of the South (*)
> Bluebird Photoplays, Inc., 1919

White, Nelia Gardner

The Little Horse (S)

> Sentimental Journey
> Twentieth Century-Fox Film Corp., 1946

> The Gift of Love
> Twentieth Century-Fox Film Corp., 1958

> Sentimental Journey (TVM)
> Lucille Ball Prod.--Smith-Richmond Prod./Columbia
> Broadcasting System, 1984

Whitehouse, Esther

The Call of the East

> The Call of the East (*) (G. B.)
> International Artists/Curry, 1922

Widdemer, Margaret

The Rose-Garden Husband

> A Wife on Trial (*)
> Universal Film Manufacturing Co.-A Butterfly
> Picture/Universal Film Manufacturing Co., 1917

Why Not?

        The Dream Lady (*)
        Bluebird Photoplays, Inc., 1918

   The Wishing Ring Man

        The Wishing Ring Man (*)
        Vitagraph Co. of America, 1919

Wier, Ester

   The Loner

        The Young Loner (TVM)
        Walt Disney Prod./National Broadcasting Co., 1968

Wiggin, Kate Douglas (also see the two entries below)

   The Bird's Christmas Carol (S)

        A Bit O' Heaven (*)
        Frieder Film Corp., 1917

   Mother Carey's Chickens

        Mother Carey's Chickens (also based on the same named
        play, by Wiggins and Rachel Crothers, which is derived
        from Wiggen's novel)
        RKO Radio Pictures, Inc., 1938

        Summer Magic
        Walt Disney Prod./Buena Vista Dist. Co., 1963

   Rebecca of Sunnybrook Farm

        Rebecca of Sunnybrook Farm (*) (also based on the play,
        Rebecca of Sunnybrook Farm, by Wiggin and Charlotte
        Thompson, which was derived from Wiggin's novel)
        Artcraft Pictures Corp./Paramount Pictures Corp., 1917

        Rebecca of Sunnybrook Farm
        Fox Film Corp., 1932

        Rebecca of Sunnybrook Farm
        Twentieth Century-Fox Film Corp., 1938

   Rose O' the River

        Rose of the River (*)
        Paramount Pictures Corp., 1919

   Timothy's Quest

                              359

Timothy's Quest (*)
Dirigo Films/American Releasing Corp., 1922

Timothy's Quest
Paramount Pictures Corp., 1936

Wiggin, Kate Douglas and Rachel Crothers (also see the entry
     above and the entry below)

Mother Carey's Chickens (P)

Mother Carey's Chickens (also based on the same named
novel, by Wiggin, from which the play was derived)
RKO Radio Pictures, Inc., 1938

Wiggin, Kate Douglas and Charlotte Thompson (also see the two
     entries above)

Rebecca of Sunnybrook Farm (P)

Rebecca of Sunnybrook Farm (*) (also based on the samed
named novel, by Wiggin, from which the play was
derived)
Mary Pickford/Artcraft Pictures Corp., 1917

Wilcox, Ella Wheeler

The Price He Paid (Po)

The Price He Paid (*)
Humanology Film Prod. Co./United Film Service, 1914

Reveries of a Station House (Po)

The Beautiful Lie (*)
Metro Pictures Corp.-Rolfe Photoplays, Inc./Metro
Pictures Corp., 1917

Wilder, Laura Ingalls

The Little House on the Prairie (NF)

The Little House on the Prairie (TVM)
NBC, 1974

Wilder, Margaret Applegate

Together

Since You Went Away

United Artists' Film Corp., 1944

Wilder, Sally and Robert Wilder

    Flamingo Road (P)

        Flamingo Road (also based on the same named novel, by
        Robert Wilder, from which the play was derived)
        Warner Brothers Pictures, Inc., 1949

Williams, Ella Gwendolen Rees (see Jean Rhys)

Williams, Margaret and Hugh Williams

    The Grass is Greener (P)

        The Grass is Greener (G. B.)
        Grandon/Universal International Motion Pictures, 1960

Williams, Mona

    May the Best Man Win (S)

        Woman's World
        Twentieth Century Fox Film Corp., 1954

Williams, Rebecca

    Father was a Handful (NF)

        The Vanishing Virginian
        Metro-Goldwyn-Mayer, Inc., 1941

Williamson, Alice Muriel (also see Dona Teresa De Savallo and the
entry below)

    Honeymoon Hate (S)

        Honeymoon Hate (*)
        Paramount Famous Lasky Corp., 1927

    The Life Mask

        The Life Mask (*)
        Petrova Picture Co./First National, 1918

    The Woman Who Dared

The Woman Who Dared (*)
California Motion Picture Corp./State Rights--Motional
Picture Corp.--Better-Than-Program Dist. Co.--Ultra
Pictures Corp., 1916

Williamson, Alice Muriel and Charles Norris Williamson (also see
    Dona Teresa de Savallo and the entry above)

The Demon

The Demon (*)
Metro Pictures Corp., 1918

The Guests of Hercules

Passion's Playground (*)
Katherine MacDonald Pictures Corp./First National-
Attractions Dist. Corp., 1920

The Lion's Mouse

The Lion's Mouse (*) (G. B.)
Granger-Binger, 1922

Lord John in New York (S)

Lord John in New York (*)
Universal Film Manufacturing Co./Universal Film
Manufacturing Co.-Gold Seal, 1915

Lord Loveland Discovers America

Lord Loveland Discovers America (*)
American Film Co./Mutual Film Corp.--Mutual
Masterpictures De Luxe Edition, 1916

The Second Latchkey

My Lady's Latchkey (*)
Katherine MacDonald Pictures Corp./Associated First
National, 1921

The Shop Girl

The Shop Girl (*)
Vitagraph Co. of America-a Blue Ribbon Feature/Greater
Vitagraph, 1916

Williamson, Maud and Andrew Soutar

The Pruning Knife (P)

Was She Justified? (*) (G. B.)
Walter West/Butcher's Film Service, 1922

Willis, Mary and Jack Willis

    But There are Always Miracles

        Some Kind of Miracle (TVM)
        Lorimar Prod./Columbia Broadcasting System, 1979

Willoughby, Florence Barrett

    Spawn of the North

        Spawn of the North
        Paramount Pictures Corp., 1938

        Alaska Seas
        Paramount Pictures Corp., 1953

Willson, Dixie

    God Gave me Twenty Cents (S)

        God Gave me Twenty Cents (*)
        Famous Players-Lasky Corp./Paramount Pictures Corp.,
        1926

        Ebb Tide (G. B.)
        Paramount Pictures Corp. British, 1932

    Help Yourself to Hay (S)

        Three Ring Marriage (*)
        First National, 1928

    Here Y'Are Brother (S)

        An Affair of the Follies (*)
        Al Rockett Prod./First National, 1927

Wilson, Augusta Jane Evans
    (also see August J. Evans)

    At the Mercy of Tiberius

        God's Witness (*)
        Thanhouser Film Corp./Mutual Film Corp.-a Mutual
        Masterpiece, 1915

        At the Mercy of Tiberius (*) (G. B.)
        Samuelson Film Manufacturing Co./General Film Dist.,
        1920

Beulah

> *Beulah* (*)
> Balboa Amusement Prod. Co./Alliance Films Corp., 1915

Infelice

> *Infelice* (*) (G. B.)
> G. B. Samuelson/Moss, 1915

Wilson, Cherry

The Branded Sombrero (S)

> *The Branded Sombrero* (*)
> Fox Film Corp., 1928

Empty Saddles

> *Empty Saddles*
> Universal Motion Pictures Co., 1936

Starr of the Southwest

> *Sandflow*
> Universal Motion Pictures Co., 1937

Stormy

> *Stormy*
> Universal Motion Pictures Co., 1935

Wilson, Dorothy Clarke

The Prince of Egypt

> *The Ten Commandments* (also based on the novel *On Eagle's Wings* , by the Rev. G. E. Southon; the novel *Pillar of Fire*, by the Rev. J. H. Ingraham; and the ancient texts of Josephus, Eusebius, Philo, and The Midrash)
> Paramount Pictures Corp., 1956

Winch, Evelyn

The Girl in the Flat (S)

> *The Girl in the Flat* (G. B.)
> British and Dominions Film Corp./Paramount Pictures Corp. British, 1934

Winsor, Kathleen

Forever Amber

Forever Amber
Twentieth Century-Fox Film Corp., 1947

Winter, Louise

The Mad Dancer (S)

The Mad Dancer (*)
Jans, 1925

The Magnificent Jacala (S)

The Brazen Beauty (*)
Bluebird Photoplays, Inc., 1918

Princess Virtue

Princess Virtue (*)
Bluebird Photoplays, Inc., 1917

The Spite Bride

The Spite Bride (*)
Selznick Pictures Corp./Select Pictures Corp., 1919

Wolfe, Winifred (Harriet)

Ask any Girl

Ask any Girl
Euterpe Prod./Metro-Goldwyn-Mayer, Inc., 1959

If a Man Answers

If a Man Answers
Ross Hunter Prod./Universal International Motion
Pictures, 1962

Wolff, Maritta Martin

Night Shift

The Man I Love
Warner Brothers Pictures, Inc., 1946

Whistle Stop

Whistle Stop
United Artist's Film Corp., 1946

Wolff, Ruth

The Abdication (P)

The Abdication (G. B.)
Warner Brothers Pictures, Inc., 1974

Wolford, Shirley and Nelson Wolford

The Southern Blade

A Time for Killing
Sage Western Pictures/Columbia Pictures Corp., 1967

Wong, Mary Gilligan

Nun: a Memoir (NF)

Shattered Vows (TVM)
Bertinelli, Inc.-River City Prod./National Broadcasting
Co., 1984

Wood, Bari and Jack Greasland

Twins

Dead Ringers (Can.)
Mantle Clinic II/Twentieth Century Prod.-Fox Film
Corp., 1988

Wood, (Mrs.) Henry [Ellen Price Wood]

The Channings

The Channings (*) (G. B.)
Master Films/Butcher's Film Service, 1920

East Lynne (also see Mary Elizabeth Braddon)

East Lynne (*) (G. B.)
Barker/ Walturdaw, 1913

East Lynne (*) (Note: sources differ about whether
this film was based on Wood's novel or Braddon's play.)
Fox Film Corp, 1916

East Lynne (*)

Hugo Ballin Prod./W. W. Hodkinson Corp., 1921

East Lynne (*)
Fox Film Corp., 1925

Ex-Flame
Liberty Pictures Corp./Tiffany Pictures, 1930

Woodrow, Mrs. Wilson ([Nancy Mann Waddel] Woodrow)

The Black Pearl

The Black Pearl (*)
Trem Carr Prod./Rayart Pictures, 1928

Burned Evidence

Burned Evidence
Continental Pictures, 1929

The Hornet's Nest

The Hornet's Nest (*)
Vitagraph Co. of America, 1919

The Second Chance

Her Second Chance (*)
First National/Vitagraph Co. of America, 1926

Woods, Madeline

Scandal House

Slander House
Progressive Pictures Corp., 1938

Woolf, Virginia

To the Lighthouse

To the Lighthouse (TVM) (G. B.)
British Broadcasting Corp. TV, 1982

Wootten, Rosemary and Robert B. Hutton

I Hate you Cat! (S)

Terror of Sheba (G. B.)
Tyburn/Fanfare, 1974

Worker, Barbara and Dwight Worker

Escape (NF)

>> Escape (TVM)
>> Henry Jaffe Enterprises/Columbia Broadcasting System,
>> 1980

Wormser, Anne

The Baby's had a Hard Day (S)

>> West Point Widow
>> Paramount Pictures Corp., 1941

Wray, Fay and Sinclair Lewis

Angela is 22 (P)

>> This is the Life
>> Universal Motion Pictures Co., 1944

Wright, Anna Maria Rose (see Anna Perrott Rose)

Wuolijoki, Hella Helsinki (see Juhani Tervapaa)

Wylie, Ida Alexa Ross

The Daughter of Brahma

>> Shattered Idols (*)
>> J. L. Frothingham Prod./Associated First National, 1922

A Feather in Her Hat

>> Feather in Her Hat
>> Columbia Productions Ltd., 1935

The Gay Banditti (aka: **The Young in Heart**)

>> Young in Heart
>> Selznick International Pictures/United Artists Film
>> Corp., 1938

Grandma Bernle Learns Her Letters (S)

>> Four Sons (*)
>> Fox Film Corp., 1928

Four Sons

 Twentieth Century-Fox Film Corp., 1940

The Hermit Doctor of Gaya

 Stronger Than Death (*)
 The Nazimova Prod./Metro Pictures Corp., 1920

The Inheritors (S)

 Gaiety Girl (*)
 Universal Motion Pictures Co., 1924

Jungle Law

 A Man Must Live (*)
 Famous Players-Lasky Corp./Paramount Pictures Corp.,
 1925

Keeper of the Flame

 Keeper of the Flame
 Metro-Goldwyn-Mayer, Inc., 1942

Melia No-Good (S)

 For Valour (*)
 Triangle Film Corp./Triangle Dist. Corp., 1917

The Paupers of Portman Square

 The Grass Orphan (*) (G. B.)
 Ideal, 1922

Pilgrimage (S)

 Pilgrimage
 Fox Film Corp., 1933

Puritan at Large

 The Road to Reno
 Universal Motion Pictures Co., 1938

The Red Mirage

 The Unknown (*)
 Jesse L. Lasky Feature Play Co./Paramount Pictures
 Corp., 1915

 The Foreign Legion (*)
 Universal Motion Pictures Co., 1928

The Temple of Dawn

369

The Price of Redemption (*)
Metro Pictures Corp., 1920

Vivacious Lady (S)

Vivacious Lady
RKO Radio Pictures, Inc., 1938

Why Should I Cry (S)

Torch Song
Metro-Goldwyn-Mayer, Inc., 1953

Widow's Evening (S)

Evenings for Sale
Paramount Pictures Corp., 1932

The Wonderful Story

The Wonderful Story (G. B.)
Fogwell/Sterling, 1932

Young Nowheres (S)

Young Nowheres
First National, 1929

Some Day (G. B.)
Warner Brothers Pictures, Inc.-First National/Warner
Brothers Pictures, Inc., 1935

That Man's Here Again
First National-Warner Brothers Pictures, Inc., 1937

Wylie, Lauri, Franz Arnold, Ernest Bach and Arthur Wimperis

A Warm Corner (P)

A Warm Corner (G. B.)
Gainsborough Prod./Ideal, 1930

Wynette, Tammy and Joan Dew

Stand by Your Man (NF)

Stand by Your Man (TVM)
Robert Papazian Prod./JNP Associates/Peter Gruber
Prod.-Jon Peters Prod./Columbia Broadcasting System,
1981

Wynn, May

The Education of Nicky

> The Education of Nicky (*) (G. B.)
> Harma-Associated Exhibitors, Inc./Walturdraw, 1921

The Little Mother

> The Little Mother (*) (G. B.)
> Ideal, 1922

A Run for his Money

> Big Money (*) (G. B.)
> Harma, 1918

Wynne, Pamela
    (pseud. of Winfred Mary Scott)

Ann's an Idiot

> Dangerous Innocence (*)
> Universal Motion Pictures Co., 1925

A Little Flat in the Temple

> Devotion
> RKO Radio Pictures, Inc., 1931

Wyse, Lois

Kiss, Inc.

> The Million Dollar Face (TVM)
> Nephi-Hamner Prod./National Broadcasting Co., 1981

Xantippe
    (believed to be the pseud. of Edith Meiser)

    Death Catches Up with Mr. Kluck

        <u>Danger</u> <u>on</u> <u>the</u> <u>Air</u>
        Universal Motion Pictures Co., 1938

Yates, Elizabeth

    Skeezer, Dog with a Mission

        <u>Skeezer</u> (TVM)
        Margie-Lee Enterprises--Blue Marble Co.--Inc.
        Television Co. Prod./National Broadcasting Co., 1982

Yezierska, Anzia

    Hungry Hearts (RS)

        <u>Hungry</u> <u>Hearts</u> (*)
        Goldwyn Pictures Corp., 1922

    Salome of the Tenements

        <u>Salome</u> <u>of</u> <u>the</u> <u>Tenements</u> (*)
        Famous Players-Lasky Corp./Paramount Pictures Corp.,
        1925

York, Susannah

    In Search of Unicorns

        <u>Images</u> (Ire.)
        Lion's Gate-Hemdale/Columbia Pictures Corp., 1972

Young, Billie (see Penelope Ashe)

Young, Miriam

    Mother Wore Tights

        <u>Mother</u> <u>Wore</u> <u>Tights</u>
        Twentieth Century-Fox Film Corp., 1947

Young, Rida Johnson [Rida Johnson] (also see the three entries
    below)

    Captain Kidd, Jr. (P)

        <u>Captain</u> <u>Kidd,</u> <u>Jr.</u> (*)

Pickford/Famous Players-Lasky Corp.--Artcraft Pictures
Corp., 1919

Glorious Betsy (P)

Glorious Betsy
Warner Brothers Pictures, Inc., 1928

Hearts Divided
Cosmopolitan/First National-Warner Brothers Pictures,
Inc., 1936

Little Old New York; a Comedy in Four Acts (P)

Little Old New York (*)
Cosmopolitan Pictures/Goldwyn Dist. Corp.-Cosmopolitian
Dist. Corp., 1923

Little Old New York
Twentieth Century-Fox Film Corp., 1940

The Lottery Man (P)

The Lottery Man (*)
F. Ray Comstock/Unity Sales Corp., 1916

The Lottery Man (*)
Famous Players-Lasky Corp./Famous Players-Lasky Corp.--
Paramount Pictures Corp.--Artcraft Pictures Corp., 1919

The Story of Mother Machree (S, inspired by Young's song
"Mother Machree")

Mother Machree (*)
Fox Film Corp., 1928

Out of the Night

Hell Harbor
Inspiration Pictures/United Artists Film Corp., 1930

Young, Rida Johnson [Rida Johnson] and Gilbert P. Coleman (also
see the entry above and the two entries below)

Brown of Harvard (P/N)

Brown of Harvard (*)
Selig Polyscope Co.-Perfection Pictures/George Kleine
System, 1918

Brown of Harvard (*)
Metro-Goldwyn-Mayer, Inc., 1926

Young, Rida Johnson [Rida Johnson], Cyrus Wood, and Sigmund
    Romberg [music] (also see the two entries above and the
    entry below)

   Maytime (O)

        Maytime (*)
        B. P. Schulberg Prod./Preferred Pictures, 1923

        Maytime
        Metro-Goldwyn-Mayer, Inc., 1937

Young, Rida Johnson and Victor Herbert   (also see the three
    entries above)

   Naughty Marietta; a Comic Opera (O)

        Naughty Marietta
        Metro-Goldwyn-Mayer, Inc., 1935

Zaharias, Babe Didrickson

    This Life I've Led (NF)

        <u>Babe</u> (TVM)
        Norman Felton-Stanley Rubin Prod.--Metro-Goldwyn-Mayer
        Television/Columbia Broadcasting System, 1975

Ziegler, Isabelle Gibson

    Nine Days of Father Serra

        <u>Seven</u> <u>Cities</u> <u>of</u> <u>Gold</u>
        Twentieth Century-Fox Film Corp., 1955

INDEX TO FILM TITLES

377

378

379

381

382

387

393

395

396

398

401

405

410

413

415

417

419

424

INDEX OF LITERARY SOURCES

434

436

442

443

444

447

449

451

453

454

457

462

467

468

469

472

473

Bibliography

Alvarez, Max Joseph (comp.) <u>Index</u> <u>to</u> <u>Motion</u> <u>Pictures</u> <u>Reviewed</u> <u>by</u> <u>Variety,</u> <u>1907-1980</u> (Metuchen, N. J. and London: The Scarecrow Press, 1982)

The American Library Association (comp.) <u>The</u> <u>National</u> <u>Union</u> <u>Catalog:</u>   <u>Pre-1956</u> <u>Imprints</u>   (Chicago: Mansell Information/Publishing, Ltd., 1971)

Anonymous <u>The</u> <u>Cumulative</u> <u>Book</u> <u>Review</u> <u>Digest</u> (vols. 1 [1905] to 84 [1988]) (Minneapolis, Minn.; then N. Y.: The H. W. Wilson Co., 1905-1989)

Aros, Andrew A. (comp.) <u>A</u> <u>Title</u> <u>Guide</u> <u>to</u> <u>the</u> <u>Talkies,</u> <u>1964</u> <u>through</u> <u>1974</u> (Metuchen, N. J.: The Scarecrow Press, Inc., 1977)

Atkinson, Frank <u>Dictionary</u> <u>of</u> <u>Literary</u> <u>Pseudonyms,</u> <u>4th</u> <u>ed.</u> (London: Library Association Pub., Ltd., 1987)

Bogart, Gary L. (comp.) <u>Short</u> <u>Story</u> <u>Index:</u> <u>Supplement</u> <u>1974-1978</u> (N. Y.: H. W. Wilson Co., 1979)

Bordman, Gerald <u>American</u> <u>Musical</u> <u>Theatre:</u> <u>a</u> <u>Chronicle</u> (N. Y.: Oxford Univ. Press, 1978)

Bordman, Gerald <u>The</u> <u>Oxford</u> <u>Companion</u> <u>to</u> <u>American</u> <u>Theatre</u> (N. Y. and Oxford: Oxford University Press, 1984)

The British Library staff (comps.) <u>General</u> <u>Catalogue</u> <u>of</u> <u>Printed</u> <u>Books:</u> <u>Five-Year</u> <u>Supplement:</u> <u>1971-1975</u> (13 vols.) (London: British Museum Pub., Ltd., 1979)

British Museum staff (comps.) <u>British</u> <u>Museum</u> <u>General</u> <u>Catalogue</u> <u>of</u> <u>Printed</u> <u>Books</u> <u>to</u> <u>1955</u> (263 vols.) (London: The Trustees of the British Museum, 1966)

British Museum staff (comps.) <u>British</u> <u>Museum</u> <u>General</u> <u>Catalogue</u> <u>of</u> <u>Printed</u> <u>Books:</u> <u>Ten-Year</u> <u>Supplement:</u> <u>1956-1965</u> (50 vols.) (London: The Trustees of the British Museum, 1968)

British Museum staff (comps.) <u>British</u> <u>Museum</u> <u>General</u> <u>Catalogue</u> <u>of</u> <u>Printed</u> <u>Books:</u> <u>Five-Year</u> <u>Supplement:</u> <u>1966-1970</u> (26 vols.) (London: The Trustees of the British Museum, 1972)

Bronner, Edwin <u>The</u> <u>Encyclopedia</u> <u>of</u> <u>the</u> <u>American</u> <u>Theatre:</u> <u>1900-</u> <u>1975</u> (San Diego: A. S. Barnes & Co., Inc., 1980)

Brown, Les <u>The</u> <u>New</u> <u>York</u> <u>Times</u> <u>Encyclopedia</u> <u>of</u> <u>Television</u> (N. Y.: Times Books, 1977)

Clarens, Carlos <u>An</u> <u>Illustrated</u> <u>History</u> <u>of</u> <u>the</u> <u>Horror</u> <u>Film</u> (N. Y.: Capricorn Books, 1967)

Contemporary Authors: A Bio-Bibliographical Guide to Current
Authors and Their Works (126 vols.) (Detroit: Gale, 1967-1989)

Contemporary Authors: New Revision Series (28 vols.) (Detroit:
Gale, 1962-1990)

Cook, Dorothy E. and Isabel S. Monro (comps.) Short Story Index
(N. Y.: H. W. Wilson Co., 1953)

Cook, Dorothy E. and Estelle A. Fidell (comps.) Short Story
Index: Supplement 1950-1954 (N. Y.: H. W. Wilson Co., 1953)

Cook, Michael L. and Stephen T. Miller (comps.) Mystery,
Detective, and Espionage Fiction: a Checklist of Fiction in U.
S. Pulp Magazines, 1915-1974 (N. Y. and London: Garland Pub.,
Inc., 1988)

Copyright Office (comp.) Catalog of Copyright Entries: Motion
Pictures, 1912-1939 (Washington, D. C.: The Library of Congress,
1951)

Copyright Office (comp.) Catalog of Copyright Entries: Motion
Pictures, 1940-1949 (Washington, D. C.: The Library of Congress,
1953)

Copyright Office (comp.) Catalog of Copyright Entries: Motion
Pictures, 1950-1959 (Washington, D. C.: The Library of
Congress, 1960)

Copyright Office (comp.) Catalog of Copyright Entries: Motion
Pictures, 1960-1969 (Washington, D. C.: The Library of
Congress, 1971)

Coven, Brenda (comp.) American Women Dramatists of the Twentieth
Century: a Bibliography (Metuchen, N. J. and London: The
Scarecrow Press, Inc., 1982)

The Cumulative Book Review Digest (Vols. 1 [1905] to 84 [1988])
(Minneapolis, Minn.; then N. Y.: H. W. Wilson Co., 1905-1989)

Cushing, Helen Grant and Adah V. Morris (eds.) Nineteenth Century
Readers' Guide to Periodical Literature: 1890-1899 (N. Y.: H.
W. Wilson Co., 1944)

Dimmitt, Richard B. (comp.) A Title Guide to the Talkies, 1929
through 1963 (Metuchen, N. J.: The Scarecrow Press, Inc., 1965)

Eames, John Douglas The Paramount Story (N. Y.: Crown, 1985)

Eames, John Douglas The MGM Story, The Complete History of
Fifty-Seven Roaring Years (N. Y.: Crown, 1985)

Emmens, Carol A. (comp.) Short Stories on Film and Video, 2nd
ed. (Littleton, Col.: Libraries Unlimited, 1985)

477

Enser, A. G. S. (comp.) <u>Filmed Books and Plays: a List of Books and Plays from which Films have been Made, 1928-1986</u> (Gower Publishing Co.: Brookfield, Vt. and Aldershot, Hampshire, Eng., 1987)

Fidell, Estelle (comp.) <u>Play Index: 1961-1967</u> (N. Y.: H. W. Wilson Co., 1968)

Fidell, Estelle (comp.) <u>Play Index: 1968-1972</u> (N. Y.: H. W. Wilson Co., 1973)

Fidell, Estelle (comp.) <u>Play Index: 1973-1977</u> (N. Y.: H. W. Wilson Co., 1978)

Fidell, Estelle (comp.) <u>Short Story Index: Supplement 1959-1963</u> (N. Y.: H. W. Wilson Co., 1965)

Fidell, Estelle (comp.) <u>Short Story Index: Supplement 1964-1968</u> (N. Y.: H. W. Wilson Co., 1969)

Fidell, Estelle (comp.) <u>Short Story Index: Supplement 1969-1973</u> (N. Y. : H. W. Wilson Co., 1979)

Fidell, Estelle and Dorothy Margaret Peake (comps.) <u>Play Index: 1953-1960</u> (N. Y.: H. W. Wilson Co., 1963)

Fidell, Estelle and Esther V. Flory (comps.) <u>Short Story Index: Supplement 1955-1958</u> (N. Y.: H. W. Wilson Co., 1956)

Firkins, Ina Ten Eyck (comp.) <u>Index to Plays: 1800-1926</u> (N. Y.: H. W. Wilson Co., 1927)

Firkins, Ina Ten Eyck (comp.) <u>Index to Plays: Supplement</u> (N. Y.: H. W. Wilson Co., 1935)

Firkins, Ina Ten Eyck (comp.) <u>Index to Short Stories, 2nd. and enlarged ed.</u> (N. Y.: H. W. Wilson Co., 1923)

Firkins, Ina Ten Eyck (comp.) <u>Index to Short Stories Supplement</u> (N. Y.: H. W. Wilson Co., 1929)

Firkins, Ina Ten Eyck (comp.) <u>Index to Short Stories, 2nd Supplement</u> (N. Y.: H. W. Wilson Co., 1929

Fisher, Kim N. <u>On the Screen: a Film, Television, and Video Research Guide</u> (Littleton, Col.: Libraries Unlimited, Inc., 1986)

Gifford, Denis (comp.) <u>The British Film Catalogue: 1895-1985: A Reference Guide</u> (N. Y. and Oxford: Facts On File Publications, 1987)

Halliwell, Leslie <u>Halliwell's Film Guide: Fourth ed.</u> (N. Y.: Charles Scribner's Sons, 1983)

Hannigan, Francis J. (comp.) The Standard Index of Short Stories: 1900-1914 (Boston: Small, Maynard & Co. Pub., 1918)

Hanson, Patricia King (ed.) The American Film Institute Catalog of Motion Pictures Produced in the United States: Feature Films: 1911-1920 (Berkeley and Los Angeles, Cal. and London: Univ. of Cal. Press, 1988)

Hardy, Phil The Encyclopedia of Horror Movies (N. Y.: Harper and Row Pub., 1986)

Holmes, Harvey (comp.) The New York Times Obituaries Index: 1969-1978 (N. Y.: The New York Times Co., 1980)

Hubin, Allen J. (comp.) Crime Fiction, 1749-1980: A Comprehensive Bibliography (N. Y. and London: Garland Pub., Inc., 1984)

Krafsur, Richard P. (ed.) The American Film Institute Catalog of Motion Pictures: Feature Films: 1961-1970 (N. Y. and London: R. R. Bowker Co., 1976)

Langman, Larry (comp.) Writers on the American Screen: A Guide to Film Adaptations of American and Foreign Literary Works (N. Y.: Garland Pub., Inc., 1976)

Leonard, William Torbert Theatre: Stage to Screen to Television (2 Vols.) (Metuchen, N. J. and London: The Scarecrow Press, Inc., 1981)

Library of Congress staff (eds.) The National Union Catalog: Pre-1956 Imprints (754 vols.) (London: Mansell Pub., 1981)

Library of Congress staff (eds.) The National Union Catalog: 1968-1972 (104 vols.) (Ann Arbor, Mich.: J. W. Edwards Pub., Inc., 1973)

Library of Congress staff (eds.) National Union Catalog: 1973-1977 (135 vols.) (Totowa, N. J.: Rowman and Littlefield, 1978)

Logasa, Hannah (comp.) Index to One-Act Plays: Fifth Supplement: 1958-1964 (Boston: F. W. Faxon Co., 1966)

Logasa, Hannah (comp.) Index to One-Act Plays: Fourth Supplement: 1948-1957 (Boston: F. W. Faxon Co., 1958)

Logasa, Hannah (comp.) Index to One-Act Plays: Second Supplement: 1932-1940 (Boston: F. W. Faxon Co., 1941)

Logasa, Hannah (comp.) Index to One-Act Plays: Third Supplement: 1941-1948 (Boston: F. W. Faxon Co., 1950)

Logasa, Hannah and Winifred Ver Nooy (comps.) An Index to One-Act Plays (Boston: F. W. Faxon Co., 1924)

Logasa, Hannah and Winifred Ver Nooy (comps.) Index to One-Act
Plays: Supplement: 1924-1931 (Boston: F. W. Faxon Co., 1932)

Mainiero, Lynn (ed.) American Women Writers, Vols. 1-4 (N. Y.:
Frederick Ungar Pub. Co., 1979-1982)

Maltin, Leonard Leonard Maltin's TV Movies and Video Guide, 1990
ed. (N. Y.: New American Library, 1989)

Marshall, Alice Kahler (comp.) Pen Names of Women Writers: From
1600 to the Present (Camp Hill, Penn.: The Alice Marshall
Collection, 1985)

McGill, Raymond D. (ed.) Notable Names in the American Theatre
(Clifton, N. J.: James T. White and Co., 1976)

Munden, Kenneth W. (ed.) The American Film Institute Catalog of
Motion Pictures Produced in the United States: Feature Films:
1921-1930 (N. Y. and London: R. R. Bowker Co., 1971)

Nash, Jay Robert and Stanley Ralph Ross The Motion Picture Guide
(10 vols.) (Chicago: Cinebooks, Inc., 1985-1986)

Nash, Jay Robert and Stanley Ralph Ross The Motion Picture
Guide: 1986 Annual (Chicago: Cinebooks, Inc., 1987)

Nash, Jay Robert and Stanley Ralph Ross The Motion Picture
Guide: 1987 Annual (Chicago: Cinebooks, Inc., 1987)

Nash, Jay Robert and Stanley Ralph Ross The Motion Picture
Guide: 1988 Annual (Chicago: Cinebooks, Inc., 1987)

Nash, Jay Robert and Stanley Ralph Ross The Motion Picture Guide:
1989 Annual (Chicago: Cinebooks, Inc., 1988)

The New York Times' staff (comps.) The New York Times Film
Reviews: 1913-1968, Vol. 6 Appendix Index (N. Y.: The New York
Times and Arno Press, 1971)

The New York Times' staff (comps.) The New York Times Index [1984
to 1986] (5 vols.) (N. Y.: The New York Times Co., 1985-1989)

O'Brien, Edward J. (ed.) The Best Short Stories of 1915 and the
Yearbook of the American Short Story (Boston: Small, Maynard &
Co. Pub., 1916)

O'Brien, Edward J. (ed.) The Best Short Stories of 1916 and the
Yearbook of the American Short Story (Boston: Small, Maynard &
Co. Pub., 1917)

O'Brien, Edward J. (ed.) The Best Short Stories of 1917 and the
Yearbook of the American Short Story (Boston: Small, Maynard &
Co. Pub., 1918)

O'Brien, Edward J. (ed.) The Best Short Stories of 1918 and the

Yearbook of the American Short Story (Boston: Small, Maynard &
Co. Pub., 1919)

O'Brien, Edward J. (ed.) The Best Short Stories of 1919 and the
Yearbook of the American Short Story (Boston: Small, Maynard &
Co. Pub., 1920)

O'Brien, Edward J. (ed.) The Best Short Stories of 1920 and the
Yearbook of the American Short Story (Boston: Small, Maynard &
Co. Pub., 1921)

O'Brien, Edward J. (ed.) The Best Short Stories of 1921 and the
Yearbook of the American Short Story (Boston: Small, Maynard &
Co. Pub., 1922)

O'Brien, Edward J. (ed.) The Best Short Stories of 1922 and the
Yearbook of the American Short Story (Boston: Small, Maynard &
Co. Pub., 1923)

O'Brien, Edward J. (ed.) The Best Short Stories of 1923 and the
Yearbook of the American Short Story (Boston: Small, Maynard &
Co. Pub., 1924)

O'Brien, Edward J. (ed.) The Best Short Stories of 1923 and the
Yearbook of the American Short Story (Boston: Small, Maynard &
Co. Pub., 1925)

Online Computer Library Center (Dublin, Ohio: Online Computer
Library Center, Inc., 1990)

Ottoson, Robert L. American International Pictures: a
Filmography (N. Y. and London: Garland Pub., Inc., 1985)

Reilly, John M. (ed.) Twentieth-Century Crime and Mystery
Writers (N. Y.: St. Martin's Press, 1980)

Richardson, Larry L. Cinema Sources: a Guide to the Film
Reference Collection of Memorial Library, University of
Wisconsin-Madison (Madison, Wisc.: The Univ. of Wisc.-Madison
Libraries, 1979)

Riley, Dick and Pam McAllister (eds.) The New Bedside, Bathtub,
and Armchair Companion to Agatha Christie, 2nd ed. (N. Y.: The
Ungar Pub. Co., 1986)

Robbins, Leonard A. (comp.) The Pulp Magazine Index: First
Series (3 vols.) (Mercer Island, Wash.: Starmont House, Inc.,
1989)

Robins, Leonard A. (comp.) The Pulp Magazine Index: Second
Series (Mercer Island, Wash.: Starmont House, Inc., 1989)

Rothman, John and Byron A. Falk, Jr. (comps.) The New York Times
Obituaries Index: 1858-1968 (N. Y.: The New York Times Co.,
1970)

R. R. Bowker Company's Department of Bibliography in collaboration with the publications Systems Department (comps.) Fiction: 1876-1983: a Bibliography of United States Editions (N. Y. and London: R. R. Bowker Co., 1983)

Sharp, Harold S. Handbook of Pseudonyms and Personal Nicknames (2 vols.) (Metuchen, N. J.: The Scarecrow Press, Inc., 1972)

Sherman, Robert L. (comp.) Drama Cyclopedia: a Bibliography of Plays and Players (Chicago: Robert L. Sherman, 1944)

Shirley, Graham and Brian Adams Australian Cinema: The First Eighty Years (Australia, Angus and Robertson Pub. in Association with Currency Press, 1983)

Silver, Alain and Elizabeth Ward (eds.) Film Noir (Woodstock, N. Y.: The Overlook Press, 1979)

Stanley, John The Creature Features Movie Guide, rev. ed. (N. Y.: Warner Books, 1984)

Steinbrunner, Chris and Otto Penzler (eds.) Encyclopedia of Mystery and Detection (San Diego, Cal. and N. Y.: Harcourt Brace Jovanovich, Pub., 1976)

Thomas, Tony and Aubrey Solomon The Films of 20th Century-Fox: 50th Aniversary Edition (Secaucus, N. J.: Citadel Press, 1985)

Thomson, Ruth Gibbons (comp.) Index to Full Length Plays: 1895 to 1925 (Boston: F. W. Faxon Co., 1956)

Thomson, Ruth Gibbons (comp.) Index to Full Length Plays: 1926 to 1944 (Boston: F. W. Faxon Co., 1946)

various editors (eds.) Contempory Authors, First Revision (vols. 1 through 126) (Detroit: Gale Research Co., 1967-1989)

various editors (eds.) Contempory Authors: New Revision Series (vols. 1 through 19) (Detroit: Gale Research Co., 1981-1987)

various editors (eds.) Readers' Guide to Periodical Literature [1900 to 1988] (48 vols.) (Minneapolis, Minn. -- then N. Y.: H. W. Wilson Co., 1905 to 1989)

West, Dorothy Herbert and Dorothy Margaret Peake (comps.) Play Index: 1949-1952 (N. Y.: H. W. Wilson Co., 1953)

Willis, Donald C. Horror and Science Fiction Films II (Metuchen, N. J. and London: The Scarecrow Press, Inc., 1982)

Willis, Donald C. Horror and Science Fiction Films III (Metuchen, N. J. and London: The Scarecrow Press, Inc., 1984)

Yaakov, Juliette (comp.) Play Index: 1978-1982 (N. Y.: H. W.

Wilson Co., 1983)

Yaakov, Juliette (comp.) <u>Short Story Index: Collections
Indexed, 1900-1978</u> (N. Y.: H. W. Wilson Co., 1979)

Yaakov, Juliette (comp.) <u>Short Story Index: Supplement 1979-
1983</u>) (N. Y.: H. W. Wilson Co., 1984)

Yaakov, Juliette (comp.) <u>Short Story Index: 1984</u> (N. Y.: H.
W. Wilson Co., 1985)

Yaakov, Juliette and John Greenfield (comps.) <u>Play Index:
1983-1987</u> (N. Y.: H. W. Wilson Co., 1988)